DEMOCRACY
AND BEAUTY

LEONARD HASTINGS SCHOFF MEMORIAL LECTURES

UNIVERSITY SEMINARS
LEONARD HASTINGS SCHOFF MEMORIAL LECTURES

The University Seminars at Columbia University sponsor an annual series of lectures, with the support of the Leonard Hastings Schoff and Suzanne Levick Schoff Memorial Fund. A member of the Columbia faculty is invited to deliver before a general audience three lectures on a topic of his or her choosing. Columbia University Press publishes the lectures.

Robert G. O'Meally, *Antagonistic Cooperation: Jazz, Collage, Fiction, and the Shaping of African American Culture*

Herbert S. Terrace, *Why Chimpanzees Can't Learn Language and Only Humans Can*

Annette Insdorf, *Cinematic Overtures*

Paige West, *Dispossession and the Environment: Rhetoric and Inequality in Papua New Guinea*

Robert L. Belknap, *Plots*

Philip Kitcher, *Deaths in Venice: The Cases of Gustav von Aschenbach*

Douglas A. Chalmers, *Reforming Democracies: Six Facts About Politics That Demand a New Agenda*

Boris Gasparov, *Beyond Pure Reason: Ferdinand de Saussure's Philosophy of Language and Its Early Romantic Antecedents*

Robert W. Hanning, *Serious Play: Desire and Authority in the Poetry of Ovid, Chaucer, and Ariosto*

Lesley A. Sharp, *Bodies, Commodities, and Biotechnologies: Death, Mourning, and Scientific Desire in the Realm of Human Organ Transfer*

George Rupp, *Globalization Challenged: Conviction, Conflict, Community*

David Rosand, *The Invention of Painting in America*

Partha Chatterjee, *The Politics of the Governed: Reflections on Popular Politics in Most of the World*

Lisa Anderson, *Pursuing Truth, Exercising Power: Social Science and Public Policy in the Twenty-First Century*

Ira Katznelson, *Desolation and Enlightenment: Political Knowledge After Total War, Totalitarianism, and the Holocaust*

For a complete list of books in the series, please see the Columbia University Press website.

DEMOCRACY AND BEAUTY

THE POLITICAL AESTHETICS OF W. E. B. DU BOIS

ROBERT GOODING-WILLIAMS

Columbia University Press *New York*

Columbia University Press
Publishers Since 1893
New York   Chichester, West Sussex

Copyright © 2025 Columbia University Press
All rights reserved

Library of Congress Cataloging-in-Publication Data
Names: Gooding-Williams, Robert, author.
Title: Democracy and beauty : the political aesthetics of W.E.B. Du Bois / Robert Gooding-Williams.
Other titles: Political aesthetics of W.E.B. Du Bois
Description: New York : Columbia University Press, [2025] | Series: Leonard Hastings Schoff memorial lectures | Includes bibliographical references and index.
Identifiers: LCCN 2024038155 (print) | LCCN 2024038156 (ebook) | ISBN 9780231220026 (hardback) | ISBN 9780231220033 (trade paperback) | ISBN 9780231563024 (ebook)
Subjects: LCSH: Du Bois, W. E. B. (William Edward Burghardt), 1868–1963 —Political and social views. | Aesthetics —Political aspects —United States. | African Americans —Politics and government. | White supremacy (Social structure) —United States. | United States —Race relations —Philosophy.
Classification: LCC E185.97.D73 G663 2025 (print) | LCC E185.97.D73 (ebook) | DDC 320.56/909 —dc23/eng/20241206

Cover design: Noah Arlow
Cover image: Norman Lewis (1909–1979), *Alabama*, 1960, oil on canvas, 48 1/8 × 72 5/8 inches / 122.2 × 184.5 cm, signed; Cleveland Museum of Art, Cleveland, OH. John L. Severance Fund 2017.1; © Estate of Norman Lewis, courtesy of Michael Rosenfeld Gallery LLC, New York, NY

GPSR Authorized Representative: Easy Access System Europe, Mustamäe tee 50, 10621 Tallinn, Estonia, gpsr.requests@easproject.com

CONTENTS

1 *Darkwater*, Democracy, and Aesthetic Education   1
2 Moral Psychology of White Supremacy   29
3 Democratic Despotism   55
4 Beauty   79
5 Propaganda   105
6 Pessimism   133
7 Du Bois's Pluralism: Unfinished Lives, Unfinished Societies   169

Acknowledgments   197
Notes   201
Index   247

DEMOCRACY AND BEAUTY

1

DARKWATER, DEMOCRACY, AND AESTHETIC EDUCATION

During the decade of the First World War (1910–1920) W. E B. Du Bois argued that white supremacy functioned, within the United States and internationally, to thwart the democratic political aspirations of the Earth's "darker peoples." During the same decade, Du Bois elaborated an aesthetics—a philosophy of beauty—that conceptualized beauty as a political force capable of supporting the struggle against white supremacy: of sustaining the moral resolve required to fight it and of undermining its grip on the individuals who perpetuated it. Du Bois believed that white supremacy is a deeply rooted feature of American political life—that it persists, despite its anti-democratic tendencies. White supremacy is a powerful cultural force that resists rational revision, he argued, because it is rooted in the entrenched habits—the moral character—of the white supremacist. Beauty has a role to play in opposing white supremacy and fostering a more inclusive democracy, first, because it can strengthen our determination to fight it, the obduracy of the white supremacist notwithstanding; and second, because it can unsettle and help to transform the pernicious habits that perpetuate it.

In *Dusk of Dawn* (1940), Du Bois's first, book-length autobiography, he describes *Darkwater* (1920), a book he published fewer than two years after the Great War ended, as the second of three "sets of thought" he had essayed "centering around the hurts and hesitancies that hem the black man in America" (the first and the third were *The Souls of Black Folk* [1903] and *Dusk of Dawn* itself). Comprising a credo, a postscript, and a litany, as well as essays, stories, and poems, *Darkwater* figures centrally in my study of Du Bois's aesthetics for two reasons.[1] One is that Du Bois explicates and exemplifies his concept of beauty in *Darkwater*. The second is that *Darkwater* establishes the historical, moral-psychological, and normative contexts that explain Du Bois's turn to beauty as a vehicle for combatting white supremacy. Du Bois's philosophy of beauty presupposes a narrative of the history of modern struggles for democracy, a normative conception of democracy, and a moral psychology of white supremacy. According to the historical narrative, the modern democratic political movement is a perpetually embattled struggle to promote the normative, democratic ideal of an unrestricted franchise against the rule of self-interested capitalists in the aftermath of the industrial revolution. Du Bois's moral psychology of white supremacy helps explain the limited success of that struggle and the correlated restriction of democratic development to white races, including the failure of Reconstruction and the advent of a new, industrial imperialism.

"Democratic movements inside groups and nations are always taking place and they are efforts to increase the beneficiaries of the ruling," Du Bois writes. The modern democratic movement has been so "broad and sweeping," he continues, as to accord that aim "universal expression." A product of the eighteenth century, it proposes "that if All ruled they would rule for All," and it seeks "Universal Good . . . through Universal Suffrage." Hoping to universalize the benefit of ruling, to grant that good to everyone, the modern democratic movement has advocated universal suffrage as an indispensable means to that end. But ignorance and selfishness have thwarted its ambitions. Initially, "ignorance about the action of men in groups and the technique of industry in general" limited democratic achievements to "restricting menial service, securing the right of property in handiwork and regulating public taxes; distributing land ownership; and freeing trade and barter." As democratic struggles met with self-interested "stubborn resistance," moreover, "a whole new organization of work suddenly appeared"—the "'Industrial Revolution' of the 19th century"—primarily if not exclusively as a consequence of the "determination of powerful and intelligent individuals to secure the benefits of privileged persons, as in the case of foreign slave trade." Accosted by this "vast and unexampled development of industry," the "new democracy stood aghast and impotent. It could not rule because it did not understand." Ultimately "an invincible kingdom of trade, business, and commerce ruled the world, and before its threshold stood the Freedom of 18th century philosophy warding the way. Some of the very ones who were freed from the tyranny of the Middle Age became the tyrants of the industrial age."[2]

In his magisterial study of the "Age of Revolution," the historian Eric Hobsbawm argued that "[i]f the economy of the nineteenth century world were formed mainly under the influence of the British Industrial Revolution, its politics and ideology were formed mainly by the French."[3] Du Bois sketches much the same argument, but additionally proposes that the tyranny of the industrial age and the "Philosophy of Democracy handed down from the 18th century" were necessarily opposed to one another.[4] Du Bois acknowledges that the "Philosophy of Democracy" can be used to rationalize tyranny, but the conflict between democracy and tyranny, be it political or industrial, was always fundamental to his thinking.[5] At the time he wrote *Darkwater*, Du Bois believed that the contradiction driving modern world history was the clash between the essentially democratic impulses propelling the French Revolution and the essentially antidemocratic, capitalist, and self-interested forces propelling the slave trade and the industrial revolution.[6] With the latter victorious, "Captains of Industry" and "Philanthropy" came to dominate the world, while meanwhile the "lowest laborers," American Negroes revolting from slavery among them, joined the democratic movement's fight for freedom.[7] Du Bois argues, however, that the Civil War was *not* "a war for Negro freedom, but a duel between two industrial systems, one of which was bound to fail because it was an anachronism, and the other bound to succeed because of the Industrial Revolution."[8] In the wake of the Civil War, the philosophy of democracy yet again took up the struggle against capitalism, for with Reconstruction there "was a chance . . . to try democratic rule in a new way, that is, against the new industrial oppression with a mass of workers who were not yet in its control, . . . a unique chance to realize a new modern democracy in industry in the southern United States which would point the way to the world."[9] But the effort to point the way to the world—by enfranchising black and white labor, by redistributing land and capital, and by establishing a public school system—failed, because the "former slave-owners" and the "owners of the industrial North" opposed it.[10] The upshot of this failure, Du Bois writes, "was the disenfranchisement of the blacks of the South and a world-wide attempt to restrict democratic development to white races and to distract them with race hatred against darker races."[11] "This program," he emphasizes, while "it helped raise the scale of white labor, in much greater proportion put wealth and power in the hands of the great European Captains of Industry and made modern industrial imperialism possible."[12]

In alluding here to the advance of white labor and, subsequently, to white European workers' "renewed efforts" democratically to "control" modern industrial imperialism, Du Bois adduces his distinctive conceptual framework for understanding the mode of rule structuring the modern world.[13] For Du Bois, the year 1877 is a pivotal moment in the history of modern struggles for democracy, marked by the end of Reconstruction and Sir Henry Morton Stanley's approach to the mouth of the Congo River.[14] Specifically, Du Bois believes that the end of Reconstruction and the start of the scramble for Africa that Stanley's journeys occasioned led to the emergence of a form of international governance essentially defined by two reciprocally connected tendencies: (1) the continuing democratic development of the white working class—its ability, that is, to alter the existing, imperialist political order by championing polices that curbed the capitalist domination and exploitation of white workers in Europe and America; and (2) the relentless stifling of the democratic development of the world's darker races—thus, their unremitting subjection to domination and exploitation by white workers united with white capitalists.[15] Du Bois describes this mode of international governance as "democratic despotism," and his moral psychology of white supremacy belongs to his attempt to explain, causally to account for, the conjunction of its constitutive tendencies: specifically, to say (1) why the norms advanced by the modern democratic movement, while effective in curbing capitalist interests when they targeted white workers, were not thus effective when they targeted the world's darker peoples; and (2) why the economic interests that targeted these peoples found their labor, in contrast to white labor, cheap and defenseless.[16] On Du Bois's account, the white supremacist moral character that imbues white Christian culture suppresses the democratic development of the world's darker peoples and helps sustain the regime of democratic despotism by permitting and even encouraging the normatively unencumbered subjection of nonwhite races to self-interested economic exploitation.

In chapter 3, I examine Du Bois arguments for this claim, and for his related account of the interplay between racial hatred and economic exploitation in the United States. For present purposes, however, I want to emphasize that Du Bois's political aesthetics—again, his idea that beauty is a political force capable of advancing the struggle against white supremacy—belongs to a larger argument about the role beauty can play in advancing the democratic development of the world's darker peoples. Given Du Bois's picture of the mode of rule structuring the modern world, circa 1915, it follows that a politics that helped to unsettle white Christian culture would assist that development, other things being equal. By the time he wrote *Darkwater*, Du Bois had come to the conclusion that the habits of mind constituting the moral character of the white supremacist resist revision through scientific inquiry and internal critique. This conclusion—Du Bois's *entrenchment thesis*—was a source of concern to him, for it implied that science and logical reasoning would not suffice to unsettle white Christian culture. During the era of the Great War, Du Bois responds to this concern by arguing that racial oppression and the restriction of darker peoples' democratic development, to the extent that they were permitted and perpetuated by the entrenched cognitive, affective, and motivational dispositions characteristic of the white supremacist, must be attacked with weapons of sudden and immediate "assault." Du Bois, I argue, thought that beauty could serve as one of those weapons. Distinguishing between natural and artistic beauty, he held that the former could help black citizens cope with their despair at the possibility of undermining racial oppression that is propped up by the stubborn resistance of white Christian culture to rational revision. Regarding the latter, he maintained that it could transform the white Christian, contesting and discomposing her religious self-understanding.[17] Du Bois allows that natural beauty can challenge the bleak picture of the social world that black citizens' pessimism-inducing despair presumes, and he proposes that artistic beauty can challenge the white Christian's understanding of what is required of a Christian life.

That said, let me immediately emphasize that Du Bois's political defense of beauty is not simply a defense of its efficacy as a weapon. In addition, it is a defense of beauty's pedagogical power, of its contribution to the cultivation of democratic citizenship. Du Bois's account of the political power of aesthetic education, whether directed toward the pessimism of the oppressed or the recalcitrant-to-reason commitments of the oppressor, depends on his normative notion of democracy no less than on his conception of beauty. In a later part of this chapter, I briefly sketch that conception, a more detailed analysis of which I offer in chapter 4. In particular, I introduce Du Bois's contention that one of beauty's defining features—its power to astonish through the revelation of what is unexpected and unfamiliar—has a critical role to play in the cultivation of a characteristically democratic civic virtue: to wit, citizens' openness, their receptivity, to possibilities of feeling, thought, and action that otherwise strike them as strange or remote. First, however, I reconstruct Du Bois defense of his "democratic ideal," his normative invocation of democracy as a standard of political excellence. I then return to the idea of beauty's pedagogical power via an analysis of his understanding of the *culture of democracy*—on his account, the culture of *the crowd*, which aesthetic education geared to the virtue of receptivity is meant to promote.

DU BOIS'S DEMOCRATIC IDEAL

Du Bois begins his defense of the democratic ideal, which is to universalize the franchise, by rebutting the reasoning typically adduced to exclude the ignorant, the inexperienced, the guarded, and the unwilling from a share in the ruling of men. Often, he tells us, this reasoning falters on a "misapprehension," on the untrue premise that the basis of the argument for universalizing the franchise is that voting is *simply* a means to satisfy the needs or wants of some group—e.g., that the franchise should be extended to white women and blacks just because meeting their needs requires it. According to Du Bois, however, the "foundation of the argument for democracy," the principle on which the case for the "rule of all" rests, is that democracy is the "method" of government required to realize "the broadest measure of justice to all human beings"; or, limiting the scope of the principle to the potentially "self-ruling" peoples of modern sovereign states, to realize "the broadest justice for all citizens." On this account, the measure of justice that rulers extend to the ruled is maximally broad *only if* all the ruled rule. Du Bois defends the proposition that democracy is needed to realize the broadest justice to a state's citizens by arguing that justice requires inclusiveness and that inclusiveness requires democracy. But what is inclusiveness, and why does justice require it?[18]

Du Bois answers the first question in political terms, conceptualizing inclusiveness as the inevitably disruptive incorporation of previously excluded perspectives and voices into the mix of considerations that determine how a body politic is to be governed: in his words, the "addition of . . . new wisdom . . . new points of view, and . . . new interests [that] must . . . be from time to time bewildering and confusing." Thus, while "those who have a voice in the body politic have expressed their wishes and sufferings . . . [t]he appearance of new interests and complaints means disarrangement and confusion to the older equilibrium." Du Bois answers the second question in epistemic terms, arguing that justice requires the accumulation of wisdom from diverse sources, and that gathering wisdom from such sources requires inclusiveness. The people of a democratic nation, he writes, "holds in the heads and hearts of its individual citizens the vast mine of knowledge, out of which it may build a just government, . . . a government built on the broadest justice to every citizen."[19]

For Du Bois, justice involves responsiveness to individual interests; it is a matter of giving appropriate weight to everyone's interests. As I read him, moreover, this is precisely the idea of justice he advances when he depicts a world where "the interests of no human soul will be neglected," when he insists that women need the ballot "to right the balance of a world sadly awry because of its brutal neglect of the rights of women and children," and when he asserts that "Negro enfranchisement" would entail that "black men in the south would have to be treated with consideration, have their wishes respected and their manhood rights recognized."[20] In Du Bois's view, the laws that make a government just ("enlightened, social legislation")[21] give due weight to (rather than disregard) the desires and concerns of all citizens, their interests in having their rights protected among them. And such laws, he proposes, convey the epistemic diversity of the citizenry—as a contemporary philosopher puts the point, they manifest "citizens' situated knowledge—the fact that citizens from different walks of life have different experiences of problems and policies of public interest, experiences that have evidential import for devising and evaluating solutions."[22] Epistemic diversity is essential to justice, for "in the last analysis," Du Bois writes, "only the sufferer knows his sufferings."[23] Just laws demand inclusiveness, for just laws reflect epistemic diversity, and because reflecting epistemic diversity requires that perspectives and insights (situated knowledge) not previously taken into account enter into the determination of the laws governing a polity. Du Bois arrives at the conclusion of his argument—that inclusiveness requires democracy, the universalization of the franchise—by reasoning that, without extending suffrage to groups previously excluded from the franchise, their members' distinctive perspectives and insights will not figure in the determination of the laws. In justifying democracy as a method for extending the broadest measure of justice, Du Bois likewise justifies inclusion as a process whereby citizens learn from one another's viewpoints and determine the law on that basis.[24]

In a passage about democratic tyrannies of the majority over permanent minorities that echoes both Tocqueville's *Democracy in America* and Mill's *On Liberty*, Du Bois relates his justice-based defense of democracy to "the democratic ideal":

> But suppose that the out-voted minority is necessarily always a minority? Women, for instance, can seldom expect to be a majority; artists must always be the few; ability is always rare, and black folk in this land are but a tenth. Yet to tyrannize over such minorities, to browbeat and insult them, to call that government a democracy which makes majority votes an excuse for crushing ideas and individuality and self-development, is manifestly a peculiarly dangerous perversion of the real democratic ideal. It is right here, in its *method* and not in its object, that democracy in America and elsewhere has so often failed. We have attempted to enthrone any chance majority and make it rule by divine right.[25]

While democracy is a necessary condition of justice, a requirement to realize the broadest justice to a state's citizens, it is not a sufficient condition. Were all blacks enfranchised, Du Bois argues, their exercise of the franchise would not guarantee that the white majority would not deprive them of "a voice in their government and their right to self-development."[26] In denying a voice to enfranchised blacks, an omnipotent white majority would be subjecting them to a tyranny that excluded their perspectives from the determination of the laws by which the American body politic was to be governed. That is, it would be subjecting black citizens to the unjust laws of an unjust government, thereby perverting the universalization of the franchise, the "real democratic ideal." Put differently, if the franchise has been universalized, but permanent majorities have turned a deaf ear to the perspectives and voices of permanent minorities (where, then, in fact, not all the ruled rule), then the real democratic ideal has been rendered impotent—that is, it has been kept from realizing its proper end ("its object"), which is maximally to broaden the measure of justice. Justice matters to Du Bois, in part because its incorporation of previously excluded perspectives and voices shapes the polity to accommodate the individuality and self-development of those whose perspectives and voices the method of democracy incorporates. The method fails when tyrannies of the majority ignore those perspectives and voices, for they consistently decline to "consider as 'men' the crankiest, humblest, poorest and blackest peoples,"[27] and so crush rather than accommodate the individuality and self-development of the members of permanent minorities.

I close this section by noting that Du Bois models his method of philosophical inquiry on the method of democracy. In the "Postscript" he appends to the beginning of *Darkwater*, Du Bois represent his book as an extended discussion of the universal themes that animate the "human drama": e.g., work and service, rule and reason, women and children, and, of course, beauty, death, and war. To received, Euro-American thought about those themes he aims to "add a point of view," as if "from a veiled corner." Adding a point a view, he continues, is tantamount to striking "here and there a halftone, newer, even if slighter, up from the heart of my problem and problems of my people." Du Bois's philosophical method, he suggests, is incrementally to improvise on the characterization of universal themes by considering them in the perspective of lives lived within the hidden nook he inhabits; that is, by advancing a view of those themes that reflects the concrete experiences of black people. Phrased as a slogan, his method is *historically and self-consciously situated hermeneutical improvisation*. There are many examples of Du Bois's implementation of this distinctive mode of philosophical inquiry, including the opening pages of the *Darkwater* chapter in which he explicates his concept of beauty. For now, however, I want simply to stress that Du Bois's philosophical method is his considered attempt, patterned on the method of democracy, not now to incorporate a previously excluded perspective and range of voices into the determination of the laws to govern a polity, but to incorporate them into the determination of the shape of a larger and largely white conversation that governs Euro-America's understanding of the human drama—an understanding that has been historically compromised and distorted, time and time again, by a chafing deafness to, a vast ignorance of, what his book's subtitle calls "voices from within the veil."[28] It perhaps goes without saying that when such attempts founder, it is often because the democratic method in philosophy, no less than the democratic method in politics, has been met with institutionally hegemonic and effectively tyrannical approaches to inquiry predicated on the *ongoing* exclusion of those voices from the conversation of philosophy.

THE DISCOVERY OF THE CROWD

In the concluding chapter of *Democracy in America*, volume 1, Tocqueville excuses his book's want of attention to "Negroes" and "Indians" by arguing that "[t]hese topics are like tangents to my subject, being American, but not democratic, and my main business has been to describe democracy."[29] In contrast to Tocqueville, Du Bois believes that part of understanding democracy in America is making sense of its failures and, especially, its exclusions.[30] And again, he believes that these exclusions stem from a democratic despotism that is sustained through the inhibition of the democratic development of the world's darker peoples by the white Christian culture prevalent in Europe and America.[31] To combat that culture, Du Bois advocates for the promotion of a democratic culture, animated in part by the pedagogical power of beauty. As the following two passages attest, if read with an eye to their ramifications for democracy in America and elsewhere, the contrast between these cultures can suitably be described as a contrast between a culture of the mob and a culture of the crowd:

> The meaning of America is the beginning of the discovery of the Crowd. The crowd is not so well-trained as a Versailles garden party of Louis XIV, but it is far better trained than the Sans-culottes and it has infinite possibilities. What a world this will be when human possibilities are freed, when we discover each other, when the stranger is no longer the potential criminal and the certain inferior!

> In fact no one knows himself but that self's own soul. The vast and wonderful knowledge of this marvelous universe is locked in the bosoms of its individual souls. To tap this mighty reservoir of experience, knowledge, beauty, love, and deed we must appeal not to the few, not to some souls, but to all. The narrower the appeal, the poorer the culture; the wider the appeal the more magnificent are the possibilities. Infinite is human nature. We make it finite by choking back the mass of men, by attempting to speak for others, to interpret and act for them, and we end by acting for ourselves and using the world as our private property.[32]

The first sentence of the first passage is ambiguous. If it is read as an historian's observation that a particular event, the beginning of the discovery of the Crowd, led to the determination of the meaning of America, it seems that Du Bois's interest is to identify the causal origins of Americans' habits, prejudices, and the like.[33] But interpreted more plausibly, as a political theorist's claim that America is defined by a normatively distinctive project—more exactly, by a founding (beginning) commitment to make known (to discover) to the world a polity organized around the concept of the crowd—it appears that Du Bois's central concern is to expose America's ongoing failure to honor that commitment.[34] The allusions to Louis XIV and the sans culottes are telling—on one hand, reference to an absolute monarch whose rule has been described as a "reign of etiquette";[35] on the other, reference to a social movement whose name signifies its repudiation of the costume and ceremonial manners of the ancien régime. In the regimented world of the Versailles garden party, strict observance of the detailed codes governing the actions of the king's courtiers entailed the regularity of routine, allowing no prospect for the play of the unfamiliar.[36] Were there no adherence to routine and little training to enforce it, however, as in the case of Du Bois's sans culottes, the background of familiar practices presupposed by the appearance of unfamiliar alternatives to routine would be missing. For Du Bois, the welcome advent of the unfamiliar, of possibilities represented by the stranger, is characteristic of the crowd, which is neither so chaotic, so un-ruly, that deviation from established rules is difficult to discern, nor so rigid, so rule-bound, as to frown on every deviation. Neither formlessly anarchic, nor demanding inflexible obedience to well-defined codes of behavior, the culture of the crowd is dynamically responsive to strange voices and to the unfamiliar, unanticipated possibilities they express.[37] If America has failed to honor its founding commitment, it is because its citizens have yet to discover one another, and so to free those possibilities.[38]

"Crowd," "stranger," and "criminal"—in conjoining these terms to explain the meaning of America, Du Bois may mean to echo Edgar Allan Poe's short story "The Man of the Crowd" (1840), but the particulars of his argument can more fruitfully be interpreted as improvising on Georg Simmel's famous essay "The Stranger" (1908).[39] In Poe's story, a convalescent in the manner of a detective shadows a stranger through a London crowd, drawn to him because he cannot find the correct category to classify him and judging him to be a criminal, a "genius of deep crime," because he "refuses to be alone" or, arguably, because he refuses legibility.[40] But Du Bois's paradigmatic stranger, the "American Negro," refuses nothing; rather the Negro is judged to be a latent criminal and an indubitable inferior because, in Simmel's terms, white Christian culture is a culture of the mob that regards "the stranger" not as a "member of the group," but as akin to a "barbarian."[41] Simmel's stranger is not "the wanderer who comes today and goes tomorrow, but . . . the man who comes today and stays tomorrow," bringing qualities into a group "that are not and cannot be indigenous to it."[42] In contrast to the peoples the Greeks dubbed "barbarians," peoples who were not Greek, not members of the group, strangers are group members who are "close by" yet "remote," for they are "not bound by roots to the . . . partisan dispositions [*einseitigen Tendenzen*] of the group."[43] Extending Simmel's conceptual framework, Du Bois distinguishes two kinds of group: the crowd, marked by a receptivity to the unfamiliar possibilities and dispositions that the group's strangers represent; and the mob, marked by a tendency to constrain an otherwise "infinite" human nature by "choking back" and usurping the voices that would express those possibilities. As he puts the point in his portrait of the life of Samuel Coleridge-Taylor, "[w]e know in America how to discourage, choke, and murder ability when it so far forgets itself so as to choose a dark skin."[44] Du Bois metonymically figures white Christian culture as a culture of the mob—more precisely, of the choking, stifling *lynch* mob—for it quashes the voices of the strangers who have chosen dark skin, projecting them as subhuman criminals, but, like the ancients' barbarians, *not* as members of the group, *not* as fellow members of the polity. If, then, Du Bois can be read as improvising on Poe as well as Simmel, perhaps we should regard him as reading Poe as allegorizing the tendency to violence that energizes the lynch mob in his depiction of a detective's maniacal pursuit of a stranger in a crowd.[45]

In the autobiographical sketch that is chapter 1 of *Darkwater*, Du Bois notes that Louis XIV "drove" two of his ancestors, "two Huguenots, Jacques and Louis Du Bois, into wild Ulster County, New York."[46] I note *this* allusion to Louis XIV, for it tells against the perhaps tempting but questionable interpretive assumption that Du Bois means to associate the American lynch mob with the sans culottes. In Du Bois's eyes, the reign of the Sun King was characterized no less by the intense persecution of the Huguenot religious minority than by its insistence on strict rules of etiquette that allow no play to unfamiliar behavior or strange voices. And that persecution, of an oppressed minority by a ruling majority, more nearly resembled the persecution of black Americans than did the sans culottes' rebellious use of violence in their struggle against the aristocracy.[47] For Du Bois, I surmise, the white Christian lynch mob had greater affinity to Louis's etiquette-driven and anti-Huguenot persecutory monarchy than to the sans culottes. America's white Christian culture perpetuates racial oppression, but Du Bois hopes that the cultivation of a democratic culture of the crowd will help to erode it and thereby to alleviate racial oppression. Du Bois's ambition to establish a polity shaped by the culture of crowd is an ambition to topple an unjust social order, as was the sans culottes' ambition to establish an egalitarian republic.[48] But the culture of the crowd is no more the culture of the sans culottes than it is the culture of the mob.

Further to clarify Du Bois's distinction between mobs and crowds, and between the culture of the crowd and the culture of the mob, it is useful to invoke Susanna Siegel's analysis of the difference between episodic and dispositional mobs. The former exist only as long as they are gathered, Siegel argues, while the latter comprise people sharing specific political dispositions, regardless of whether these people, said to belong to a mob, "gather together at a single place or time."[49] Du Bois's thinking, I suggest, involves both dispositional and episodic ideas of the mob and the crowd. When he conceptualizes white Christian culture as a culture of the mob, for example, he implies that white Christian culture derives its essential character from the viciousness of white supremacists who stand ready, ever disposed to silence the stranger, or at least to ignore what she has to say, even if they have yet to gather together to form an episodic mob intent on lynching him or her through the activation of the racist temperament uniting them. And when he conceptualizes the culture of democracy as a culture of the crowd, he suggests that the culture of democracy derives its essential character from the receptivity of citizens who stand ready, ever disposed to lend an ear to the stranger, even if they have yet to gather together to form an episodic crowd intent on discovering him or them through the activation of the democratic sensibilities uniting them.

Du Bois's notions of the culture of the crowd and the culture of the mob are ideal types, conceptual constructs that generally serve him as tools for imagining the possibility of advancing America's founding normative project while keeping attuned to the recurrent upsurge of attitudes that threaten to suffocate that possibility. I conclude this section by considering Du Bois's short story "The Second Coming" as an example of this general serviceability. Within *Darkwater*, Du Bois places "The Second Coming" immediately after the chapter that introduces the concept of the crowd—in part, to help him illustrate that concept, in both its dispositional and its episodic aspects, but also to show the importance of tethering a democratic and emancipatory political imagination to an acknowledgment of the power of the forces that oppose it.

Reworking the New Testament's account of the Epiphany, "The Second Coming," tells the tale of the arrival of three bishops in

Valdosta, Georgia, where a black Christ has been born to Lucy, a young black girl who could pass for white. Each of the bishops—one white, one black, and one yellow—has received a formal letter summoning him to Valdosta.[50] When the black bishop receives his missive, he says, "I must go down there. Those colored folk are acting strangely." And when the yellow bishop receives his, he writes, "I have been strangely bidden to the Val d'Osta." As the story unfolds we learn that the white bishop was already on his way to Valdosta, to attend the wedding of Marguerite, the daughter of the "governor" (of Georgia?). After the white bishop arrives, the governor states that he "never saw niggers act so," opining that "they seem to be expecting something." "What's the crowd, Jim?" the governor asks his chauffeur. Later we hear that when a "wag in the surging crowd" yelled "Fire," "all laughed and ran." Finally, as the governor hurries the white bishop to his waiting limousine, after the latter has discovered that Lucy and her baby are black, he asks, "Did you hear anything? Do you hear that noise? The crowd is growing strangely on the streets and there seems to be a fire over toward the East. I never saw so many people here—I fear violence—a mob—a lynching—I fear—hark!"[51]

The coming of a black Christ causes black folk to behave strangely and an Asian bishop to feel the pull of a strange event. A similar feeling enlivens the crowd, apparently, for it is "growing strangely."[52] In keeping with his concept of the crowd, and perhaps with an eye to Matthew 25:42–46, Du Bois depicts a particular, surging episodic crowd as soon to welcome and accommodate the strange appearance of a black Christ. But is that what will happen?—a question that is prompted by the governor's fearful suggestion that the crowd is potentially a mob, that it could well *become* a violent lynch mob. To be sure, I do not suggest that the Du Bois's governor means to discriminate between the concepts of the crowd and the mob. I do suggest, however, that Du Bois means to discriminate between them and, more importantly, to highlight the fragility of America's normatively distinctive project, its ever-present vulnerability to the dispositional, Christian white supremacist mob. Fully to appreciate Du Bois's point, we need only notice that, by setting "The Second Coming" in Valdosta, Georgia, he frames his fiction as a retelling of the story of Mary Turner, the black victim of a white mob that hung her upside down from a tree, set her clothes afire with gasoline, cut from her womb the baby with whom she was eight months pregnant, and then crushed the baby's head under foot before spraying her body with bullets—all because Turner dared to protest the lynching of her husband the day before. Turner's husband was lynched for allegedly conspiring to kill Hampton Smith, a white farmer, but Turner herself was murdered, literally in order to silence her speech—because, as the *Savannah Morning News* reported the incident, she "made statements . . . about the execution of her husband and the people in their indignant mood took exception to her remarks as well as her attitude and took her to the river where she was hanged."[53] Du Bois envisions a gathering crowd intent on welcoming the strange arrival of a black baby Jesus, but his political imagination is troubled by the brutal murder of another black baby and his black mother just north of Valdosta, and just a little less than two years before *Darkwater* was published. Recognizing that an episodic crowd can easily grow and mutate into an episodic mob, thus that the project of shaping a polity around the idea of the crowd is ever pregnable, he reminds us that our effort to create a culture that welcomes the stranger and her pronouncements is a precarious enterprise that can be undone by a resurgence of the culture it seeks to displace.[54] If Mary Turner's child could not escape the violence of the mob, there is no assurance that Lucy's child will escape it to survive a modern day, Valdosta version of the "massacre of the innocents," even as the sound of "music,—some strong and mighty chord," announces his coming.[55]

"In the treatment of the child," Du Bois writes, "the world foreshadows its own future and faith. All words and all thinking lead to the child,—to that vast immortality and the wide sweep of infinite possibility which the child represents." In explaining the immortality and infinite possibility that the child represents, Du Bois invokes Wordsworth's intimations of immortality (from the "Ode"), remarking that "[t]he heaven that lies about our infancy is but the ideals come true which every generation of children is capable of bringing." In this particular context, a *Darkwater* chapter titled "The Immortal Child," Du Bois's ideals are educational aims, first among which is the aim to achieve "freedom" through the development of "human souls." That the thought of fulfilling these ideals involves an intimation of heavenly immortality suggests that the ideals are universal and enduring, bound neither by place nor by time. More important to Du Bois, however, is the prospect of an earthly, "practical immortality," an ongoing cultivation of freedom and self-development that "continues through the endless life of children's children." For Du Bois, the work of educating children is a multigenerational project to free the "infinite possibilities" of human self-development that the white Christian mob "chokes back." It is part of a struggle to create a polity shaped by the democratic culture of the crowd. As "The Second Coming" shows, the work of educating black children compounds that struggle, for the culture of the mob ever threatens to "crucify" these children's "souls," and so ever puts black peoples' future at risk and their faith in question. How can a faith in black peoples' future be sustained? How can it be protected from creeping feelings of despair and pessimism at the prospect of a practical immortality of *black souls*? Beginning with "A Litany of Atlanta" and its anguish over God's silence, and continuing through "The Princess of the Hither Isles," with its suicidal ending, and "The Second Coming," with its anxious, ambiguous ending, *Darkwater* tacitly but repeatedly poses these questions, but only addresses them explicitly in "Of Beauty and Death." Here, Du Bois philosophically affirms that establishing a polity shaped by the culture of the crowd requires not only a radical transformation of the souls of the members of the mob, the souls of white folk, but resistance to despair and pessimism at the possibility of establishing such a polity.[56]

AESTHETIC EDUCATION

In this last section, I begin by turning to Friedrich Schiller's *Letters on the Aesthetic Education of Man* (1795), still a critical point of reference in ongoing, philosophical discussions of politics in relation to aesthetics.[57] Schiller writes in the wake of the overthrow of the despotic ancien régime and in reaction to the reign of terror. In contrast, Du Bois writes in advance of the (hoped-for) overthrow of a despotic form of democracy and in reaction to racial oppression. Heir to the tradition of modern republican political thought (Machiavelli, Montesquieu, Rousseau, and so forth), Schiller responds to the Terror by defending aesthetic education, *after* the revolution, as a vehicle for cultivating the moral and civic virtue required to ensure "the stability and duration of the new French republic."[58] Heir to the same tradition, Du Bois responds to the terror of despotism itself by defending aesthetic education *before* the revolution, so to speak—as a means the oppressed, wishing to overthrow their oppressors, might deploy against them. For Schiller, art facilitates the integration of our sensible and intellectual natures, thus enabling us to achieve the autonomy that moral and civic virtue demand. In the words of one commentator, it "frees us from subservience to our immediate needs and stimulates us to exercise our fledgling powers of thinking and deciding."[59] In the perspective of Schiller's *Letters*, the integrative power of aesthetic experience helps secure political stability. On this point, however, Du Bois inverts Schiller, arguing for forms of aesthetic education that, by dis-integrating the self-understanding of the Christian white supremacist and highlighting the possibility of subverting racial oppression, threaten political stability.[60]

The key to Du Bois's defense of aesthetic education is his concept of beauty. For present purposes I restrict myself to encapsulating the elements of the concept, which, again, I consider in detail in chapter 4. In Du Bois's view, an event—a natural occurrence, a work of art, a religious vision, or a life—counts as beautiful only if it comes to an apt end (like the ending of a good story, for example) that casts the event in an unfamiliar, astonishing light—in a strange light. The completion of an event, its coming to a suitable end, he suggests, is necessary for the event's unfamiliarity to come into view. Due to their power to reveal what is unexpected and unfamiliar, Du Bois argues, artistic and natural beauties can enhance citizens' receptivity to strange and unfamiliar possibilities of thought, feeling, and action, and in this way promote democracy and the democratic culture of the crowd.

For Du Bois, receptivity to unfamiliar possibilities is a form of alertness to those possibilities that involves a desire to hold oneself accountable to them, to answer to them. Where the democratic culture of the crowd tends to prevail, citizens embody the virtue of receptivity, which is why the culture of the crowd is dynamically responsive to strange voices and the unfamiliar possibilities they express. Or, more exactly, why it is dynamically responsive to unfamiliar, possible considerations that stem from strangers' "reservoir of experience," to considerations that can and ought to be brought to bear in determining how the polity is governed. Receptivity requires that citizens desire to respond to strangers' experience-based, atypical insights, which is to require that citizens desire to answer to those insights by considering them as potentially bearing on their deliberations about how the polity should be governed.[61]

Where the antidemocratic, white Christian culture of the mob tends to prevail, white citizens lack the receptivity characteristic of the crowd, which is why that culture "chokes back" strange voices and remains oblivious to possibilities that should have been brought to bear in determining how the polity is governed. Where that culture tends to prevail, moreover, it can erode resistant black citizens' capacity for receptivity, *not* now to the unfamiliar possibilities to which that culture is itself oblivious, but to the seemingly remote and to that extent unfamiliar possibility of acting to subvert racial oppression. When white Christian habits of mind have become so deeply entrenched that they appear to preclude the possibility of subverting racial oppression, resistant black citizens may *cease to see* that possibility as existing for them, *relinquish* their desire to answer to it, *and hopelessly quit* their efforts at subversion.

For these reasons, then, Du Bois believes that aesthetic education meant to combat white supremacist mob culture and to promote the culture of the crowd must proceed along at least two tracks, each of which is premised on the assumption that receptivity to possibilities is, to borrow a phrase from a contemporary political theorist, "disclosure-dependent."[62] To desire to answer to a range of unfamiliar, possible considerations that bear on her understanding of what the "broadest justice" requires, the Christian white supremacist must come to view those considerations as belonging to, in Martha Nussbaum's felicitous phrasing, her "circle of concern"—that is, as deriving from voices and lives that morally matter to her.[63] Similarly, to desire to answer to the remote possibility of subverting racial oppression, when the penetrating grip of racial oppression on black lives and the future of blacks' "children's children" seems to preclude the possibility of subversion, the despairing and pessimistic opponents of racial oppression must come anew to view that possibility as a prospect that exists for them, as a possibility that, because it has not been removed from their social world, they could enact. Regarding the first case, the function of aesthetic education, through the medium of artistic beauty, is radically to transform (again, to dis-integrate) the Christian white supremacist's self-understanding by disclosing to her, to her astonishment, that the circle of Christian moral concern, *properly understood*, comprehends black lives and voices. Regarding the second, the function of aesthetic education, through the medium of natural beauty, is to relieve blacks of their tendency to despair of and quit the struggle by disclosing to them, to their astonishment, that the regularities that structure their social world are susceptible to interruption and so do not rule out the prospect of action that subverts racial oppression.

Two theses summarize Du Bois's account of the role aesthetic education can play in combatting democratic despotism. The first thesis, the focus of chapter 5, is that artistic beauty can enhance the Christian white supremacist's receptivity to the unfamiliar possibilities black strangers voice by showing her that she can enlarge her circle of concern and, indeed, that she ought to do so. The second, the focus of chapter 6, is that natural beauty can enhance despairing blacks' receptivity to the remote possibility of subverting racial oppression by letting them see that they themselves can transform their social world. The idea linking these theses, and that runs throughout Du Bois's defense of aesthetic education, is that beauty is a pedagogical force that can activate the destabilizing power of human agency to renovate our moral and institutional lives—a power that the political theorist Roberto Unger, following the poet John Keats, calls "negative capability."[64]

THE ARGUMENT

I conclude by noting that, broadly speaking, my argument falls into two halves.

Chapters 1–3 explore what in chapter 1—the present chapter—I have described as the presuppositions of Du Bois's philosophy of beauty: his narrative history of modern struggles for democracy; his normative conception of democracy; and his moral psychology of white supremacy. The present chapter limns the contours of Du Bois's narrative history and analyzes his defense of his democratic ideal. Chapter 2 examines Du Bois's moral psychology, while chapter 3 explores his idea that the character and culture of the Christian white supremacist inhibit the realization of his democratic ideal. In addition, chapter 2 relates Du Bois's critique of Christian white supremacist culture to some recent discussions of the politics of the religious right. Taken in tandem, finally, chapters 2 and 3 also explain why, given his moral psychology of white supremacy and the causal significance he attributes to Christian white supremacist character and culture, Du Bois thought that combatting white supremacist habits of mind could help to undo racial oppression.

This and the next chapter (chapters 1 and 2) include brief discussions of Du Bois's accounts of beauty generally and of artistic and natural beauty specifically, but only in chapters 4, 5, and 6 do I turn to the particulars of Du Bois's philosophy of beauty. Chapter 4 highlights the tension between Du Bois's belief that beautiful events must be complete and his belief that they must disclose unfamiliar possibilities. In this connection, I argue that Du Bois's notion of beauty is temporally bipolar, pointing at once to the past and the future, and that it is beauty's forward-looking power to reveal unfamiliar possibilities—of reforming our moral characters and culture (artistic beauty) and of acting to transform an oppressive social order (natural beauty)—that he takes to be most *politically* significant. That said, it is critical to emphasize Du Bois's commitment to the claim that beauty requires completeness. The ultimate roots of that commitment, I suggest, are (1) his understanding of beauty in general with reference to the paradigm of a beautiful life; and (2) his seemingly religious faith that we redeem our lives and render them beautiful only if, at the end, it is possible for us, or, better, our contemporaries, to look back at them, regard them as coherent wholes, and say, "Well done." In the background, here, is Du Bois's reading of the New Testament Parable of the Talents, a text he echoes in *Darkwater*'s "Credo," his politically inflected version of the Apostles' Creed, and in his narrative of the life of Alexander Crummell, which best exemplifies his notion of a beautiful life.

Chapters 5 and 6 explore Du Bois's conceptions of artistic and natural beauty in detail, and chapter 7 returns to his conception of a beautiful life. Chapter 5 explains Du Bois's conception of artistic beauty with reference to his short story "Jesus Christ in Texas," his 1909 biography *John Brown*, and, briefly, two recent artworks and an example of political theater. Du Bois's aesthetics show that art can challenge received morality, I argue, but they also run the risk of moralism—a risk that, when combined with the assumption that beauty requires completeness, cuts against his desire to promote a democratic culture of the crowd. Chapter 6 analyzes Du Bois's understanding of natural beauty as a romantic, natural supernaturalist antidote to the pessimistic despair haunting the lives of those who would struggle against entrenched democratic despotism.

Chapter 7 builds on the arguments of chapters 5 and 6. Specifically, it invokes *Darkwater*'s essay "The Damnation of Women," as well as Du Bois's infamous book review of novels by Nella Larsen and Claude McKay, to show how his religiously rooted celebration of beautiful, complete, and morally redeemed lives sponsors a form of praise that compromises his democratic political commitments. In its application to his fellow, female citizens, I argue, Du Bois's philosophy of beauty cuts against his politics. By way of a discussion of contemporary, apocalyptic Afropessimism, chapter 7 likewise proposes that Du Bois's account of natural beauty and his rejection of pessimism depend on a pluralist (in William James's sense) social theory that parallels the pluralist idea of human agency his political commitments require. Chapter 7 concludes by noting the affinities between Du Bois's reliance on a pluralist social theory and some recent contributions to black aesthetics that echo Du Bois—specifically, work by Fred Moten and Saidiya Hartman.

2

MORAL PSYCHOLOGY OF WHITE SUPREMACY

In *Dusk of Dawn* (1940), Du Bois describes his social theory of racial oppression as evolving through three phases: from thinking that ignorance alone caused racial oppression, where ignorance is a lack of the sort of knowledge that can be obtained through rational inquiry; to thinking that ignorance in tandem with ill-will caused racial oppression; to thinking that ignorance in tandem with ill-will, economic interests, and unconscious motives caused racial oppression. In addition, he remarks that each of these three explanatory frameworks entailed a different account of the political strategies the darker races required to dismantle racial oppression. When Du Bois thought that ignorance alone was the problem, he argued that reason and scientific education sufficed to end racial injustice. But when he realized that ill-will, or malice, was also a cause, he held that blacks "must fight for freedom," adding that rational inquiry and scientific education should be supplemented by boycott, propaganda, and mob frenzy, the weapons of "sudden" and "immediate" assault. When, finally, Du Bois recognized that economic interest and unconscious motive contribute to the perpetuation of racial oppression, he argued that rational inquiry and the fight for freedom must be supplemented with a "long siege," carried out through "careful planning and subtle campaign."[1]

In the present chapter, I examine the white supremacist ill-will that is central to the second explanatory framework, and that is foundational to Du Bois's political aesthetics. Here, as in chapter 1, I concentrate on *Darkwater*, which, in keeping with the spirit of the second explanatory framework, Du Bois describes as "an exposition and militant challenge, defiant with dogged hope"—in essence, as a call to arms.[2] In particular, I focus on "The Souls of White Folk," the book's second chapter, for it is Du Bois's detailed assessment of the malicious moral character of the white supremacists comprising the bulk of Europe's and America's white folk. "The Souls of White Folk" is Du Bois's primary contribution to the moral psychology of white supremacy—that is, to the study and analysis of the habits of mind that, he maintains, the souls of white folk typically exhibit.[3]

Before proceeding further, some preliminary thoughts:

1. First, that while Du Bois's ill-will-centered explanatory framework is manifest throughout *Darkwater*, it would be a mistake to regard the book as belonging exclusively to his second phase of intellectual development. In *Dusk of Dawn*, Du Bois claims that his commitment to the ill-will-centered framework was well established before World War I began, but that the war, "the lesson of fighting," transformed his thinking in the direction of the third explanatory framework.[4] These remarks are significant, for they suggest that *Darkwater*, which incorporated materials written before as well as during the war —"The Souls of White Folk" includes work belonging to both periods (see below)—and which Du Bois continued to revise after the November 1919 armistice, straddles the second and third phases.[5] I shall be arguing, in fact, that Du Bois relies on his characterization of capitalist economic interests no less than on his moral psychology of white supremacy to explain racial oppression in *Darkwater*—and, moreover, in other war-era

writings—arguing, for example, that the profit motive operates in tandem with ill-will and the other vices entangling it to bring about Europe's exploitation of the world's darker peoples. What is yet to appear in *Darkwater*, however, is Du Bois's later, Freudian turn to explanation in terms of "unconscious" or "subconscious" impulses, which he only explicitly embraces in *Dusk of Dawn*.

2. Second, that Du Bois's belief that the moral character of the white supremacist is recalcitrant to reason depends on his equation of reason with the use of rational methods of inquiry. In denying that the elimination of ignorance will suffice to subvert racial oppression, Du Bois holds that the acquisition of knowledge through specifically rational means is by itself helpless against ill-will, and that reason requires the assistance of forces that direct an "appeal" to the white supremacist.[6] Part of my interest here is in Du Bois's idea of an appeal, in the distinction he draws between "reason" and "appeal," and in the idea that beauty can be the source of an appeal. For Du Bois, knowledge acquired through rational means is knowledge obtained through either empirical-evidence-based scientific research or logical argument. On his view, then, to say that the moral character of the white supremacist is recalcitrant to reason, or to rational revision, is to say that it is susceptible neither to "scientific proof that neither color nor race limits a man's capacity or desert" nor to "logical method[s]" that expose hypocrisy (see below). But the character of the white supremacist *is* susceptible to a sort of *moral* entreaty, Du Bois believes—at least in what I have been calling the second phase of his intellectual development—and Du Bois has in mind precisely this sort of entreaty, I propose, when he suggests that white supremacist ill-will is susceptible to appeal. Thus understood, an appeal is a plea for moral self-reflection, not the assertion of a conclusion predicated on scientific research or logical reasoning. Du Bois thinks that beauty's appeal to the white supremacist stems from its power to reveal moral truths that dramatically challenge our understanding of

what we are doing, not from the implementation of rational modes of inquiry. Beauty calls the white supremacist critically to question his conception of what it is to live an ethical life. It addresses the white supremacist as an agent capable of practical deliberation informed by moral insight.[7]

3. Third, that Du Bois means his moral psychology to serve two purposes. The first is social-scientific explanation—specifically, the social-scientific explanation of the domination and exploitation of the world's darker peoples. The second is to articulate the Christian white supremacist's ideal conception of his life as a Christian, for it is in virtue of this conception that the Christian white supremacist is vulnerable to the power of beauty.

SOCIAL SCIENTIFIC EXPLANATION

In *Black Reconstruction* (1935), published fifteen years after *Darkwater*, Du Bois criticizes histories that approach slavery with moral impartiality, depicting America as helpless and the South as blameless, while explaining the difference in development between North and South as "a ... working out of cosmic social and economic law." An example of this approach is Charles and Mary Beard's *The Rise of American Civilization*, which represents the contest between North and South as if it were a "clash" between striving winds and waters. In the Beards' "sweeping mechanistic interpretation" of history, Du Bois writes, "there is no room for the real plot of the story, for the clear mistake and guilt of rebuilding a new slavery of the working class in the midst of a fateful experiment in democracy; for the triumph of sheer moral courage and sacrifice in the abolition crusade; and for the hurt and struggle of degraded black millions in their fight for freedom and their attempt to enter democracy. Can all this be omitted and half suppressed in a treatise that calls itself scientific?"[8]

To count as scientific, Du Bois argues, historical explanation cannot ignore the human significance of human history. If historiography is to contribute to the science of human action, rather than model its knowledge claims on the mechanistic explanations characteristic of the sciences of nature, then it must take account of the purposes informing human actions and events—of the morally praise or blameworthy motives that constitute the "real plot" of the stories the historian narrates. Echoing Max Weber, Du Bois suggests that the historian's primary charge is a form of *Verstehen*, explanatory understanding that takes account of human motivation by placing our individual actions, in Weber's words, "in an intelligible and more inclusive context of [subjective] meaning." Du Bois stresses the importance of explanatory understanding because he is committed to the view that moral judgment is a critical component of historiography. Unlike Weber, he is a moral realist who believes that historical knowledge includes a knowledge of the moral worth of the motives that explain human action—thus, not only the knowledge that such-and-such actions are right or wrong, but that the motives which explain those actions are morally blameworthy (guilty) or, again, that they are morally praiseworthy (like moral courage).[9]

In *Black Reconstruction*, Du Bois explicitly defends the thesis that the moral evaluation of human motives is critical to historical explanation. In *Darkwater*'s "The Souls of White Folk," I suggest, he takes this thesis for granted. A part of the point, then, of that essay's moral psychology of white supremacy is to sketch a general profile of white folks' morally deplorable habits of mind, and then to show how these habits of mind help explain the domination and exploitation of the world's darker peoples. That said, two caveats are in order here. One is that Du Bois's explanation is complex—that the causal/explanatory significance he attributes to the motivational disposition to do ill to black life, and to the beliefs and feelings that support that disposition, is part of a larger explanation that, as I note above, also emphasizes the role of capitalist economic interests in explaining racial domination and exploitation.[10] The second is that his construction of a profile of white souls does not require that he deny "that there are many white folk who feel the unfairness and crime of color and race prejudice and have toiled and sacrificed to counteract it." In *Dusk of Dawn*, Du Bois candidly admits that the "action of England" toward the darker races has "not involved the guilt of all Britons" (e.g., it has excluded the abolitionists, men like "William Wilberforce and Granville Sharpe"). Still, echoing *Black Reconstruction*, he also writes that "we cannot jump to the opposite and equally fallacious conclusion that there has been no guilt; that the development of the British Empire is a sort of cosmic process with no individual human being at fault." What matters, Du Bois argues, is "the balance of public opinion," so that in the United States, where neither "the philosophy of Jefferson nor the crusade of Garrison nor the reason of Sumner was able to counterbalance the race superiority doctrines of Calhoun, the imperialism of Jefferson Davis, nor the race hate of Bill Tillman," white America, "[a]s a result, . . . has crucified, enslaved, and oppressed the Negro group." When, then, Du Bois writes in general, typifying terms of white souls, or a white world, he means to be attributing "effective social action" to the prevalent psychological tendencies shaping European and American culture.[11] Du Bois's study of white souls attributes racial domination and exploitation to the malicious moral character of white supremacists. He believed that white supremacists may be morally blamed for racial oppression because racial oppression stems, in part, from their morally culpable habits of mind.

THE IDEA OF A GUIDING CONCEPTION

In recent work the philosopher Tamar Schapiro has distinguished between two standpoints from which to study human agency. One, "the scientific standpoint," is that of the natural or social-scientific inquirer who ascribes actions to agents, and of the philosopher who asks why such attributions make sense. It is a "third-person" point of view. The other, "the participant standpoint," is that of the investigator who reflects on an activity in which she is already participating and asks, "what am I doing insofar as I am engaging in this activity?" It is a "first-person" point of view.

To answer the participant question is to say neither what causes an action nor what happens when someone acts, but to articulate an agent's ideal conception of what she is doing. When you ask, "what am I doing insofar as I am engaging in journalism?," for example, you are asking for an ideal conception of journalism. In Schapiro's words, "you are interested in showing yourself how journalism could be the worthwhile undertaking" you take it to be. An ideal conception, she writes, "is a description under which you value the activity in which you are engaged, a description under which you see it as worth undertaking." Importantly, an ideal conception is likewise a "guiding conception," for it is in light of such a conception that a participant in an activity "takes responsibility for doing what she is doing." An ideal conception guides the performance of an activity, for it "sets a standard of the integrity of the activity, with reference to which the participant can judge whether she is engaging in it properly, and whether she is thereby achieving what she is striving to achieve by engaging in it." When, then, a journalist articulates an ideal conception of journalism she is describing her activity in normative terms to which she holds herself accountable.[12]

Schapiro's work is relevant to the present discussion, because Du Bois's moral psychology of white supremacy relies on *both* third- and first-person perspectives. As I have already suggested, his moral psychology is in part intended to contribute to a social-scientific explanation of racial domination and exploitation. In particular, as I show in chapter 3, he means his study of white souls to help causally to account for the persistent suppression of the democratic development of nonwhite peoples. But Du Bois's moral psychology is more complex than a third-person perspective geared to social-scientific explanation can accommodate, for it imputes to the white supremacist an ideal conception—specifically, an ideal conception of Christian ethical life—to which the white supremacist holds herself accountable. Du Bois considers the souls of white folk not only with an eye to identifying the vicious qualities of character that explain malicious individual and collective behavior (e.g., the "action of England"), but also with a view to the conception of Christianity that ethically guides and orients the white supremacist. To put the point a little differently, a signal purpose of Du Bois's moral psychology is an account of the white supremacist's first-person answer to the question "what am I doing insofar as I am living my life as a Christian?" As I argue in chapter 5, Du Bois believes that artistic beauty can help subvert white supremacy because it can challenge the white supremacist to transform her ideal conception of a Christian life.

Throughout *Darkwater*, Du Bois's explores the interplay between modern racial oppression and the emergence of a global political and economic order shaped by Euro-American imperialism and World War I. Du Bois believed that white supremacist habits of mind functioned to secure and stabilize that order against political threats to capitalist economic interests.[13] In addition, he believed that part of understanding why beauty matters to politics is recognizing not only how moral vice can lead to racial oppression, but how an aesthetic appeal to the guiding conceptions embraced by the vicious can undermine it. Accordingly, I divide the remainder of the present chapter into three parts. In the first, I sketch Du Bois's moral psychology in very general terms, and I emphasize his notion of "white Christianity." In the moral character of the white supremacist, he argues, white supremacist habits of mind qualify and delimit the scope of Christian habits of mind. In the second, I turn to Du Bois's portrait of the white supremacist—that is, to his detailed analysis of the ill-will and other qualities of character to which he attributes causal/explanatory significance. In the third part, finally, I revisit Du Bois's discussion of white Christianity in order to examine the "first-person" dimension of his moral psychology of white souls.

WHITE MORAL CHARACTER AND WHITE CHRISTIANITY

The version of "The Souls of White Folk" that appears in *Darkwater* is an amalgam of two previously written essays. One, also titled "The Souls of White Folk," is a short essay that Du Bois published in *The Independent* in August 1910.[14] The other, "Of the Culture of White Folk," he published in *The Journal of Race Development* in April 1917.[15] While the 1920 version of "Souls" incorporated elements of the earlier 1910 version, most notably in its opening several pages and its concluding depiction of a white Prometheus, bound by the fable of white supremacy, the main body of the later essay is drawn from "Of the Culture of White Folk." In what follows, I draw on all three essays, including passages from journal publications that Du Bois excluded from the *Darkwater*.[16]

I begin with Du Bois's claims regarding white religion and white Christianity. Du Bois writes that white religion is an "utter failure."[17] He adds that a "nation's religion is its life and as such white Christianity is a miserable failure."[18] What, however, is white Christianity? As I read Du Bois, he holds that white Christianity is the substance of European and American culture—what he sometimes calls "white culture"[19]—and that it is a syncretic religion, a fusion of Christianity and a white supremacist "new religion of whiteness."[20] In the *Darkwater* version of "Souls," which combines the 1910 essay's analysis of white (American) psyches with the 1917, World War I–era essay's reflections on white (European) culture, Du Bois represents white Christianity and white culture as widespread, socially pervasive manifestations of white folks' moral character. In addition, he represents his moral psychology of white folks' moral character as a diagnosis of the failure of a white Christian culture that, because it unites Europe and America, determines the life not only of one nation, but of many.

White Christianity is a failure, Du Bois believes, because the behavior of white Christian nations and their white citizens so often neglects to express the Christian virtues of unselfishness, charity, and adherence to the golden rule. Du Bois explains this sort of morally deficient behavior by noting that "we have injected into our creed a gospel of human hatred and prejudice, a despising of our less fortunate fellows, not to speak of our reverence for wealth, which flatly contradicts the Christian ideal." In effect, he argues that the amalgamation of the virtues endorsed by Christianity and the vices embraced by the new religion of whiteness (e.g., hatred and prejudice, about which more below) has produced a religion—white Christianity—that sanctions behavior contradicting the Christian ideal. That "there is absolutely no logical method by which the treatment of black folk by white folk . . . can be squared with any reasonable statement or practice of the Christian ideal" Du Bois takes to be obvious. Yet he also knows that few who practice white Christianity regard their behavior as hypocritical, and that a "widely accepted" view "attempts to reconcile Color Caste and Christianity and sees or affects to see no incongruity." Du Bois is genuinely puzzled when he asks, "what ails the religion of a land when its strongholds of orthodoxy are to be found in those regions where race prejudice is most uncompromising, vindictive, and cruel? where human brotherhood is a lie?"[21]

In "The Souls of White Folk" (1920) and throughout *Darkwater*, Du Bois addresses this question. In the case of the person who sees no incongruity, reasoning that faults practice for contradicting principle is not likely to help. Indeed, any such argumentation, or "logical method," will beg the question, precisely because Du Bois's interlocutor will reject a critical premise of the hypocrisy charge—namely, that the moral demands of Christian brotherhood require "the application of the golden rule between White and Black Folk."[22] The issue dividing Du Bois and the Christian white supremacist is not logical so much as metaphysical; it is a question of what Christianity *is*, of what it does and does not require of those who embrace it as a truthful revelation.

A PORTRAIT OF THE WHITE SUPREMACIST

Of the souls of white folk, Du Bois tells us, he is singularly clairvoyant, an epistemic claim he defends by proclaiming that he is "native, not foreign, bone of their thought and flesh of their language." If the "bone" of the souls of white folk is their thought and the "flesh" of those souls is their language, then Du Bois in essence asserts here, echoing Genesis 2:23, that his thought and language are of a piece with theirs. His claim to clairvoyance is justified, he suggests, because he is a cultural insider who has seen through white folks' pretenses—their clutching at "rags of facts and fancies to hide their nakedness"—to observe "undressed . . . the working of their entrails." Du Bois's moral psychology of white supremacy is, in part, a description of those entrails—again, an account of the ill-will and other qualities of character to which he attributes causal significance.

Now, among contemporary moral philosophers it is not unusual to regard moral virtues as character traits that dispose agents, in Peter Barry's words, "to perform certain actions in certain circumstances for certain constitutive reasons with certain constitutive feelings."[23] On this account, "virtues are partly constituted by motivational dispositions but also affective and cognitive ones—say to have certain beliefs about other people and feelings about them."[24] Du Bois, I suggest, has a similar view of the moral vices—thus, of the entrails of white souls. In particular, he takes the moral vice of white supremacy to be constituted by a complex of motivational, cognitive, and affective dispositions.

Consider, for example, Du Bois's description of that vice in the third chapter of *Darkwater*, titled "The Hands of Ethiopia." Due to "a world campaign beginning with the slave-trade and ending with the refusal to capitalize the word 'Negro,' leading through a passionate defense of slavery by attributing every bestiality to blacks, and finally culminating in the evident modern profit which lies in degrading blacks—all this," he remarks, "has unconsciously trained millions of honest modern men into the belief that black folk are sub-human."[25] This belief, he continues,

> is not based on science, else it would be a postulate of the most tentative kind, ready at any time to be withdrawn in the face of facts; the belief is not based on history, for it is absolutely contradicted by Egyptian Greek, Roman, Byzantine and Arabian experience; nor is the belief based on any careful survey of the social development of men of Negro blood to-day in Africa and America. It is simply passionate deep-seated heritage, and as such can be moved by neither argument nor fact. . . . our modern contempt of Negroes rests upon no scientific foundation. . . . It is nothing more than a vicious habit of mind.[26]

For Du Bois, this vicious habit of mind, the evil that is white supremacy, involves affective and cognitive components alike—both contempt for blacks and the belief that blacks are subhuman.[27] Specifically, he suggests that the habits of despising blacks and taking them to be subhuman are inherited qualities of character: entrenched ("deep seated") and strongly felt ("passionate") dispositions acquired through a long, relentless drilling of white souls that began with the slave trade, and that has been perpetuated through antiblack defenses of slavery and the profitable degradation of black life.[28] In Du Bois's view, the modern "discovery" of personal whiteness—what he somewhat sarcastically describes as a "sudden, emotional conversion," the world's awakening to see and feel itself as "white and by that token, wonderful"[29]—is in fact the result of an historically extended process of subject formation, a story of the progressive de-formation of the moral character of white folk. Individual white subjects have come habitually to disdain blacks and to regard them as subhuman, even as they have come to affirm and to take delight in their own superiority, not because science and historical inquiry support their views—in fact, they speak against them—but because the *long durée* of modern slavery, its ideological justifications, and the ongoing abasement of black life have trained their psyches, endowing them with a distinctively modern mode of moral viciousness that is impervious to argument and to the evidence that speaks against it.[30]

In the *Darkwater* version of "The Souls of White Folk," Du Bois's synthesis of the 1910 and 1917 essays paints a complex portrait of the white supremacist's cognitive, affective, and motivational dispositions.[31] With respect to his cognitive traits, Du Bois claims that the white supremacist is disposed to believe not simply (1) that blacks are subhuman, but (2) that whites have the exclusive right to possess, enjoy, and dispose of the earth in perpetuity ("that whiteness is ownership of the earth forever and ever, Amen!"),[32] and (3) that whites' right of ownership is, to borrow Jeremy Waldron's term, a "responsibility-right"[33]—in essence, a right that carries with it certain obligations, including the philanthropic duty to advance the welfare of the world's dark, "ignoble" races and the colonial duty "to divide up the darker world and administer it for Europe's good."[34] Picturing himself as a triumphant, "world-mastering" demigod, the white supremacist proudly endorses these beliefs with "disconcerting seriousness."[35]

With respect to the white supremacist's affective dispositions, the 1920 "Souls" several times mentions the white supremacist's contempt for nonwhites, repeatedly emphasizing his tendency to despise them, but saves its most vivid treatment of white supremacist affect for its depiction of hatred:

> the descent into hell is easy. On the pale, white faces which the great billows whirl upward to my tower I see again and again . . . a writing of human hatred, a deep and passionate hatred, vast by the very vagueness of its expressions. Down through the green waters, on the bottom of the world, where men move to and fro, I have seen a man—an educated gentleman—grow livid with anger because a little, silent, black woman was sitting by herself in a Pullman car. He was a white man. I have seen a great, grown man curse a little child, who had wandered into the wrong waiting room, searching for its mother: "Here, you damned black—" He was white. In Central Park I have seen the upper lip of a quiet, peaceful man curl back in a tigerish snarl of rage because black folk rode by in a motor car. He was a white man. We have seen, you and I, city after city drunk with ungovernable lust of blood; mad with murder, destroying, killing, and cursing; torturing human victims because somebody accused of crime happened to be the same color as the mob's innocent victim and because that color was not white! We have seen . . . what have we not seen, right here in

America, of orgy, cruelty, barbarism, and murder done to men and women of Negro descent.

Up through the foam of green and weltering waters wells this great mass of hatred, in wilder, fiercer violence, until I look down and know that today that to the millions of my people no misfortune could happen,—of death and pestilence, failure and defeat—that would not make the hearts of millions of their fellow beat with fierce, vindictive joy.[36]

In Du Bois's view, white supremacist hatred is a feeling attended by other character traits that the white supremacist tends to express when he acts—as when one hateful man shows disdain for a child he curses, and as when another expresses his belief that it is the prerogative of whites, the owners of the Earth, to remind blacks where they may sit. And that feeling, like antiblack contempt and the belief in black subhumanity, appears to be an entrenched ("deep") and strongly felt ("passionate") quality of character that is impervious to argument and evidence. But white supremacist hatred is not simply a feeling, Du Bois suggests, not simply an affective tendency, for it is also a propensity to act from a particular motive: specifically, it is a motivational disposition to act from ill-will. For Du Bois, white supremacist hatred is at once a feeling of intense dislike for blacks *and* a tendency to act from ill-will toward them. In his description of his descent into hell, he artfully characterizes white supremacist ill-will as a desire to injure and do violence to black life.[37]

Consider, again, Du Bois's examples: the appearance of a black woman, out of place in a car reserved for whites, prompts the white supremacist to react furiously; the sight of a black child, wandering into a waiting room similarly reserved for whites, fills him with animosity; and the picture of Negroes riding in car—an activity not formally reserved for whites, but surely not meant for blacks—incites him to rage. Du Bois has seen white men manifest their hostility toward blacks for failing to comply with the requirements of racial subordination. But at the bottom of the world, at the bottom of the hell into which he has descended, he has also discovered that the driving force behind white men's displeasure with rule-breaking blacks is a desire to do them harm. Cursing and growling aggressively at black life is continuous with destroying and killing it. The disposition to act out of a desire to injure and do violence to black life, Du Bois implies, is no less evident in a segregated waiting room or along the way in Central Park than it is when white mobs cruelly torture "human victims." In its more "benign" expressions, white supremacist malevolence motivates livid looks, imprecations, and snarls; but in its "wilder, fiercer" forms, it leads to murderous violence and to whites gleefully celebrating black misfortune.

Du Bois's depiction of the white supremacist's moral character is nuanced and complicated. The white supremacist's tendency to act from anti-black malevolence, whether his ill-will finds expression in nasty displays of hostility or explicit acts of murder, is an essential feature of the portrait. Certain cognitive and affective tendencies are equally essential, however, for when the white supremacist acts malevolently he is (1) assuming the truth of a wide range of firmly held beliefs (that blacks are subhuman, that whiteness is ownership of the Earth, and so forth) that he regards as authorizing his actions, and (2) expressing a wide range of intensely felt affects (contempt, hatred, and so forth) that lend emotional texture to his actions. In Du Bois's view, a combination of interrelated motivational, cognitive, and affective dispositions—including but not limited to ill-will directed against blacks—comprises the white supremacist's morally vicious character, a formation of habits and character traits that is implicated whenever the white supremacist mistreats black people.

WHITE CHRISTIANITY IN THE PERSPECTIVE OF THE FIRST PERSON

Let me return now to Du Bois's analysis of white Christianity. Du Bois's white supremacist is a white Christian in whose moral character the virtues of charity and unselfishness sit amicably, side by side, with the dispositions to hate blacks and to consider them to be subhuman. In the eyes of the white Christian, white supremacist vice is in fact no vice at all, but itself an expression of virtue consonant with Christian moral virtue and endorsed by the new religion of whiteness. Du Bois describes the souls of black folk as divided by "two unreconciled strivings," but in the souls of white folk there is no want of reconciliation between striving to be a good Christian and striving to injure and do violence to black life; there is no conflict between "warring ideals."[38] In other words, Du Bois's Christian white supremacist is not ambivalently torn between living as a Christian and living as a white supremacist, for enacting Christianity, as he understands it, is a matter of demonstrating the demands of Christian virtue in his transactions with whites, while ignoring them in his transactions with blacks. For the Christian white supremacist, the Christian ideal is, in essence, the Christian white supremacist ideal of endorsing the golden rule in one's dealings with other whites while disavowing the golden rule in one's dealings with blacks.[39]

The soul of the Christian white supremacist is not in the least at odds with itself. Herman Melville makes a similar and relevantly illuminating point about the soul of the Indian-hater, whose "instinct of antipathy against an Indian grows ... with the sense of good and bad, right and wrong." In "one breath," Melville tells us, the Indian-hating backwoodsman "learns that a brother is to be loved, and an Indian to be hated."[40] Melville's point, here, is that the backwoodsman's love and hate fit seamlessly together. Each limits and restricts the other, but without contradiction, for to hate where love is required would be no less absurd than to love where hate is required. It would make no more sense to the Indian-hater to hate his brother, or other whites, than it would make to the Christian white supremacist to treat whites as he treats blacks. And it would make no more sense to the Christian white supremacist to behave charitably toward blacks than it would make to the Indian-hater to treat an Indian as a brother. For Melville there is no dissonance in the soul of the Indiahater, and for Du Bois there is no dissonance in the soul of the Christian white supremacist.

Du Bois's treatment of Christian white supremacy is compelling, but it may be objected that it oversimplifies a rather complex racial formation. Afterall, not all white Christians are white supremacists, and white supremacy itself has historically degraded whites as well as blacks. As the historian Matthew Frye Jacobson has observed, in a discussion of American Anglo-Saxonism, the trajectory of American racial thought from the mid-nineteenth century to the early twentieth century "represents a shift from one brand of bedrock racism to another—from the unquestionable hegemony of a unified race of 'white persons' to a contest over 'political fitness' among a now fragmented, hierarchically arranged series of distinct 'white races.'"[41] Regarding the first objection, Du Bois could again reply that what matters is the balance of public opinion, and so acknowledge that the action of Christianity toward the darker races no more involves the guilt of all Christians than the action of England toward them involves the guilt of all Britons. Regarding the second, he would have admitted that corresponding to the world's darker races are different lighter, whiter races, but he also would have argued that distinct and hierarchically ranked white peoples, including Anglo-Saxons, southern Europeans, and so on, notwithstanding the hostilities among them, all too often find common ground in their antipathy to blacker, darker races.[42] But more than that, I surmise that Du Bois would have emphasized his particular interest in the white supremacist, religious consciousness animating what Jacobson himself describes as the Jim Crow South's "unforgiving, *binary* caste system of white-over-black."[43] Again, recall Du Bois's sincere puzzlement when he asks, "what ails the religion of a land when its strongholds of orthodoxy are to be found in those regions where race prejudice is most uncompromising, vindictive, and cruel? where human brotherhood is a lie?" In a study titled "Feast of Blood," the sociologist Orlando Patterson reminds us that Jim Crow "rose to power on, was suffused with, and had as the very center of its doctrine not just the permanent segregation and subjugation of Afro-Americans but their demonization, terrorization, and humiliation." "The central ritual of this version of the Southern civil religion," he writes, "was the human sacrifice of the lynch mob."[44] Patterson quotes one Southern clergyman, a Protestant minister, as forthrightly and unabashedly pronouncing his commitment to the religion of the lynch mob: "I joined the Knights of the Ku Klux Klan," the clergyman proclaims," because I believed in Jesus Christ and his church; I believed in a militant Christianity; I believed in the Cross—a symbol of service and sacrifice for the right. If there is not enough in that to challenge a real red-blooded, virile minister to a sense of duty, he has lost his vision."[45] In "A Litany of Atlanta" (1906), which Du Bois initially wrote in the wake of the Atlanta race riots and republished as part of the first chapter of *Darkwater*, he expresses his anguish at the thought of just this sort of murderous, mob-endorsing Southern religious consciousness when he desperately intones, "Lord God, deaf to our prayer and dumb to our dumb suffering. Surely Thou, too are not white, O Lord, a pale, bloodless, heartless thing! *Ah! Christ of all the Pities!* Forgive the thought! Forgive these wild, blasphemous words. . . . But whisper—speak—call, great God, for Thy silence is white terror to our hearts!"[46]

Because Christianity as the white Christian understands it disavows the applicability of moral considerations to the treatment of blacks, a putatively internal critique of his behavior, an attempt to alter his actions by showing that *his* understanding of Christian principle contradicts them, cannot but fail to unsettle his white supremacist commitments.[47] And because these commitments—his white supremacist beliefs, feelings, and motivational dispositions—are so deeply ingrained in him, so fundamentally entrenched and intensely felt that he attributes to them an unimpeachable authority that is recalcitrant to the results of scientific inquiry, any attempt to alter his behavior by invoking such results must likewise fail. If white supremacist commitments are immune to rational revision through internal critique and scientific inquiry alike, how, then, can they be dislodged?

Here, I have posed Du Bois's question as what philosophers sometimes call a "how possibly" question. How is it possible that such-and-such is the case, they ask, *given (or supposing)* a set of considerations that *appear to exclude*—that is, to rule out—the possibility that such-and-such is the case. For example, and famously, we may ask "how is it possible to know anything given that it is logically possible that we are dreaming?"—one way to interpret the question Descartes poses in his *First Meditation*. Or, to take another example, how is it possible for us to have free will, given that all acts are causally determined?—a question Kant engages by distinguishing between noumena and phenomena. Philosophers of various stripes —Descartes and Kant, but also Nietzsche, Foucault, and others—tend to answer "how possibly" questions by attempting to show how it is possible for such-and-such to be the case, notwithstanding the considerations that appear to rule out that possibility. The "how possibly" question Du Bois poses—how is it possible to unsettle white supremacist beliefs, feelings, and motivational dispositions, given that their immunity to rational revision through internal critique and scientific inquiry seems to rule out that possibility?—he answers by attempting to show that the white supremacist's insusceptibility to the results of rational inquiry notwithstanding, he is vulnerable to an appeal to his normative conception, his guiding conception, of what it is properly to live his life as a Christian.[48]

Consider in this connection Patterson's Southern clergyman. His Christianity, it seems, is the source of his sense of duty. His conception of what Christianity is, of what it requires of him, led him to join the Ku Klux Klan, which suggests not only that he takes lynching to be compatible with his guiding conception of what it is to be a Christian, but that he regards anti-black racial violence as *expressing* that conception. Now Du Bois himself, we know, is committed to an idea of Christianity that aligns it, not with mob, but with democracy and the ethos of the (dispositional) crowd. "The number of white individuals who are practicing with even reasonable approximation the democracy and unselfishness of Jesus Christ," he writes, "is so small and unimportant as to be fit subject for jest in Sunday supplements and in *Punch, Le Rire,* and *Fliegende Blätter.*"[49] For Du Bois, then, the point of an appeal to Christian white supremacists like Patterson's Southern clergyman is to persuade them to embrace an alternative, guiding conception of the moral demands of a Christian life that, because it expresses the democracy and unselfishness of Jesus Christ, calls them to repudiate their racist character traits. Du Bois argues that artistic beauty can be persuasive in just this way, for it can serve as the vehicle of a call to moral self-reflection. Such a call, such an appeal, can be effective, Du Bois will suggest, if it conveys a moral authority that the addressee of the appeal acknowledges. On this view, artistic beauty can function as a medium of second-person, dialogic address that holds the addressee—here, the Christian white supremacist—accountable for the conception of her conduct in light of which she or he takes responsibility for it.

I conclude my account of Du Bois's analysis of first-personal white Christianity by highlighting its perhaps startling relevance to contemporary debates. More to the point, I propose that evaluating

Du Bois's analysis in the perspective of recent discussions of the "religious right" lets us see not only the pertinence of his voice to contemporary conversations, but how these conversations could benefit from his treatment of their central themes. Here, in particular, I consider the relevance of Du Bois's analysis to the critique of a form of contemporary Christianity that scholars describe variously—as, e.g., "white Christian nationalism" or "white evangelicalism"—that is, as a form of antidemocratic, exclusionary Christianity that is historically continuous with the Jim Crow–era Christianity that, I have suggested, especially interested Du Bois.[50] This is a Christianity for which America is blessed by God, that imagines Jesus in the virile image of John Wayne, and for which "un-American" influences threaten the nation from within and without.[51]

Consider, in this connection, Philip S. Gorski and Samuel L. Perry's *The Flag and the Cross* (2022), a sociological study that strongly echoes Du Bois in its analysis of white Christian nationalism and the threat it presents to American democracy.[52] Recalling Du Bois's account of white Christianity, for example, Gorski and Perry argue that white Christian nationalism is a syncretic social formation that ties "whiteness" to "Christian nationalism" through the "conflation" of "white" and "Christian" social identities to form "a single identity—'white-Christian.'"[53] Adducing the relevant sociological evidence for these claims, they emphasize that, for white Americans, "indicators of Christian nationalism . . . are powerful predictors of ultra-conservatism, especially on any issues involving race, discrimination, xenophobia, or justice."[54] Gorski and Perry likewise echo Du Bois when they show that white Christian nationalists disavow the applicability of important moral considerations to blacks and other nonwhites, sometimes regarding these "others" as "zombies" and "rodents" who are "unworthy of help," who have no claim on their empathy, and to whom a philosophy of "unequal rights" applies:

"rights for me, not for thee."[55] When, however, they address themselves to white Christian nationalists, to answer the question "what can be done?," they insist that "conservative white Christians might start by confronting their own history," emphasizing that "Reckoning with white Christian nationalism means more than 'looking into one's heart'; it also means reckoning with your tribe's history. It means confronting, not just your own sins, but also 'the sins of the fathers.'"[56] Here, in other words, Gorski and Perry invoke the language of sin to chastise the Christian white nationalist, and so imply that the problem for which they seek a solution ("What can be done?) is a hypocritical conflict between the white Christian nationalist's beliefs—specifically, her ideal conception of Christian conduct—and her and her fathers' sinful behavior, their racism and ultraconservatism. Having read Du Bois, however, it is difficult to suppose that this question-begging response to white Christian nationalists can do justice to the challenge that their conception of properly Christian conduct presents.

What arguably is at issue for many white Christian nationalists, as for Du Bois's white Christians, is, again, the metaphysical question of what Christianity is, of what it requires of those who embrace it. In *Christianity's American Fate* (2022), the historian David Hollinger, in keeping with this insight, writes that "What matters about religion for the health of democracy is not belief in God but what believers say God authorizes them to do."[57] And he could well have added: what they say God permits, what they say God counts as sin, and what they say God expects of us. For Hollinger, the evangelicalism animating white Christian nationalism has "created a safe harbor for white people who wanted to be counted as Christians without having to accept what ecumenical leaders said were the social obligations demanded by the gospel, especially the imperative to extend civil equality to nonwhites."[58] But these white people should not be left to themselves where they have dropped anchor, he argues; rather they should be brought into the storm of public, political debate through public "critical engagement" with their religious ideas.[59] Faced with what Kristen Kobes Du Mez, also an historian, calls "contradictory understandings of the Christian faith,"[60] Hollinger, like Du Bois, believes that contesting antiblack and other exclusionary conceptions of the moral requirements of Christian faith is critical to the defense of democracy.[61] For Du Bois, artistic beauty has a role to play in this defense, a claim that, again, I will substantiate in chapter 5.

In chapter 1, I offered a general account of Du Bois's conception of democracy, and of the role that aesthetic education can play in advancing the ends of democracy. Where the antidemocratic, white Christian culture of the mob tends to prevail, I argued, white citizens lack the receptivity of the crowd, which is why that culture "chokes back" the unfamiliar points of view of the black citizens whose insights must figure in the determination of just laws. To acquire the crowd's receptivity to strangers, I added, white supremacist Christians had to come to regard those insights as stemming from what, following Martha Nussbaum, I called their "circle of concern"—or, in other words, as deriving from voices and lives that morally mattered to them. But black lives and voices don't matter to the white supremacist Christian, not because she or he is an atheist, or an adherent to some non-Christian religious faith, but because her Christian ethical ideal is to endorse the golden rule in her dealings with other whites while repudiating it in her dealings with blacks. In a case such as this, the function of aesthetic education, through the medium of artistic beauty, is radically to transform the Christian white supremacist's self-understanding by disclosing to her that her circle of concern should include black lives and voices. I have characterized that function more precisely in the present chapter, proposing that it is to advance an alternative conception of the moral character of a genuinely Christian life—a conception that requires of the white Christian that she recognize and reject as evil the beliefs, feelings, and ill-will that have prompted her to exclude black lives and voices from her circle of concern to begin with, and that help causally to explain the suppression of the democratic development of the world's darker peoples.

3

DEMOCRATIC DESPOTISM

One reason beauty matters to the political struggle against racial oppression, Du Bois believed, is that the moral character of the white supremacist mattered to the perpetuation of racial oppression. But *how*, exactly, did the white supremacist's moral viciousness matter in this way? In chapter 2, I elaborated Du Bois's moral psychology of white supremacy, which includes a general profile of white folks' morally deplorable habits of mind. In the present chapter, I elucidate the causal/explanatory significance he attributes to these habits of mind. More exactly, I show that, for Du Bois, the moral character of the white supremacist mattered to the perpetuation of racial oppression because it helped causally to explain the domination and exploitation of the world's darker peoples. In showing how Du Bois's causal explanations work, I shall again emphasize aspects of his argument with affinities to Max Weber's social thought—here, and in particular, to Weber's emphasis on the importance of "world views" to social-scientific causal analysis. In specifying the content of these explanations, I shall also emphasize their affinities to and differences from J. A. Hobson's and some then-current Marxist theories of imperialism, including the role that the notion of a "labor aristocracy" plays in these explanations. Methodologically Weberian in some respects, but also intent on demonstrating the role of capitalist economic interests in explaining racial oppression abroad and at home, Du Bois presents a distinctive account of the ongoing, causal efficacy of white Christian culture in inhibiting the democratic development of the world's darker peoples. In the first part of the chapter I focus on Du Bois's explanation of European imperialism. In the second, I connect the theoretical outlook which frames that explanation to his analysis of racial subordination in the United States.

DU BOIS, HOBSON, AND THE NEW IMPERIALISM

Quoting Pliny the Elder's pronouncement that out of Africa there is always something new—"Semper novi quid ex Africa"—Du Bois opens "The African Roots of War" by remarking that "the Roman proconsul . . . voiced the verdict of forty centuries." Published in the May 1915 issue of *Atlantic Monthly*, Du Bois's essay makes the case that the cause of the then-ongoing world war was to be sought in Africa—and, indeed, in the advent of something *new* in Africa. While Pliny's proclamation has been historically verified through any number of events, including, the essay argues, the first welding of iron and the emergence of Christianity as a world religion, Du Bois's interest is the comparatively recent event of Europe's colonial expansion into Africa, a "prime cause" of the world war and a world-historical catastrophe of "lying treaties, rivers of rum, murder, assassination, mutilation, rape, and torture [which] have marked the progress of Englishman, German, Frenchman, and Belgian on the dark continent." Like J. A. Hobson, with whom he attended the "First Universal Races Congress," held at the University of London in 1911, Du Bois described this catastrophe as "the new imperialism."[1]

Nine years earlier, in his book on the new imperialism, Hobson had argued that "the novelty of recent Imperialism regarded as a policy consists chiefly in its adoption by several nations." Hobson's epitome of the "root idea of empire," of the "conception of a *single empire* wielding political authority over the civilized world," was the hegemony that Rome exercised over the entire "recognized world . . . under the so-called pax Romana." With the fall of Rome, he tells us, this conception "did not disappear," but survived in the ambitions of Charlemagne, Rudolph of Hapsburg, and Charles V, as well as in "the policy of Peter the Great, Catherine, and Napoleon." In contrast to the initially Roman idea of empire, Hobson's "essentially modern" notion is exemplified by the competitive "scramble" of several European nations (Belgium, Britain, France, Germany) politically to absorb "tropical or sub-tropical lands in which white men will not settle with their families." The "new imperialism," Hobson writes, is "driven more and more into the annexation and administration of tropical countries."[2]

With his opening reference to Pliny, who, during the early years of the Roman Empire, seems to have spent part of his career as a procurator in Africa, Du Bois tacitly echoes Hobson in contrasting an older, Roman imperialism to "the new Imperialism": that is, to the efforts of England, France, Germany, and Portugal, in the aftermath of the Franco-Prussian War, to seek "power and dominion away from Europe." The upshot of these efforts, of the "scramble for Africa," he argues, is that "a continent where Europe claimed but a tenth of the land in 1875, was in twenty-five more years practically absorbed." Du Bois reminds us that the scramble for Africa began with Stanley's explorations of Central Africa and King Leopold's establishment of the Congo Free State, whose murder, mutilation, and robbery of black Africans "differed only in degree and concentration from the tale of all Africa in this rape of a continent already furiously mangled by the slave trade." But while Stanley's explorations were "the occasion" of European nations seeking dominion away from Europe, "the cause lay deeper." "Why was this?," Du Bois asks, "What was the new call for dominion?"[3]

The new imperialism caused the war, Du Bois will argue, but what caused the new imperialism? In what follows, I argue that Du Bois's answers to these questions, his accounting for the new imperialism, involves two components. The first is his explanation of the impetus to European imperial expansion, of the new call for dominion, per se. The second is his explanation of Europe's realization of this impulse through its amoral, antidemocratic expansion into territories occupied by black and other darker peoples notwithstanding the modern democratic movement's success in promoting moral norms that had otherwise been effective in taming capitalist self-interest. Conceptually, we can think of the distinction between these components of Du Bois's accounting for the new imperialism in terms that Max Weber famously invokes, arguing that "material and ideal interests, not ideas, directly dominate the actions of human beings. But the 'world views' created by 'ideas' have often served as switches, setting the tracks along which the dynamics of interest moved the actions forward."[4] For Weber, the valid attribution of causal significance to a particular world view relied on counterfactual reasoning to show how that world view, through its embodiment in our practices, had made a difference to the determination of the actual course of events through which material or ideal interests had been realized; or, to put the point otherwise, *to establish that the direction of historical development would have diverged from the actual course of events had that world view not acquired efficacy.*[5] Now, Du Bois explains the impulse to European expansion per se in terms of material economic interests. But the targeting of black Africa and other areas inhabited by darker peoples for imperial expansion he explains in terms of the beliefs and affects constituting the moral character of the Christian white supremacist—her "world view."

Absent the historical efficacy of Christian white supremacy, Du Bois argues, Europe would not have expanded into Africa, or, if it did, its expansion would not have been at the expense of the democratic development of the world's darker peoples. In terms of Weber's "train switches" metaphor, he proposes that Christian white supremacy was the "switch" that accounts for Europe's anti-democratic, imperialist involvement in Africa, for, absent the cultural practice of Christian white supremacy, that involvement, had it still occurred, would not have been a moral disaster.[6] More precisely, and as we shall see, he argues that the "switch" of Christian white supremacy functioned as a "switch off" as well as a "switch on"—that it served not only to trigger violence against black Africans, but effectively to rule out the application of the moral norms the modern democratic movement had advanced to curb the domination and exploitation of white workers to white Europeans' treatment of black Africans.

"It is admitted by all business men," Hobson writes, "that the growth of the powers of production in their country exceeds the grown in consumption, that more goods can be produced than can be sold at a profit, and that more capital exists than can find remunerative investment." It is "this economic condition of affairs," he adds, "that forms the taproot of Imperialism." Owing to deficient demand—to underconsumption—among Europe's domestic working classes, capitalists and financiers have a material, economic interest in opening up new markets for goods that can be sold at a profit. In each of several nations, these potential beneficiaries of investment abroad press the nation, the state, to annex foreign territory for the purpose of satisfying that interest. When this pressure succeeds, when, more exactly, the capitalists and financiers "secure the active co-operation of statesmen and political cliques," persuading them to confound class-specific economic interests with the nation's interests, the upshot is the nation's acquiescence to imperialist foreign policies and a consequent "fight" among European nations "for foreign markets or foreign areas of investment." This dynamic could be halted, Hobson proposes, were each nation to follow the lead of the trade unionists and the socialists by redistributing income to the working class, or to public expenditure, thus raising "the general standard of home consumption" and abating "the pressure for foreign markets."[7]

Like Hobson, Du Bois conceptualizes the nation as an agent of material, economic interests. On three critical points, however, Du Bois breaks with Hobson. The first is Du Bois's rejection of Hobson's explanation of the genesis of the new imperialism. The second is his rejection of Hobson's analysis of the relationship between nations' interests and the material interests that drive the new imperialism. For example, Du Bois denies that European imperialism is driven by a false identification of the interests of the nation with the interests of capitalists and financiers. The third is Du Bois's rejection of Hobson's view of the sort of remedy the dynamic of the new imperialism requires. In Du Bois's argument these three points belong together, for each of them stems from his effort in "The African Roots of War" clearly to formulate "the theory" of the "new democratic despotism."[8]

Du Bois presents his formulation of that theory as the solution to a philosophical paradox. "Most philosophers," he writes, "see the ship of state launched on the broad, irresistible tide of democracy, with only delaying eddies here and there." "Others," however, "looking closer, are more disturbed. Are we, they ask, reverting to aristocracy and despotism—the rule of might?" The paradox is not simply conceptual, but readily observable in the world, for it has "reconciled the Imperialists and captains of industry to any amount of 'Democracy,'" while allowing "in America the most rapid advance of democracy to go hand in hand ... with increased aristocracy and hatred toward darker races." Du Bois's solution is straightforward: "The paradox is easily explained," he writes, "the white workingman has been asked to share the spoil of exploiting 'chinks and niggers.'"[9]

As we have seen, Du Bois conceptualizes democratic political movements as "efforts to increase the number of beneficiaries of the ruling [of men]."[10] In "The African Roots of War," he argues in a related vein that from the eighteenth through the twentieth centuries the advance of European democratic movements has led to an *increase* in the numbers of those who benefit from government, with the "dipping of more and grimier hands into the wealth bag of the nation, until to-day only the ultra stubborn fail to see that democracy in determining income is the next inevitable step to Democracy in political power."[11] Economic democracy is an ideal that Du Bois explicitly endorses, but the intra-European tendency toward the realization of that ideal has, in practice, nationalized and radically altered the structure of exploitation: it is no longer the "merchant prince" or the "aristocratic monopoly" or simply "the employing class" that dominates and exploits the world in order to reap "dividends," but "the nation; a *new democratic nation* composed of united capital and labor."[12] For Du Bois, the paradox of modern democracy is explained by the circumstance that democratic progress within Europe and America for white laborers has entailed the despotic exploitation in America and elsewhere of "chinks' and 'niggers.'" "The present world war," he maintains, is "the result of jealousies engendered by the recent rise of armed national associations of labor and capital whose aim is the exploitation of the wealth of the world mainly outside the European circle of nations."[13]

According to the theory of democratic despotism, material interests in the accumulation of profits through foreign investment gave rise to the new imperialism and explain the impetus to European expansion. Against Hobson, however, Du Bois's theory claims that European nations have become the agents of imperialist economic interests not because underconsumption has led capitalists and financiers to secure the assistance of statesmen and other political allies to advance them, but because the democratic gains of white workers have eliminated the possibility of extracting inordinate profit through the exploitation of those workers. Against Hobson, Du Bois also argues that the material interests sustaining the new imperialism are the true interests of the new democratic nations, each constituted through a unification of capital and labor, not the interests of capitalists and financiers that have been mistaken for these nations' true interests. And against Hobson, finally, Du Bois implies that a downward redistribution of income from white capitalists to white workers cannot possibly remedy the new imperialism, for precisely that sort of democratic redistribution has led to the emergence of democratic despotism and the new imperialism in the first place.[14]

I turn now to a more detailed analysis of Du Bois's explanation of Europe's expansion into Africa and elsewhere in terms of white supremacist beliefs, feelings, and motivational dispositions. Consider first a paragraph from "The African Roots of War," which focuses on beliefs:

> Whence comes this new wealth and on what does its accumulation depend? It comes primarily from the darker nations of the world—Asia and Africa, South and Central America, the West Indies and the islands of the South Seas. There are still, we may well believe, many parts of white countries like Russia and North America, not to mention Europe itself, where the older exploitation still holds. But the knell has sounded faint and far, even there. In the lands of darker folk, however, no knell has sounded. Chinese, East Indians, Negroes, and South American Indians are by common consent for governance by white folk and economic subjection to them. To the furtherance of this highly profitable economic dictum has been brought every

available resource of science and religion. Thus arises the astonishing doctrine of the natural inferiority of most men to the few, and the interpretation of "Christian brotherhood" as meaning anything that one of the "brothers" may at any time want it to mean.[15]

The new imperialism generated stupendous wealth from the darker nations (the answer to the "Whence . . ." question), but, Du Bois suggests, the targeting of those nations for the extraction of wealth depended on beliefs about the world's darker peoples (the answer to the "on what . . ." question). As the older exploitation (of the merchant prince, aristocratic monopoly, and so on) waned in Europe, the knell tolling its demise likewise sounded in other, predominately white areas of the globe—like Russia and North America. But in the land of the "darker folk"—of the Chinese, East Indians, Negroes, and South American Indian—no such knell was even softly heard; indeed, it is precisely the exploitation of the nonwhite peoples inhabiting these lands that generated stupendous wealth for the European metropoles. Why, then, did the knell that otherwise tolled faint and far sound *not at all* in these lands? Du Bois's rejoinder is that the new democratic nations have given their common consent to the profit-yielding dictum that nonwhite peoples are *for* governance by white folk and *for* economic subjection to them. New democratic nations targeted nonwhite peoples for exploitation, while slowly ceasing to exploit their white inhabitants, because the citizens of these nations held that their core, white supremacist beliefs—that nonwhites may be directed and used as whites are pleased to direct and use them; that they are naturally inferior to whites; and that they need not be regarded as the virtue of Christian brotherhood would dictate[16]—entailed that the moral considerations that had gradually persuaded them to repudiate the "rule of might," to curtail their exploitation of one another, and more and more to embrace the egalitarian demands of the modern democratic movement simply *did not apply to the treatment of nonwhites*. Again, Du Bois's reasoning is counterfactual: causal significance can be attributed to the new democratic citizens' core, white supremacist beliefs, he suggests, for absent those beliefs, and thus absent the limitation of valid moral judgments to the treatment of whites, the knell would likewise have sounded in the lands of darker folk, thus precluding Europe's realization of its material economic interests though an amoral, antidemocratic expansion into these lands.[17]

The larger story Du Bois tells is complex. As we have seen, he believed that the demise of Reconstruction and the advent of the scramble for Africa engendered a mode of global governance featuring the democratic development of the white working class and the suppression of the democratic development of the world's darker races. In *The Negro* (1915), published the same year as the "The African Roots of War," Du Bois elaborates this thesis in terms that resonate with his analysis of democratic despotism. "The middle of the nineteenth century saw the beginning of the rise of the modern [white] working class," he observes, for by means of "political power the laborers slowly but surely began to demand a larger share in the profiting industry." It was "natural to assume" that the "uplift" of emancipated "dark workers" would follow the same path, he adds, but the "new colonial theory" shaping the "new" colonialism "transferred the reign of commercial privilege and extraordinary profit from the exploitation of the European working class to the exploitation of backward races under the political domination of Europe."[18] In "Of the Culture of White Folk," published just two years later, Du Bois not only elaborates his understanding of modern global governance, but explicitly recurs to his earlier suggestion that white supremacist beliefs help causally to explain it:

> It is plain to modern white civilization that the subjection of the white working classes cannot much longer be maintained. Education,

political power, and increased knowledge of the technique and meaning of the industrial process are destined to make a more and more equitable distribution of wealth in the near future. The day of the very rich is drawing to a close, so far as individual white nations are concerned. But there is a loophole. There is a chance for exploitation on an immense scale for inordinate profit, not simply to the very rich, but to the middle class and to the laborers. This chance lies in the exploitation of darker peoples. It is here that the golden hand beckons. Here are no labor unions or votes or questioning onlookers or inconvenient consciences. These men may be used down to the very bone, and shot and maimed in "punitive" expeditions when they revolt. In these dark lands "industrial development" may repeat in exaggerated form every horror of the industrial history of Europe, from slavery and rape to disease and maiming, with only one test of success,—dividends!

This theory of human culture and its aims has worked itself through warp and woof of our daily thought with a thoroughness that few realize. Everything great, good, efficient, fair, and honorable is "white"; everything mean, bad, blundering, cheating, and dishonorable is "yellow"; a bad taste is "brown"; and the devil is "black." The changes of this theme are continually rung in picture and story, in newspaper heading and moving-picture, in sermon and school book, until, of course, the King can do no wrong,—a White Man is always right and a Black Man has no rights which a white man is bound to respect.[19]

As the white working class inevitably advances, through political power, but also through education and so on, and as it wins an increasingly equitable distribution of wealth—as it dips its ever "grimier" hands into the wealth bags of the nations, in the words of "The African Roots of War"—European capitalists' interest in accumulating "extraordinary," now "inordinate" profit through the exploitation of the European white working class ceases to be viable. But there is "loophole," the essence of which was expressed in Judge

Taney's remark, in the Dred Scott decision, that "a Black man has no rights which a white man is bound to respect." On Du Bois's account, white culture, in all its varied, quotidian manifestations (school books, newspapers, moving pictures, etc.), denies that the moral considerations that animated and won wide acceptance through the modern democratic movement—that supported white workers' rights to organize and to vote and, more generally, that supported the protection of white workers from the murderous exploitation required to extract inordinate profit—bear on whites' actions regarding blacks. Put differently, he maintains that white culture places all such actions beyond the pale of moral scrutiny—for, again, blacks have no rights that whites must respect. Echoing "The African Roots of War," Du Bois further suggests that by so limiting the scope of legitimate moral judgment, white culture's loophole allows for levels of exploitation that would not have obtained had blacks enjoyed moral standing in the eyes of whites. But because blacks enjoyed no moral standing, because whites regarded blacks as right-less subjects to be directed and used as white whim dictated, European capitalists looked to black Africans and other darker peoples to realize their material interests in inordinate profits with a vengeance. White workers benefited from European imperialism, for in addition to winning larger and larger shares of the profits that European capitalists extracted from their labor, they were "practically invited to share in this new exploitation," and "flattered by popular appeals to their inherent superiority to 'Dagoes,' 'Chinks,' 'Japs,' and 'Niggers.'"[20] Accepting the "invitation," white labor entered into alliance with white capital, thus forging and strengthening the armed, national associations of labor and capital that sustained the new imperialism.[21]

I conclude my analysis of Du Bois's explanation of Europe's expansion into Africa and elsewhere by considering two paragraphs, versions of which appear both in "Of the Culture of White Folk" and the *Darkwater* version of "The Souls of White Folk." Like "The African Roots of War," the first focuses on the Christian white supremacists' cognitive commitments. The second focuses on his feelings and motivational dispositions:

> With the dog-in-the-manger theory of trade, with the determination to reap inordinate profits and to exploit the weakest to the utmost there came a new imperialism,—the rage for one's own nation to own the earth or, at least, a large enough portion of it to insure as big profits as the next nation. Where sections could not be owned by one dominant nation there came a policy of "open door," but the "door" was open to "white people only." As to the darkest and weakest of peoples there was but one unanimity in Europe,—that which Herr Dernburg of the German Colonial Office called the agreement with England to maintain white "prestige" in Africa,—the doctrine of the divine right of white people to steal.
>
> Thus the world market most wildly and desperately sought today is the market where labor is cheapest and most helpless and profit is most abundant. This labor is kept cheap and helpless because the white world despises "darkies." If one has the temerity to suggest that these workingmen may walk the way of white workingmen and climb by votes and self-assertion and education to the rank of men, he is howled out of court. They cannot do it and if they could, they shall not, for they are the enemies of the white race and the whites shall rule forever and forever and everywhere. Thus the hatred and despising of human beings from whom Europe wishes to extort her luxuries has led to such jealousy and bickering between European nations that they have fallen afoul of each other and have fought like crazed beasts. Such is the fruit of human hatred.[22]

The new imperialism was a competition among multiple new democratic nations to own and profit from the ownership of as much of the Earth as possible; but where no nation could establish exclusive control over some section of the Earth, the competing nations agreed to a nonprotectionist (non-dog-in-the-manger), "open-door" trade policy that allowed them *jointly* to exploit it. Du Bois characterizes the open-door policy as for "white people only," for it extended only to white nations—the new democratic nations—not to "the darker nations." The dynamic of interests driving the new imperialism dictated that, where no nation was dominant enough to own some part of the Earth, an open-door trade policy was needed. Why, however, did white European nations limit the scope of the trade policy on the basis of race? Why did they decide to realize their interests by opting to exclude rather than include the darker nations under the aegis of the open-door policy?

With respect to the scramble for Africa, Du Bois replies to these questions by referencing a December 1915 speech delivered by a former German colonial minister, Bernhard Dernburg. During the course of the war, Dernburg argued, England had undermined the "prestige" of the white race (in essence, colored peoples' sense that "the will of the white man is good, unshakeable, unconquerable"), as well as its solidarity against black Africans, by bringing black colonial subjects to fight in Europe.[23] In Du Bois's eyes, Dernburg's plea on behalf of white prestige and antiblack solidarity was predicated on the belief that white people have a "divine right . . . to steal" from "the darkest and weakest of peoples," a sarcastic formulation alluding to the white supremacist's supposition that "whiteness is ownership of the earth," or, as I have put it, that whites have an exclusive right to possess, enjoy, and dispose of the Earth. That belief, Du Bois now suggests, explains why the new democratic nations endorsed a racially discriminatory trade policy during the scramble for Africa. Material interests gave an impetus to a nonprotectionist trade policy where ownership by a single nation was impossible, but a belief that black Africa belongs to and is to be exploited by whites alone explains why that policy followed the path of excluding rather than including nonwhites. Had the denizens of the darker nations been white, Du Bois implies, those nations would have been welcome to participate in the open-door trade policy.

Christian white supremacist beliefs about darker peoples and about blacks, specifically, may have functioned as switches, conditioning the realization of capitalist economic interests, but the satisfaction of those interests had prerequisites. Thus, the satisfaction of an interest in "inordinate," "big," or "abundant" profits required a market where labor is cheap and helpless. Under the rule of democratic despotism, the new democratic nation was a profit seeking enterprise that pursued profit in Africa because African labor was cheap and helpless. But African labor was not *naturally* cheap and helpless, Du Bois reminds us; rather it was *kept* cheap and helpless "because the white world despises 'darkies'"; or, more expansively, due to its "hatred and despising of human beings from whom Europe wishes to extort her luxuries."

In "Of the Culture of White Folk," Du Bois claims that African labor had been kept cheap and helpless through policies that denied it the opportunities—educational, political (the vote), and self-assertive (unionization?)—that the European and American white working classes had used to advance democracy. With this observation, I suggest, he extends an argument, already evident in "The African Roots of War," that African labor had been kept cheap and helpless through the ongoing violence of primitive accumulation, what Karl Marx famously characterized as "the historical process of divorcing the producer from the means of production."[24] Thus, Du Bois observes that "all over Africa" there has been a "shameless monopolizing of land and resources to force poverty on the masses and reduce them to the dumb-driven-cattle stage of labor activity," adding that "the Union of South Africa has refused natives even the right to *buy* land . . . a deliberate attempt to force the Negroes to work on farms and in mines and kitchens for low wages."²⁵ In stressing the coercive role of primitive accumulation through white Europeans' expropriation of the lands, resources, and labor that black Africans used to sustain themselves, Du Bois echoes Rudolph Hilferding's and Rosa Luxemburg's prewar, Marxist theories of imperialism more than Hobson. For Hilferding, capital "has recourse to the power of the state and uses it for forcible expropriation in order to create the required free wage proletariat.... These violent methods are of the essence of colonial policy." For Luxemburg, "each new colonial expansion is accompanied ... by a relentless battle of capital against the social and economic ties of the natives, who are forcibly robbed of their means of production and labour power."²⁶

Importantly, Du Bois differs from Hilferding and Luxemburg in maintaining that the attempt to keep black labor helpless and cheap—whether through primitive accumulation or policies that denied black labor opportunities enjoyed by white labor—is impelled by the ill-will animating the affects of contempt and hatred: that is, by the desire to injure and do violence to black life. The white world despises darkies, and the destruction of black life required to make darkies profitable, no less than the jealousy and bickering that led to the Great War, is part of the "fruit of human hatred." Here again, then, we find Du Bois arguing that the moral character of the Christian white supremacist, of which white culture is the expression, plays a key role in explaining the new imperialism. Once more, it seems, Du Bois's causal reasoning entails a counterfactual: that had the moral character animating white culture been defined by different tendencies—in this case, had it not been defined by antiblack contempt, hatred, and ill-will—then African labor would not have been kept sufficiently cheap and helpless to incentivize armed associations of white capital and labor to boost their profits through the exploitation of African labor. It is difficult, of course, to know exactly on what alternative paths European capital would have embarked to realize its material interests had the "switch off" of white supremacist belief not functioned, historically, to rule out the application of the moral considerations embraced by modern democratic movements to white Europeans' treatment of black Africans; or had the "switch on" of white supremacist hatred and ill-will toward blacks not triggered the violence of primitive accumulation. Perhaps the result would have been a dissolution of the union of white labor and white capital, as white capital struggled to extract higher profits notwithstanding the moral norms animating modern democracy. Or, perhaps, as I suggested above, European capital would have found its way into Africa, but with less morally disastrous consequences. Or, perhaps, and finally, and as Du Bois seems to envision in "The African Roots of War," democratic movements would have progressed by leaps and bounds as the "principle of home rule" was extended to "groups, nations, and races" throughout the world and the advance of freedom at the expense of unfreedom met its demise.[27]

DEMOCRATIC DESPOTISM IN EAST ST. LOUIS

When Du Bois took the floor at the "First Universal Races Congress," for a session devoted to "Inter-Racial Economics" and "Peaceful Contact" in which he and Hobson participated, he tacitly took issue with Hobson's optimistic claim that "the main current of economic forces" provides a "basis of sympathy and unity of interests between white and coloured, advanced and backward peoples," arguing rather that "economic intercourse between two countries or groups was of benefit to both only if the income arising from it was equally distributed between both." In contrast to Hobson, Du Bois raises the question of distributive justice as it pertains to trade unions' discrimination against black Americans in the United States and to the "economic intercourse between backward and forward nations." In contrast to some of his own later writings, however—including some that came with the advent of World War I—he declines to pursue the question further, or to elaborate a general theoretical framework for connecting and comparing racial subordination in the United States to forward nations' domination and exploitation of backward nations.[28] In the second part of this chapter I argue that Du Bois's theory of the new democratic despotism, as he outlines it in "The African Roots of War," afforded him such a framework. To make my case, I focus on chapter 4 of *Darkwater*, Du Bois's analysis of the 1917 East St. Louis race riots.

According to the theory of democratic despotism, the armed associations of capital and labor that constitute the modern nation are, strictly speaking, armed associations of capital and an "aristocracy of labor," the notion of which Du Bois may well have derived from Frederick Engels's book on the working class in England, or, perhaps, from the writings of Karl Kautsky, the leading theorist of the Second International.[29] Today, Du Bois argues, only the aristocracy of white labor—"the more intelligent and shrewder and cannier workingmen" in contrast to "ignorant" and "unskilled" laborers—has been admitted "to a share in the spoils of capital." The point of the theory of democratic despotism is to show that democracy and despotism have advanced in tandem because democratic progress in Europe and America for white laborers has meant the violent exploitation in America and elsewhere of "chinks' and 'niggers.'" In Du Bois's analysis of the new imperialism, he illustrates the theory by showing that democratic advances in Europe helped to consolidated the domination and exploitation of black and other darker peoples. In his analysis of the East St. Louis race riots, he further elaborates and illustrates the theory by showing how a white labor aristocracy can effectively exploit a competition between black and white unskilled labor to protect the advantages it enjoys over both through its privileged association with capital.

"On July 2 and 3, 1917," writes the historian Charles L. Lumpkins, "rampaging white men and women looted and torched black homes and businesses and assaulted African Americans in the small industrial city of East St. Louis, Illinois." The white mob included police officers and National Guardsman, and "when the terror ended, white attackers had destroyed property worth three million dollars, razed several neighborhoods, injured hundreds, and forced at least seven thousand black townspeople to seek refuge across the Mississippi River in St. Louis, Missouri."[30] Du Bois's account of these events, and of the role that white supremacist habits of mind—specifically, white supremacist affect—played in their unfolding, highlights the reaction of skilled union labor, the labor aristocracy, to the intensification of the interracial competition for jobs that had resulted from the movement of Southern blacks to East St. Louis during the Great Migration and the United States' declaration of war against Germany in April 1917.

Before the war, Du Bois tells us, increasing democracy in the determination of income meant wage growth for East St. Louis's skilled laborers, who, "banding themselves" through unionization, "had threatened the coffers of the mighty and the mighty had disgorged." Even "common workers" struggled for modest gains, but a result of the war was to strengthen the ties between capital and the labor aristocracy while sharpening the divide between the labor aristocracy and other, poorer white laborers: "the skilled and intelligent, banding themselves even better than before, bargained with the men of might and held them by bitter threats; the less skilled and more ignorant seethed at the bottom and tried, as of old, to bring it about that the ignorant and unlettered should learn to stand together against both capital and skilled labor." Finally, because "new murder" had "opened new markets over all the world to American industry," as the "stream of immigrants" declined, East St. Louis's white labor aristocracy, no less than its counterparts in Europe's new democratic nations, benefited from a national wealth bag that grew ever richer. Within the United States, as well as within Europe, increasing democracy in the determination of income was perpetuated through violence done to human life elsewhere. As the labor aristocracy continued its assault on the coffers of the mighty, squeezing still more "reluctant dollars" from them, it dreamed of a day when labor "as they knew it" would come into its own, "with justice and with right, save for one thing, and that was the sound of the moan of the Disinherited who still lay without the walls."[31]

The story Du Bois tells is complex, but, at the risk of simplification, I suggest that its main lines are clear. The "Disinherited," the Southern blacks who migrated to East St. Louis, threatened to end the labor aristocracy's dream of, in effect, consolidating its proper share in the spoils of capital. Reacting to that threat, the skilled laborers (builders, printers, machinists, and the like) excluded blacks from their unions, which had flourished at the expense of the unskilled, unintelligent laborers who worked the aluminum works and the stockyards and who invited blacks to join their unions. When black and white aluminum workers struck in October 1916, they won "higher wages and better working hours." But when they struck again the following spring, after the United States entered the war, the government "stepped in and ordered no hesitation, no strike; the work must go on." At this point, unskilled white workers began to seek a scapegoat for their frustrations. The anger they directed against the government was "impotent," for the government supported their employers, so they turned their anger toward "entrenched union labor," the labor aristocracy. Fearing the mass of white workers, and "knowing their own guilt ... in ... the matter of bidding their way to power across the weakness of their less fortunate fellows," the leaders of this aristocracy "leaped quickly" to redirect that anger. The thing they wanted, Du Bois writes, "was even at their hands ... the oldest and nastiest form of human oppression,—race hatred." Thus, the skilled laborers argued that black men were not only guilty of bidding for white men's jobs, but "guilty of being black. It was at this blackness that the unions pointed an accusing finger. It was here that they committed the unpardonable crime. It was here that they entered the Shadow of Hell." So, Du Bois writes, "hell flamed in East St. Louis . . . white men drove even black union men out of their unions . . . they killed and beat, and murdered; they dashed out the brains of children . . . they drove victims into flames and hanged the helpless to their lighting poles."[32]

In Du Bois's view, the East St. Louis labor aristocracy took advantage of white common workers' hatred of blacks to add insult to the injury. The injury was the simple fact that other men, new comers from the South, were underbidding them for their jobs. The insult was that these other men were black. Du Bois implies here, I believe, that because white common workers held white supremacist beliefs about blacks (earlier in the essay he notes that they held blacks to be "inhuman")[33] the thought that *black men* (men "guilty of being black") could usurp their jobs and threaten their livelihood, when whites alone had the right to possess, enjoy, and dispose of all good things, was especially infuriating and intensified their desire to injure black life. Race hatred was "translated into murder" for white workers felt insulted by the fact that the threat to their economic security was posed by human beings they believed to be their inferiors. But the impulse to translate race hatred into murder would not have arisen in the first place, Du Bois suggests, had white workers not been economically injured by black workers underbidding them because they had not been able to earn a "decent living" in the South.[34]

In applying his theory of democratic despotism to account for the new imperialism, Du Bois adduces his moral psychology to explain the domination and exploitation of black Africans by armed, national associations of labor and capital. The moral vice constituting the souls and culture of white folk led to racial oppression, he argues, for

(1) it created a moral loophole permitting the brutal violence needed to accumulate inordinate profit to be directed against black Africans, and (2) the violence it motivated transformed black laborers into the defenseless victims of a predatory capitalism. In extending the theory of democratic despotism to narrate the history of the East St. Louis race riots, Du Bois again adduces his moral psychology, first, to show how labor aristocracy can exploit the moral vice of white supremacy, and especially the tendency to racial hatred, to redirect against black workers anger that promises to expose labor aristocracy's alliance with capital; and second, to show how labor aristocracy can encourage the translation of milder expressions of racial hatred into wilder, fiercer expressions of the same by representing blacks as a threat to white jobs (an injury) and by representing that threat as an offense to white superiority (an insult). Thus, where Du Bois's treatment of the new imperialism shows how moral vice can engender racial oppression by making racial difference make a difference to the determination of the course of events through which capitalists advance their interests, his discussion of East St. Louis shows how the cynical manipulation of moral vice, of antiblack affect and ill-will that breeds racial violence, serves not simply to secure the stability of a democratically despotic political regime, forged through the alliance of aristocratic labor and capital, but to intensify those very qualities of character.

To be sure, none of this is meant to suggest that Du Bois, with his theory of democratic despotism, provided a systematic and comprehensive account of how, during the Great War, white supremacist habits of mind operated domestically as well as internationally to aggravate the vulnerability of the world's darker peoples to political domination, economic exploitation, and mob violence. Rather the point is to show, if only partially, why he might reasonably have believed that combatting these habits of mind would help to undo the racial oppression that had restricted the democratic development of darker peoples. Because the moral vice of white supremacy led to and sustained racial oppression, it was plausible to think that combatting it could help to thwart racial oppression. And because the manipulation of that vice protected a political economy that dominated and exploited black and unskilled white workers alike, it was equally plausible to believe that fighting it would make it harder for capitalists and the labor aristocracy to deploy it as a means to divide workers along racial lines.[35] Finally, because the economically self-serving manipulation of racial hatred is one of the powerful social "currents" that, like other forces that have deformed the moral character of white folk, intensify racial hatred and help perpetuate it, Du Bois also suggests that the struggle against capitalism and the labor aristocracy can advance the struggle against white supremacist habits of mind and, implicitly, racial oppression.[36] For Du Bois, then, the struggles against racial oppression, against the vice of white supremacy, and against capitalism and aristocratic labor can be mutually reinforcing.[37]

4

BEAUTY

What about beauty interests Du Bois? More exactly, what about the phenomenon of beauty is salient for him, and *why* is what is salient for him salient for him? Answering these questions will enable us to see the distinctive point of Du Bois's philosophical inquiry into the nature of beauty.

I begin by noting that a recurrent tendency of Du Bois's philosophical writing is a movement from a description of an historical circumstance he shares with others to a recounting of a personal experience—or vice versa. This tendency is clearly on display in "Of Beauty and Death," and specifically in the movement from the essay's first to its second paragraph.[1]

In the essay's first paragraph, Du Bois recalls the carnage caused by the Great War: "For long years we of the world gone wild have looked into the face of death and smiled. Through all our bitter tears we knew how beautiful it was to die for that which our souls called sufficient. Like all true beauty this thing of dying was so simple, so matter-of-fact. The boy clothed in his splendid youth ... went and was gone."[2]

"Suddenly the world was full of the fragrance of sacrifice," Du Bois adds, including the more than "ordinary sacrifice" that he called his fellow African Americans to embrace when, in his "Close

Ranks" editorial of 1918, he urged them "to forget . . . [their] special grievances and close . . . ranks shoulder to shoulder with . . . [their] white fellow citizens" in the fight for democracy. The fight for democracy sufficed to justify sacrifice, and justified sacrifice seemed beautiful to all. When, however, the smell of sacrifice, though sweet, seems suddenly to fill the world, Du Bois and his contemporaries find themselves led to reflect on the nature of death and to reconsider the validity of their aesthetic judgment: "We left our digging and burden bearing; we turned from our scraping and twisting of things and words; we paused from our hurrying thither and hither and walking up and down, and asked in a half-whisper: this Death—is this Life? And is its Beauty real or false?" It is of this "heart questioning," Du Bois tells us, that he is writing.[3]

In the essay's second paragraph Du Bois shifts focus, moving from the first paragraph's generalized, worldly wise, first-person-plural references—to what "we knew," "our bitter tears," "our scraping and twisting," and so forth—to a recollection of a conversation that immediately followed a white friend's accusation just the day before: "MY FRIEND, who is pale and positive, said to me yesterday, as the tired sun was nodding: 'You are too sensitive.'" Du Bois's initial reply to his friend's charge ("I admit, I am—sensitive. I am artificial. I cringe or am bumptious or immobile. I am intellectually dishonest, art-blind, and I lack humor") is sardonic and curt. But after she rejoins his reply, demanding that he "stop all this" and importuning that he exaggerates when he says that he will not stop because "You won't let us," he answers her accusation by recounting the kinds of experience that have persistently characterized his life, "not always, but ever, not each day, but each week, each month, each year." Ranging from his references to the neglectful milkman and the truculent policeman to his complaint about discrimination in the sciences and the arts, Du Bois's descriptions of the race-based slights and indignities he has suffered concludes with a story that relates the infuriating prejudice he encountered when he sought to buy orchestra tickets to see a Charlie Chaplin movie. Alluding, perhaps, to Chaplin's 1919 short "A Day's Pleasure," which recounts the anything-but-pleasurable excursion by car and by boat of a white middle-class family, stymied by seasickness, a traffic cop, and hot tar, Du Bois bitterly complains of the contemptuousness to which he has fallen victim, echoing the sarcasm implicit in the title of Chaplin's movie: "God! *What a night of pleasure.*"[4]

Du Bois considers his essay's shift from a color-blind description of the world's experience of war and sacrifice to a personal conversation touching on his personal experience of the ugliness of racial oppression by complicating the reflections he proposes in his essay's first paragraph.

> Here, then, is beauty and ugliness, a whole vision of the world-sacrifice, a fierce gleam of world-hate. Which is life and what is death and how shall we face so tantalizing a contradiction? Any explanation must necessarily be subtle and involved. No pert and easy word of encouragement, no merely dark despair, can lay hold of the roots of these things. And first and before all, we cannot forget that this world is beautiful. Grant all its ugliness and sin—the petty, horrible snarl of its putrid threads, which few have seen more near or more often than I—notwithstanding all this, the beauty of this world is not to be denied.[5]

In chapter 6, I shall have more to say about these complicating reflections and their relation to Du Bois's discussion of natural beauty. For the purposes of the present chapter, however, I wish only to highlight his insistence that ugliness and sin do not pervade the world. Yes, ugliness abounds, but beauty exists, and so far as it exists it restricts what he later describes as "the volume and force" of ugliness. What interests Du Bois about beauty, then, what motivates his inquiry into the nature of beauty, is that its presence effectively curtails the extent to which the snarling and putrid threads of hate spread themselves throughout the world. Put otherwise, the point of Du Bois's inquiry into the nature of beauty is to identify features of beauty in virtue of which its presence in the world contradicts, limits, and reduces the presence of ugliness.[6]

In chapter 1, I described Du Bois's philosophical method as historically and self-consciously situated hermeneutical improvisation. That method, I argued, is incrementally to improvise on the characterization of universal themes by considering them in the perspective of lives lived within a "veiled" corner: that is, by advancing an account of those themes that reflects the concrete experiences of black people. It is not insignificant, then, that Du Bois introduces his explicit analysis of the nature of beauty, near the end of "Of Beauty and Death," by recurring to the figure of the veil and thus reminding his readers of the perspectival origin and specificity of his analysis: "Listen, O Isles, to these voices within the Veil, for they portray the most human hurt of the Twentieth Cycle of that poor Jesus who was called the Christ!"[7] Perceptual salience can be a function of what we "evaluate as mattering," and because the denizens of the veiled corner evaluate the hurt caused by the ugliness of racial prejudice and antiblack violence as mattering to them, that hurt and the ugliness that causes it are salient to them.[8]

But beauty is similarly salient to the point of view of the veiled corner, precisely to the extent that it functions to circumscribe and curtail the scope and the power of hurtful ugliness. Writing from that point of view, Du Bois will improvise on a received, Euro-American conversation about the universal theme of beauty; taking his bearing from the problems of his people, he will modify (add a "half-tone" to) that conversation by saying what matters about beauty from the outlook of those problems, which is, again, its power to constrain the sway of ugliness in the world. Reminiscent of the

British philosopher Edmund Burke, Du Bois conceptualizes beauty in terms of properties that have a certain causal, functional efficacy. But where Burke analyzes beauty in terms of properties that "excite love . . . or some correspondent affection" (smallness, smoothness, and the like), Du Bois analyzes it in terms of properties that render it salient to the perspective of the veiled corner: that is, in terms of properties that explain its capacity to limit ugliness.[9]

In the present chapter, I layout Du Bois's conceptualization of the phenomenon of beauty—or, more exactly, of the phenomenon of a beautiful event—*from within the confines of the veiled corner*.[10] If we use the term "event" to characterize the whole range of possibly beautiful occurrences—for Du Bois, this includes, among other things, lives and sunsets, as well as religious visions—then the nub of his contribution to the Euro-American conversation about beauty is the thesis that the features essential to a beautiful event that explain its power to limit the spread of ugliness are (1) the aptness of its ending and (2) the casting of the event, through its completion, in a new and unexpected light.

Schematically:

1. An event counts as beautiful only if it comes to an apt end.
2. An event counts as beautiful only if, through its completion, it presents itself in a new and unexpected light.

We may think of (1) and (2) as expressing criteria of beauty that pick out perspectively salient aspects of the phenomenon that explain how beauty functions as a sort of antidote to ugliness. By coming to an apt end, a beautiful event defeats and effectively destroys the ugliness that characterizes the beginnings and unfoldings of events generally and, in the instance of an individual human life, the birth and unfolding of that life. By presenting itself in a new and unexpected light, through its completion, a beautiful event can reveal unforeseen possibilities of action that could stymie and interrupt the perpetuation of ugliness.

In the next section of the present chapter, I make the case that Du Bois endorses (1), and in the section following that he endorses (2).

APT ENDINGS

Du Bois analysis of the nature of beauty comes near the conclusion of "Of Beauty and Death":

> There is something in the nature of Beauty that demands an end. Ugliness may be indefinite. It may trail off into gray endlessness. But Beauty must be complete—whether it be a field of poppies or a great life,—it must end, and the End is part and triumph of the Beauty. I know there are those who envisage a beauty eternal. But I cannot. I can dream of great and never-ending processions of beautiful things and visions and acts. But each must be complete or it cannot for me exist.
>
> On the other hand, Ugliness to me is eternal, not in the essence but in its incompleteness; but its eternity does not daunt me, for its eternal unfulfillment is a cause of joy. There is in it nothing new or unexpected; it is the old evil, stretching out and ever seeking the end it cannot find; it may coil and writhe and recur in endless battle to days without end, but it is the same human ill and bitter hurt. But Beauty is fulfillment. It satisfies. It is always new and strange. It is the reasonable thing. Its end is Death—the sweet silence of perfection, the calm and balance of utter music. Therein is the triumph of Beauty.
>
> So strong is the spell of beauty that there are those who, contradicting their own knowledge and experience, try to say that all is beauty. They are called optimists, and they lie. All is not beauty. Ugliness and hate and ill are here with all their contradiction and illogic; they will always be here—perhaps, God send, with lessened volume

and force, but here and eternal, while beauty triumphs in its great completion—Death. We cannot conjure the end of all ugliness in eternal beauty, for beauty by its very being and definition has in each definition its ends and limits; but while beauty lies implicit and revealed in its end, ugliness writhes on in darkness forever. So the ugliness of continual birth fulfils itself and conquers gloriously only in the beautiful end, Death.[11]

As a young man recounting his travels to primarily black audiences, Du Bois spoke of "the infinite beauty of the other world," of "the Eternally Beautiful," and of "Eternal Beauty."[12] By the time he published "Of Beauty and Death," however, he seems to have had second thoughts regarding the view these remarks express. Beauty, he now suggests, is essentially related to death; it is essentially a temporal phenomenon. Du Bois writes about great lives, which must *literally* meet their demise to become beautiful, but also about beautiful acts, visions, and things—a field of poppies, for example. But strictly speaking, neither acts, nor visions, nor poppy fields lose their lives.[13] To apply Du Bois's argument beyond the case of a beautiful life we must suppose that by "end" he means not only death but, more generally, cessation. An action, when it is done, ceases to be, and a vision eventually comes to a conclusion. The case of a field of poppies is no doubt more difficult, for here Du Bois seems to have in mind spatial, not temporal, limits. Notice, however, that the implied claim that a field of poppies, to be beautiful, *must not trail off into gray endlessness* envisions the field's spatial limits with reference to a temporally extended *act* of "trailing off" that comes to an end.

Not all beautiful things die, yet living things, which do, figure centrally in Du Bois's inquiry into the nature of beauty. One sees this clearly if one examines the notes Du Bois wrote when he was formulating the argument of "Of Beauty and Death"—for these jottings recurrently oppose optimism to pessimism, where the former is associated with beauty and death, the latter with ugliness and birth; where ugliness and birth are emblematic of discontent (or "utter discontent") with life; and where "Life" is characterized as "birth & death." In the spirit of a searching, philosophical meditation on the conditions of human flourishing, Du Bois's reflections on beauty are intimately bound up with the question of what renders human lives, including the lives of friends he mentions in these notes, fulfilling and worthy of endorsement. It is a question, he thinks, of determining the "attitude" he should take towards life.[14] In this chapter, then, in examining Du Bois's *Darkwater* remarks about beauty, I focus on the example of a beautiful life, which, I suggest, provides the paradigm, the basis, for his general account of the nature of beauty.

A beautiful life comes to an end, in more than one sense it seems, for "end" indicates a temporal limit, while "End," as Du Bois uses the term, indicates a triumphant end that teleologically fulfills or, in other words, *completes* the life in question.[15] Here I take Du Bois to be invoking two claims, from which he derives criterion (1): first, that to count as beautiful a life must fulfill (complete) itself in death and thereby defeat (conquer/triumph over) its ugliness; and second, that a life fulfills itself in death and thereby defeats its ugliness only if it comes to an apt end, *where an apt end is an end that coheres with what has come beforehand in that life, thus fulfilling it and allowing us to regard it as a unified whole*. In tandem, these claims entail Du Bois's first criterion of beauty, articulated with reference to the paradigm case of a beautiful life: that to count as beautiful a life must come to an apt end.

Claim 1

Regarding the first claim, Du Bois's thinking pivots around the thesis that ugliness is eternal "not in the essence but in its incompleteness." Although incompleteness is constitutive of and thus essential to the occurrence, in each instance, of ugly lives, acts, and visions, everlastingness, the property of being eternal, is not. Ugly individual lives, acts, and other incidents come and go, and so their occurrence does not require that they last forever. Yet ugliness will "always be here . . . here and eternal," Du Bois writes, because the occurrence of *at least some measure of ugliness* (of at least some ugly lives, acts, and the like) *is* a constitutive and thus essential feature of the world. Ugliness is eternal in its incompleteness, he infers, for ugliness is an eternal feature of the world and incompleteness is a constitutive feature of ugliness. Put differently, because ugliness will always (eternally) be here, and because incompleteness is constitutive of ugliness, ugliness will always (eternally) be here *in its incompleteness* (with incompleteness as one of its attributes).

"We cannot conjure the end of all ugliness in eternal beauty," Du Bois maintains, for that would require the existence of an immortal, undying beauty—thus, a beauty that is not a beauty because "beauty by its very being and definition" is limited in its duration. Still, beauty can interrupt if not eliminate the persistence of the ugliness and incompleteness that must always be here, Du Bois argues, thus curtailing and circumscribing their quantity (their volume) and intensity (their force). In particular, beautiful lives can interrupt the persistence of ugliness when, he writes, "the ugliness of continual birth fulfils itself and conquers gloriously only in the beautiful end, Death."[16] The importance of this last remark cannot be overstated, for it points to the teleology animating Du Bois's argument. The fact of natality, Du Bois thinks, is subjection to a condition of ugliness that tasks the newborn with the purpose and project of living a life through which that condition "fulfils itself"—more exactly, of living a life that, through death, conquers and overcomes its original and to that point ongoing ugliness and incompleteness.[17] As if in response to his Calvinist upbringing, Du Bois suggests that though steeped in ugliness and sin from birth a human life can in fact become beautiful, yet only if it fulfills itself in death, thereby defeating and destroying the ugliness that previously characterized it.[18]

It may appear that Du Bois's commitment to this view contradicts his claim that ugliness is eternally unfulfilled. But there is no contradiction, for the claim that ugliness is eternally unfulfilled is just a restatement of Du Bois's belief that some measure of ugliness will always (eternally) be here in, or along with, its incompleteness, or, we could say, in, or along with, its unfulfillment; and that claim, which affirms that the world will never be without ugliness and incompleteness, is consistent with the thesis that an individual life, ugly from birth, could fulfill itself, become beautiful, and interrupt the persistence of ugliness and incompleteness. To say that ugliness is eternally unfulfilled is not to deny that a life ugly from birth could ever achieve fulfillment (clearly Du Bois believes that there are "great" lives that do indeed achieve fulfillment), but to insist that unfulfilled ugliness, in some measure, will ever appear in the world.

Claim 2

To consider the second claim—that a life fulfills itself in death and defeats its ugliness only if it comes to an end that coheres with what has come beforehand in that life, thus fulfilling it—I begin with a question Max Weber poses in his famous 1917 lecture "Science as a Vocation," a question Weber derives from the novels of Leo Tolstoy. The issue is whether death can be a meaningful event for individuals belonging to a civilization that is driven by scientific progress. Weber poses his question by distinguishing between the biblical Abraham and a modern, civilized man. The former, he writes, "died 'old and fulfilled by life' because he was a part of an organic life cycle, because in the evening of his days his life had given him whatever it had to offer and because there were no riddles that he still wanted to solve."[19] By contrast, the latter, the civilized man, "inserted into a never-ending process by which civilization is enriched with ideas, knowledge, and problems may become 'tired of life,' but not fulfilled by it. For he can seize hold of only the minutest portion of the new ideas that the life of the mind continually produces, what remains in his grasp is always merely provisional, never definitive."[20] Weber envisions Abraham's life as complete and fulfilled because it proceeded through a finite set of life-stages, a *complete cycle*, including, presumably, birth; childhood; young adulthood; mature, married adulthood; old age; and, ultimately, death. Thus, as Abraham approached the end of his life, he could intelligibly and meaningfully regard his death as the final stage in a series of stages that encompassed all that life had to offer. But no such self-understanding is available to the human being caught up in the ethos of scientific progress, Weber argues, for the civilized man realizes that whatever he has come to know and appreciate about life is but the smallest fragment of what life in the "infinite" long run of scientific progress will make available in the way of enriching ideas and experience. As the civilized man approaches the end of his life, he cannot regard it as the final stage of a comprehensive series of stages, not because his life will trail off into gray endlessness, but because no life can catch up with and take the measure of the gray endlessness of scientific progress.

Here, I have summarized Weber's interpretation of Tolstoy, for it throws into relief Du Bois's answer to Weber's question, which is premised on a rejection of Tolstoy's "life-stages" conception of a fulfilled life. For Du Bois, I suggest, living a fulfilled life, a complete life, requires not that one acquaint oneself with all the significant kinds of experience that life has to offer, but that one bring one's life to an end that lends it a satisfactory shape—for Du Bois, a coherent shape.[21] As we have seen, Du Bois envisions human lives as quests for fulfillment that may or may not succeed in achieving the fulfillment they seek. Put otherwise, he thinks of human lives as having the form of a story that extends from birth to death and that may or may not end on a note of triumph. What, then, distinguishes a life that is triumphant and coherent from a life that is ugly and incoherent? What is the mark of such a life? Relying on the "story analysis" of the philosopher W. B. Gallie, I propose that, for Du Bois, a triumphant and coherent life concludes just the way we would expect *any* good story to conclude: not with an ending that could have been predicted or deduced from earlier episodes, but with an ending that conquers ugliness because it is *apt* ("acceptable" is Gallie's term)—in other words, with an ending that conquers ugliness because it is neither "ill-prepared" nor "far-fetched" and hence coheres with those earlier episodes.[22] Ugliness is inseparable from all its "contradiction and illogic," Du Bois suggests, by which I take him to mean that incoherence makes for ugliness and ugliness for incoherence. As I read him, then, Du Bois believes that a life fulfills itself in death and defeats its ugliness only if it comes to an apt end—that is, only if it comes to an end that is congruent with what has come beforehand in that life and thereby overcomes its contradiction and illogic. In addition, he believes that it is precisely by coming to an apt end, and thereby overcoming its contradiction and illogic, that a life fulfills itself in death and defeats its ugliness. For Du Bois, in short, a life fulfills itself and triumphs over its ugliness only if it comes to an end that coheres with earlier episodes, thus fulfilling that life in death and letting us see all its episodes as forming a coherent whole.[23]

The logical upshot of Du Bois's first and second claims is the criterion of beauty they entail, which is (1) above, articulated with reference to the paradigm case of a beautiful life: in fine, that a life counts as beautiful only if it comes to an apt end. For Du Bois, whether a person's life counts as beautiful depends on the way it ends, on the quality of her death. A comparison to Aristotle helps to illuminate Du Bois's position, for while Aristotle similarly holds that endings matter, that whether a life counts as happy, as *eudaimōn*, may depend on the way it ends, the tenor of his concern with lives' endings sets him at odds with Du Bois. Considering the case of Priam, the Trojan king that the *Iliad* depicts as foreseeing that he will be "stabbed or beaten to death . . . then torn to pieces by 'ravening dogs at [his] own gates—the very dogs that [he himself] fed at table and trained to guard [his] gates,'"[24] Aristotle proposes "that happiness requires both complete excellence and a complete life. For many changes occur in a life, and all sorts of things happen: it is possible for a person who flourishes to the highest degree to encounter great disasters in old age, as happened to Priam in the story of events at Troy; and no one who has had a fate like that, and died miserably, is counted happy by anyone."[25] In extreme circumstances, Aristotle asserts, an actively virtuous, flourishing life may meet with a horrible and wretched end, and so forfeit its claim to have been a happy life. What engages Aristotle is the person who suffers a late-in-life, tragic reversal that negatively affects the (ethical) appraisal of his life as a whole. What engages Du Bois, on the contrary, is the individual, not likely a king, who has had to cope with ugly, tragedy-inducing circumstances through all or most of his life and whose ability to fulfill and redeem his life is never guaranteed.

Consider, in this connection, a couple of examples, the first of which is Du Bois's depiction of the life of the "mixed-blooded" English composer Samuel Coleridge-Taylor:

> When such a man dies, it must bring pause to a reasoning world. We may call his death-sickness pneumonia, but we all know that it was sheer overwork,—the using of a delicately-tuned instrument too commonly and continuously and carelessly to let it last its normal life. We may well talk of the waste of wood and water, of food and fire, but the real and unforgivable waste of modern civilization is the waste of ability and genius. . . .

Coleridge-Taylor's life work was not finished,—it was but well begun. He lived only his first period of creative genius, when melody and harmony flashed and fluttered in subtle, compelling, and more than promising profusion. He did not live to do the organized, constructive work in the full, calm power of noonday,—the reflective finishing of evening. . . .

Deep as was the primal tragedy in the life of Coleridge-Taylor, there lay another still deeper. He smiled at it lightly, as we all do,—we who live within the veil,—to hide the deeper hurt.[26]

Samuel Coleridge-Taylor never brought his life, his life work, to a fitting conclusion. To be sure, it was well begun, but it never acquired "the full, calm power of noonday," let alone the beautifying luster, "the reflective finishing," suitable to the "evening" of such a life. Coleridge-Taylor's death was premature; it was incongruous with the creative genius he demonstrated as a young man, for it left the promise of that genius unfulfilled. Considering Coleridge-Taylor in general terms, Du Bois suggests that the composer's life fell prey to a wasteful, tragedy-inducing ugliness caused by modern civilization, a tendency to overwork that is perhaps symptomatic of the relentless pursuit of progress that Weber identifies. Considering the composer from the "added" perspective of the veiled corner, Du Bois likewise asserts that the tragedy of Coleridge-Taylor's life resulted from the hurt, the ugliness, caused by racial oppression. Coleridge-Taylor's life remained tragically incomplete when it ended, because he never defeated the ugliness tainting it by finishing his life's work. Du Bois found much to admire in Coleridge-Taylor's life, but the composer's untimely death made it impossible for Du Bois to regard his life as a unified story that had come to an apt conclusion.

Du Bois's portrait of Coleridge-Taylor comes from a chapter of *Darkwater* titled "The Immortal Child." My second example, his portrait of Alexander Crummell, comes from the eponymously named, twelfth chapter of *The Souls of Black Folk*. As readers of *Souls* will remember, Du Bois's narrative of Crummell's life is a story of the life of a solitary pilgrim and a persecuted martyr—a tale of doubt and despair, of death and rebirth ("The Valley of the Shadow of Death gives few of its pilgrims back to the world. But Alexander Crummell it gave back"), of a wanderer who finally finds his place in the world, and, ultimately, at the end of his life, a greeting from Christ, the first and prototypical Christian martyr: "I wonder where he is today? I wonder if in that dim world beyond, as he came gliding in, there rose on some wan throne a King,—a dark and pierced Jew, who knows the writhings of the earthly damned, saying, as he laid those heart-wrung talents down, 'Well done!' while round about the morning stars sat singing." Alluding to the New Testament's "parable of the talents" (Matthew 25:14–30), Du Bois completes his narrative of Crummell's life by depicting a black ("dark") and persecuted ("pierced") Christ welcoming Crummell to heaven and praising him, presumably, for his beneficent righteousness. Having lived and worked his whole life within the Veil, Crummell receives the recognition he deserves just when he dies, explicitly from Du Bois in the tale he tells ("And now that he is gone, I sweep the Veil away and cry, Lo! the soul to whose dear memory I bring this little tribute"), and, more importantly, from Christ himself ("Well done!").[27] In contrast to Samuel Coleridge-Taylor, Du Bois's Alexander Crummell overcomes the tragedy of his life by bringing it to an end that coheres with earlier episodes and that shows it to have been a unified enterprise that triumphed over tragedy and ugliness. Crummell's story comes to a finale that the reader is bound to regard as apt, for it follows the traditional, Christian plotting of human existence. As Northrop Frye remarks, "Christianity . . . sees tragedy as an episode in the divine comedy, the larger scheme of redemption and resurrection. The sense of a tragedy as a prelude to comedy seems almost inseparable from anything explicitly Christian."[28] In a similar vein,

Du Bois sees the persecution Crummell suffered throughout his life as giving way, in the end, to a quintessentially Christian vision of the wanderer in heaven, finally fulfilled and triumphant over human woe. Here, it appears, the divinely comic and, in the perspective of *Darkwater*, *beautiful* image of a resurrected and redeemed Protestant martyr displaces and even banishes the spirit of tragedy.[29]

UNFAMILIAR POSSIBILITIES

When Du Bois writes that the eternal unfulfillment of ugliness is a cause of joy, I take him *not* to be arguing that he finds joy in the fact that unfulfilled ugliness will ever appear in the world. Rather his point, as the lines following imply, is that ugliness, because it is always unfulfilled, is never new or unexpected. And because it is never new or unexpected, because it is always a recurrence of the same, of "the old evil . . . the same human ill and bitter hurt," it never daunts him; rather than overwhelm him with fear, as it would if the ill and hurt it expressed were always expressed differently than in the past, it bores him. When Du Bois maintains that the eternal unfulfillment of ugliness causes him joy, and that he remains undaunted because of that joy, he means to affirm that the fact of the qualitative sameness of ugliness in each and every one of its instances joyfully relieves him of his fear of ugliness.

Du Bois holds that ugliness will never be new or unexpected because unfulfillment, or incompleteness, is constitutive of ugliness. But beauty is always new and unexpected, or, as he also writes, new and strange. To count as beautiful, then, a life, or, more generally, an act, vision, or other event, must, through its fulfillment, its completion, present itself in a strange, an unfamiliar light—Du Bois's second criterion of beauty. As I read Du Bois, he implies that each occurrence of beauty is, as such, unique: that in contrast to the qualitative sameness of numerically distinct instances of ugliness, numerically distinct instances of beauty are qualitatively different from one another; indeed, each occurrence of beauty distinguishes itself by casting itself in a new and unfamiliar light. Of a life whose beauty arises and becomes manifest through its death, then, we may say that it presents its beauty as a beauty particular to that life precisely by presenting itself, through its fulfillment, through its completion, in a new and unfamiliar light.

For an example that illuminates both of Du Bois's criteria of beauty—both (1) and (2)—I turn to Keith Lehrer, whose recent, philosophical account of the relationship between beauty and death echoes Du Bois in several respects. In his reflections on a line of Wallace Stevens's poetry, "Death is the mother of all beauty," Lehrer comments on the death of his friend Glorya. "The life of Glorya," he reminisces, "was a thing of beauty. My appreciation of the beauty of that life depended in part . . . on the wholeness of it, on its being what it was. I could not appreciate the beauty of that life, though I admired the way Glorya lived, until her death. Death gave birth to the beauty of that life."[30] Glorya's life became beautiful when it ended, and when it ended Lehrer came to see it as a coherent whole. For Lehrer, as for Du Bois, the beauty of a beautiful life comes into view only through death. Lehrer also suggests that perceiving Glorya's life as a coherent whole was a matter not simply of appreciating the connections among different parts of her life—for example, that "her wonderful creation of an environment of her unique hacienda . . . connected with her own sense of death at the end of life, her acceptance of it"—but, as Du Bois might have argued, of seeing that her life had come to an apt ending: Glorya "died well," Lehrer recalls, "sipping some wine with family the night before her death."[31] As we have seen, Du Bois believes not that some lives never end, but that some ends are not "Ends," or, in other words, that not all lives end as Crummell's and Glorya's ended—that is, by way of a conclusion that presented the life of the deceased as a beautiful, integrated whole. Had Glorya not died well, had she been taken hostage and then tortured for months on end before her kidnappers finally murdered her, thus suffering a fate as wretched as Priam's, it may have been difficult for Lehrer to regard her death as cohering with the rest of her life, and her life as a unified "thing of beauty."[32] Lives like Glorya's interrupt the recurrence of ugliness, hate, and ill, but the ability to live such lives is often stymied by the particular ugliness of antiblack race prejudice. Coleridge-Taylor's life is a case in point, even though racial oppression in England inhibited his development to a lesser extent than it would have had he been born and come of age in America, where "we know . . . how to discourage, choke, and murder ability when it so far forgets itself as to choose a dark skin."[33]

"Artists," Lehrer writes, "try to show you what flowers can be, trees can be, colors can be, and lines can be as they have never been before."[34] Thus, "the content of everything is changed. . . . Sunflowers will never be the same after seeing Van Gogh."[35] Presupposing that a "life and the closure of it with death is an artwork," Lehrer similarly argues that where "the painting of flowers changes your conception of flowers and what flowers mean . . . [t]he end of life changes your conception of a life and what life means."[36] Here, as before, I interpret Lehrer as echoing Du Bois—specifically, Du Bois's contention that in presenting itself as a coherent whole, a life that comes to an end and becomes beautiful likewise presents itself in a new and unexpected light. Consider, again, Du Bois's portrait of Alexander Crummell:

> They who live without knew not nor dreamed of that full power within, that mighty inspiration which the dull gauze of caste decreed that most men should not know. And now that he is gone I sweep the Veil way and cry, Lo! the soul to whose dear memory I bring this little

tribute. I can see his face still, dark and heavy-lined beneath his snowy hair; lighting and shading, now with inspiration for the future, now in some innocent pain at some human wickedness, now with sorrow at some hard memory from the past.[37]

Du Bois's chiaroscuro miniature of Crummell's face, like the twelfth chapter of *Souls* to which it belongs, is itself a tribute to his mentor's life as a whole. With Crummell gone, Du Bois's chapter and his portrait commemorate the man's life, depicting it, after it is finished, as a coherent if multidimensional enterprise, ultimately with the aim of presenting it in a light that is new and unfamiliar to those "without," those who "knew not nor dreamed of that full power within, that *mighty inspiration*." By twice highlighting the power of inspiration, Du Bois envisions Crummell's life as pointing beyond itself, inviting those who knew and know little of his life to discover in it new expectations and possibilities that they can carry into the future. For Du Bois, then, seeing Glorya's life in a new light would be tantamount to seeing it as revealing possibilities heretofore unfamiliar to us, not only possibilities over and beyond the expectations we have been used to attributing to her and to others, but possibilities that we ourselves have never before anticipated, possibilities that eclipse the horizon of our expectations for ourselves. In Lehrer's terms, we would be seeing her life as expressing sensibilities, aspirations, and hopes that enriched our conception of what her life had been about, as well as our sense of what human life more generally might be about. When a life becomes beautiful through death, Du Bois argues, it comes into view as a coherent undertaking that encompasses its past even as it augments our vision of the future. From within the perspective of the veiled corner, Du Bois suggests, the perception of beauty pulls us temporally in opposed directions.

To the triumph of beauty in death, Du Bois attributes "the sweet silence of perfection, the calm and balance of utter music." By invoking the notion of "absolute" or "utter" music, Du Bois appears to attribute to all beauty the beauty of music that expresses nothing, that says nothing, so to speak, about the world. And by attributing "sweet silence" to all beauty, he seems similarly to propose that all beauty is essentially indifferent to the world, that it exists exclusively for the sake of the perfection (the fulfillment) it manifests.[38] When a life like Glorya's or Crummell's becomes beautiful, through death, its beauty comes into view as pertaining to nothing outside itself and as affording its beholder a retrospective apprehension of tranquil and proportionate fulfillment that Du Bois describes as satisfying—as satisfying our reason, he suggests. But beauty is not only satisfying, it is captivating, and its disturbing spell is sufficiently strong to prompt the utopian (optimistic) belief that conjuring "the end of ugliness in eternal beauty" is possible. Inherent in the manifestation of beauty, Du Bois implies, is the promise of a future different from the past, a future that is not simply a recurrence of the same old ugliness that has dominated the past. As we have seen, Du Bois believes that the utopian interpretation of this promise is false. But he likewise believes that a more moderate interpretation is plausible—that it is possible, again, to realize the promise implicit in the apprehension of beauty by curtailing and circumscribing its volume and force in the future. Both interpretations express an experience of beauty as involving both a satisfying, backward-looking contemplation of perfection—e.g., of fulfilled lives (like Glorya's and Crummell's) that have succeeded in conquering and eradicating ugliness—*and*, at the same time, an enchanted, forward-looking sense of being called to conjure a future less ugly and more beautiful than the past—e.g., by taking up the new possibilities that these lives have revealed.

In tying beauty to the perception of perfection, Du Bois sketched an account of aesthetic judgment with long, historical roots, extending to the German rationalist aesthetics of the eighteenth century (e.g., Alexander Baumgarten's well-known claim that judgments of beauty involve a [confused] concept of perfection), but likewise with affinities to the views of his contemporary and teacher George Santayana, who described beauty as the "the clearest manifestation of perfection, and the best evidence of its possibility."[39] As I have been suggesting, however, Du Bois is after more than a theory of aesthetic judgment: for while Du Boisian beauty satisfies our reason and elicits contemplation, it also calls us beyond ourselves. The manifestation of beauty may well arrest our attention and give us pause to contemplate a particular object or person. It may distract us from our daily involvements and immediately invite scrutiny and judgment. But beyond that, Du Bois proposes, it points to the future. In words that Edmund Burke used to describe the power of the *sublime*, Du Boisian beauty entertains the imagination "with the promise of something more."[40] Echoing Burke further, we could say that Du Boisian beauty involves an aspect of the sublime precisely to the extent that, despite its satisfying completeness, it impels us not to "acquiesce in the present object of sense," but to want to rid the world of ugliness.[41]

Among contemporary philosophers, Alexander Nehamas has similarly emphasized the "forward-looking" element in our experience of the spell beauty casts, arguing that beauty promises more than it offers. For Nehamas, "interpretation, the effort to understand what it [beauty] promises, is forever a work in progress." "[U]nderstanding comes into full blossom as attraction withers, as it always does," he adds, "unless death comes first."[42] Here, Nehamas envisions the demise of a beautiful person whose beauty is manifest before he dies, but whose life will cease and beauty vanish before interpretation, driven by the promise of beauty, causes it to wither. In contrast, Du Bois envisions the deaths of beautiful persons who *become* beautiful through death, thus enabling us to interpret their lives as coherent triumphs over ugliness. Nehamas says that the forward-looking promise of beauty should be met with ever more interpretation. In contrast, Du Bois holds that it should be met with ever more future efforts to interrupt the eternal recurrence of ugliness. That, in part, explains why Du Bois's aesthetics is *political*, for it suggests that the point of beauty is to change the world, to delimit the spread of ugliness, not simply to interpret it.

CONCLUSION

In this chapter I have argued that Du Bois conceptualizes beauty in terms of two criteria. One is that an event counts as beautiful only if it comes to an apt end. With reference to the paradigm case of a beautiful life, Du Bois derives this criterion from two claims: that to count as beautiful a life must fulfill itself in death and thereby defeat its ugliness (claim 1); and that a life fulfills itself in death and thereby defeats its ugliness only if it comes to an apt end (claim 2). Unlike Leo Tolstoy (as Max Weber interprets him), Du Bois believes that the fulfillment of a life depends on its shape, not on whether it has come to the conclusion of a preordained cycle of life-stages. And unlike Aristotle, he believes that the ending of a life matters, not because it can effect a tragic reversal, but because it can overcome tragedy and ugliness, though with no guarantees. Du Bois's second criterion says that an event counts as beautiful only if, through its completion, it presents itself in a new and unexpected light. With regard to the case of a beautiful life, I have taken this criterion to mean that beautiful lives project possibilities that we have never before foreseen, possibilities beyond the horizon of our expectations for ourselves. Examples of such lives plausibly include Du Bois's Crummell and Lehrer's Glorya. Du Bois's conception of beauty is temporally bipolar, I have argued, for each of these criteria points in a different temporal direction: one toward the unity of a life that is past, the other toward an enriched vision of the future.

Methodologically speaking, I have proposed that Du Bois aimed to develop an account of beauty that identified attributes essential to the phenomenon which, because they explained beauty's power to limit the spread of ugliness—again, to curtail and circumscribe its presence in the world—were also salient to the perspective of the veiled corner. The point of Du Bois's method of inquiry, then, was not to elaborate a comprehensive account of the nature of beauty, but to stress features of the phenomenon, the emphasis on which would make a distinctive contribution to the conversation about beauty he inherited. Du Bois identifies two such features, each of which corresponds to one of his two criteria of a beautiful event. The first is beautiful events' attribute of coming to an apt end. The second is beautiful events' attribute of presenting themselves in a light that reveals unforeseen possibilities for realizing beauty's promise of a future different from the past. In the case of the beautiful event of Alexander Crummell's life, these attributes were evident to Du Bois in that life's coming to an end that triumphed over the tragedy and ugliness that had otherwise haunted it, and in that life's revelation of inspiring new expectations and possibilities—among them, no doubt, new expectations and possibilities that inspired Du Bois himself.

In the following two chapters, I take up Du Bois's concept of beauty as he applies it to his analysis of artistic and natural beauty. Thus, I turn from my examination of Du Bois's conceptualization of beauty to his political application of the concept he articulates. Du Bois's aesthetics is political, because he believes that beauty can contribute to the struggle against democratic despotism, and thus curtail and circumscribe the sway of the ugliness *it* embodies. As I established in chapter 3, he also believes that the white supremacist moral character imbuing white Christian culture functions to sustain the rule of democratic despotism by permitting and encouraging the subjection of nonwhite races to self-interested economic exploitation. Beauty and, specifically, artistic beauty can contribute to the struggle against democratic despotism, he thinks, because, as I argued in chapter 2, it can persuade the white Christian to question her idea of what Christianity requires of her and to reject as evil the beliefs, feelings, and ill-will that have prompted her to exclude black lives and voices from her circle of concern. In fine, artistic beauty can promote the culture of the crowd by undermining the moral sensibility and the culture that help to uphold democratic despotism. Natural beauty can contribute to the same struggle, by enabling black citizens to cope with their despair at the prospect of undermining a system of oppression that is propped up by a culture that is stubborn to rational revision.

In considering the case of artistic beauty, chapter 5 examines an argument, rooted in *Darkwater*'s "Postscript," wherein Du Bois retrospectively reflects on his book's poetic contents: "Between the sterner flights of logic," he writes, "I have sought to set some little alightings of what may be called poetry. They are tributes to Beauty, unworthy to stand alone; yet perversely, in my mind, now at the end, I know not whether I meant the Thought for the Fancy—or the Fancy for the Thought."[43] When Du Bois contrasts "sterner flights of logic" to "little alightings of what may be called poetry," he implies that he initially intended his book's imaginative, literary interludes to embellish its more austere, philosophically rigorous conceptual designs. Serious chapters of thought would constitute the book's main acts, while slight perches of fancy, pauses in the unfolding of *Darkwater*'s larger intellectual agenda, would function, intermittently, to relieve thought of the stricter demands of rational inquiry. Thus would fancy and its tributes to beauty serve thought. In retrospect, however, Du Bois sees things differently, even perversely, recognizing that *Darkwater*'s thought could be regarded as serving its fancy. For the purposes of the present argument, Du Bois's shift in perspective is noteworthy, for it already hints at an argument that he will later elaborate in "Criteria of Negro

Art"—namely, that the Negro artist is duty bound to deploy the primary objects of classical philosophical thought, truth and moral goodness, as handmaidens of the imagination, that she should use truth and moral goodness to expand our cognitive and moral horizons by representing them *as beautiful*. In the "Postscript" to *Darkwater*, Du Bois anticipates the central argument of "Criteria" *in nuce*. And in "Jesus Christ in Texas," a compelling tribute to beauty and the primary subject of chapter 5, he explores the implications of the argument. Specifically, he shows how an artistically crafted religious vision can come to an apt end that manifests the calm perfection of utter (absolute) music, even as it opens the entrenched moral perspective of a Christian white supremacist to new and unexpected possibilities, demanding that she expand the circle of her moral concern, and so realize the promise implicit in the experience of beauty by creating a more inclusive democratic citizenship.

In chapter 6, I consider the theme of natural beauty, and I argue that Du Bois's account of natural beauty, no less than his account artistic beauty, gives pride of place to poetic tributes to beauty—not now to the imagination of the visual or literary artist to whom he alludes in "Criteria" and elsewhere, but to the imagination of ordinary individuals seeking to perceive beauty in nature. Where the visual or literary artist employs fancy to enrich our conception of the demands of moral goodness, and thus to broaden the circle of our moral sympathies, the ordinary individual can use her imagination to enrich her conception of perceptible nature, and thus to widen her sense of the range of possibilities she could enact. When Du Bois travels to Jamaica, to renew his flagging spirit by exercising his powers of poetic imagination, he sees the Montego Bay sunset as following a narrative arc to an apt ending that presents it as something remarkable. Considering the sunset in the perspective of science, Du Bois like everyone else perceives it as predictably according with the laws of nature. But when he considers it from a different point of view—from the point of view of his practically engaged powers of poetic imagination—he sees in it an enchanting miracle that reveals the unexpected and unfamiliar possibility of causally undetermined action that effectively interrupts and subverts the rule of the ugly regularities that govern a racially oppressive social order. As we shall see, part of what connects Du Bois's belief that artistic beauty can undermine white supremacist habits to his belief that natural beauty can successfully counter the force of black pessimism is his deeply felt Romantic faith in the creative and cognitive powers of the imagination.

5

PROPAGANDA

In the present chapter, I interpret Du Bois's argument that "all art is propaganda" with reference to his analysis of the nature of beauty in the perspective of the veiled corner. By so interpreting Du Bois's argument, I am able to show how that analysis captures the notion of beauty that is implicit, recent commentary suggests, in his defense of his thesis about "all art."

In addition, I discuss Du Bois's short story "Jesus Christ in Texas," and I argue that Du Bois uses the story to illustrate the thesis that artistic beauty can transform the Christian white supremacist, demanding that she revise her guiding conception of the moral requirements of a Christian life. Here, then, I elaborate on my suggestion (see chapter 2) that, for Du Bois, artistic beauty can function as a medium of second-person, dialogic address, or appeal, that, by conveying a moral authority that the Christian addressee of the appeal (think, again, of Orlando Patterson's Southern clergyman, or perhaps of the Christian nationalists discussed by David Hollinger and Kristen Kobes Du Mez) acknowledges, holds her accountable to the conception of her conduct in light of which she assumes responsibility for it. I argue that the religious specificity of his short story notwithstanding, Du Bois also held that artistic beauty can convey moral authority without relying on religious doctrine.

PROPAGANDA AND BEAUTY

I turn now to "Criteria of Negro Art," Du Bois's clearest statement of his disagreement with the philosopher and so-called "Dean" of the Harlem Renaissance, Alain Locke, about the relation between art and propaganda. In chapter 4 I suggested that the central argument of "Criteria" develops one of Du Bois's earlier insights, evident in the "Postscript" of *Darkwater*, to the effect that thought can serve the aims of fancy. If this suggestion is correct, then Du Bois's account of the role of imagination in creating artistic beauty must be critical to his argument, and to understanding why he was not able to embrace Locke's view that genius and talent "must choose art and put aside propaganda."[1] Here, I concentrate on Du Bois's side of the argument and, in particular, on his explanation of the relation between art and propaganda in terms of the relation between imagination and beauty. This is the critical passage:

> [I]t is the bounden duty of black America to begin this great work of the creation of Beauty, of the preservation of Beauty, of the realization of Beauty, and we must use in this work all the methods that men have used before. And what have been the tools of the artist in times gone by? First of all, he has used the Truth—not for the sake of truth, not as a scientist seeking truth, but as one upon whom Truth eternally thrusts itself as the highest handmaid of the imagination, as the one great vehicle of universal understanding. Again artists have used Goodness—goodness in all its aspects of justice, honor and right—not for the sake of ethical sanction but as the one true method of gaining sympathy and human interest.
>
> The apostle of Beauty thus becomes the apostle of Truth and Right, not by choice but by inner and outer compulsion. Free he is, but his freedom is ever bounded by Truth and Justice. . . .

Thus all Art is propaganda and ever must be, despite the wailing of the purists.[2]

By rendering truth and goodness beautiful, Du Bois argues, the imaginative artist uses truth and goodness to advance the ends of universal understanding in the first instance and sympathy and human interest in the second. Put differently, Du Bois's artist promotes these ends by using truth and goodness to create beauty that manifests truth and goodness. She creates beauty, one could say, by exercising her power of imagination to cast truth and goodness as beautiful.

In recent work, two philosophers have commented, helpfully, on the particulars of Du Bois's argument. One, Melvin Rogers, reads "Criteria" in the perspective of *The Souls of Black Folk*. This is equally a strength and a weakness of Rogers's reading. Rogers rightly sees that "[w]hen Du Bois weds truth and goodness to the work of the artist and art to propaganda, he means for the reader to understand art as a vehicle for expanding the horizons of the recipient. The recipient is brought to a wider view of the world and his or her place in it than is currently on offer."[3] Through the communication of truth, art can expand our cognitive horizons, the sweep of our understanding; and through the communication of goodness it can expand our ethical horizons, the scope of our sympathy and human interest. But how does art do this? Rogers answers this question by turning to *Souls*, and by interpreting that text as the work of "an artist of letters" that exemplifies "the aims stipulated . . . in 'Criteria.'"[4] Significantly, Rogers characterizes *Souls*'s author and "artist of letters" not as "a creator of beauty," but as "a rhetorician."[5] And although he never conflates the concepts of beauty and rhetoric, the upshot of his characterization is an analysis of Du Bois's aesthetics in which the concept of rhetoric displaces the concept of beauty and the apostle of rhetoric displaces the apostle of beauty. Rogers's reading of "Criteria" is well served by these displacements, for it shows the relevance of "Criteria" to understanding *Souls*. But it is equally ill served, for it omits to interrogate Du Bois's concept of beauty and to show how *beauty*, or *beautiful* art, can expand our cognitive and ethical horizons through the communication of truth and goodness.

Paul Taylor's account of Du Bois's argument also deserves attention. According to Taylor, Du Bois endorses an expressivist picture of the world, the crux of which "is his determination to think of things as determinate but provisional expressions of an evolving world." On this account, "the world unfolds into new forms the way a seed unfolds into a tree . . . by clarifying, over time, what was inchoate and implicit: by actualizing in history what formerly existed only *in potentia*."[6] Considered in the perspective of Marx's and Dewey's revisions of Hegel's expressivism, Taylor's Du Bois envisions ethical life as a work-in-progress—that is, as an ongoing project of holistic self-cultivation, of individuals forming themselves by creatively responding to the histories, languages, and economic structures that encumber their lives.

Du Bois's expressivism is evident in his philosophy of art, Taylor shows, for the premise from which Du Bois infers that all art is and must be propaganda—that the apostle of beauty enjoys a freedom that is ever bounded by truth and justice—is the expressivist claim that artists are "dialectically enmeshed in wider webs of meaning concerning the true and the just, and must create themselves as individuals by working out their orientation to these networks."[7] The artist is at once outwardly and inwardly compelled by the webs of meaning that encumber her, for though these webs of meaning impose themselves from "without" the artist suffers them as parameters constituting her "within." As Taylor construes Du Bois, the freedom the apostle of truth and right can claim in relation to these parameters is akin to self-legislation, because it is a freedom she realizes in creatively responding to them, in working out her relationship to them, and, eventually, in genuinely making them her own.

But, again, how does beauty figure here? Or, more exactly, what about the nature of beauty explains how an artist can use the true and the just (for Du Bois, a mode of the morally good) and the other values that encumber her to make beauty that manifests those values? Taylor omits to say how beauty features in his appraisal of Du Bois's aesthetics, but his interpretation of Du Bois as an expressivist provides a clue. Specifically, it suggests that beauty expresses and clarifies the values of truth and right precisely in virtue of its determinateness. Thus, where Rogers shows that Du Boisian artistic beauty has to have the capacity to extend the range of our understanding and sympathies, Taylor proposes that it must realize that capacity through the actualization of the limits that define it. Du Bois's "Of Beauty and Death" analysis of the nature of beauty captures both these insights, for it explains *how* beauty can expand our cognitive and ethical horizons, and *how* a beautiful event could become determinate and thus clarify the values of truth and right.

Recall that Du Bois's analysis identifies attributes essential to beauty that, because they explain beauty's power to curtail and circumscribe the presence of ugliness, are salient to the perspective of the veiled corner. One attribute is a beautiful event coming to an apt ending. The other is a beautiful event presenting itself in a light that reveals unforeseen possibilities for fulfilling the promise of a future different from the past. Accordingly, Du Bois's first criterion of beauty stipulates that an event—an action, a life, or, for example, and as we shall see in the present chapter, an artistically crafted vision—counts as beautiful only if it comes to an apt ending. The second stipulates that an event counts as beautiful only if, through its completion, it reveals possibilities heretofore unfamiliar to us.

The second criterion captures Rogers's insights, for it lets us see that a beautiful event could expand our cognitive and ethical horizons by presenting the truth or moral goodness it embodies as inviting us to embrace new, unforeseen possibilities of understanding and human sympathy. The first criterion captures Taylor's idea of determinateness, for it lets us see that a beautiful event could become determinate by coming to an apt and definite end.

Now for Du Bois, I argued in chapter 1, receptivity to unfamiliar possibilities is a form of alertness to those possibilities involving a desire to answer to them. Where the democratic culture of the crowd tends to prevail, I added, citizens embody the virtue of receptivity, and so they desire to answer to strangers' insights by considering how they bear on their deliberations as to how the polity should be governed. In the case, then, of the Christian white supremacist, the function of an aesthetic education that would promote such a culture—of an aesthetic education through Du Boisian propaganda as Rogers and Taylor so usefully conceptualize it—is to cultivate her capacity for receptivity by prompting her to see that the circle of Christian moral concern (in Rogers's terms, the compass of her ethical horizon) properly comprehends black voices and insights. Beautiful art can mandate an alternative conception of a genuinely Christian life, Du Bois believes, and thereby call on the Christian white supremacist to repudiate the beliefs, feelings, and ill-will that have led her to exclude black voices from her circle of concern, and that have causally contributed to the domination and exploitation of the world's darker peoples—as we saw in chapter 3. It is perhaps not surprising, then, that Du Bois places "Jesus Christ in Texas," the *Darkwater* "tribute to beauty" to which I now turn, immediately before his defense of his democratic ideal in "Of the Ruling of Men," for the realization of that ideal presupposes that the Christian white supremacist has repudiated her white supremacist commitments.[8]

PROPAGANDA ⚭ 111

FIGURE 5.1 Albrecht Dürer, Adoration of the Kings, 1504. Galleria degli Uffizi, Florence.

"JESUS CHRIST IN TEXAS"

Among Du Bois scholars it is well known that "Jesus Christ in Texas" first appeared with the title "Jesus Christ in Georgia," in the December 1911 issue of the *Crisis*, and that by changing the title and setting the story in Waco, Texas, Du Bois relates its ending, which features a lynching, to the 1916 lynching of a black teenager, Jesse Washington, in Waco, Texas.[9] Less well known, however, is that the heading of the cover of the December 1911 journal issue was emblazoned with the title "Christmas Crisis," that below that heading Du

FIGURE 5.2 The front page of "Jesus Christ in Georgia," from the December, 1911, Christmas Crisis.

THE convict guard laughed. "I don't know," he said, "I hadn't thought of that——"

He hesitated and looked at the stranger curiously. In the solemn twilight he got an impression of unusual height and soft dark eyes.

"Curious sort of acquaintance for the Colonel," he thought; then he continued aloud: "But that nigger there is bad; a born thief and ought to be sent up for life; is practically; got ten years last time——"

Here the voice of the promoter talking within interrupted; he was bending over his figures, sitting by the Colonel. He was slight, with a sharp nose.

"The convicts," he said, "would cost us $96 a year and board. Well, we can squeeze that so that it won't be over $125 apiece. Now, if these fellows are driven, they can build this line within twelve months. It will be running next April. Freights will fall fifty per cent. Why, man, you will be a millionaire in less than ten years."

The Colonel started. He was a thick, short man, with clean-shaven face, and a certain air of breeding about the lines of his countenance; the word millionaire sounded well in his ears. He thought— he thought a great deal; he almost heard the puff of the fearfully costly automobile that was coming up the road, and he said:

"I suppose we might as well hire them."

"Of course," answered the promoter.

The voice of the tall stranger in the corner broke in here:

"It will be a good thing for them?" he said, half in question.

The Colonel moved. "The guard makes strange friends," he thought to himself. "What's this man doing here, anyway?" He looked at him, or rather, looked at his eyes, and then somehow felt a warming toward him. He said:

"Well, at least it can't harm them— they're beyond that."

"It will do them good, then," said the stranger again. The promoter shrugged his shoulders.

"It will do us good," he said.

But the Colonel shook his head impatiently. He felt a desire to justify him-

Bois set an image of Albrecht Dürer's 1504 painting of the epiphany, "Adoration of the Kings"; and that Du Bois alluded to the painting and foreshadowed the conclusion of the story by placing the image of a crucified Christ, looking down and to his left at a lynched black man, atop the page on which the story begins. Drawing on these less familiar considerations, I read "Jesus Christ in Texas" as Du Bois's argument, relating his aesthetics to his moral psychology, that a beautiful, artistic vision can subvert the Christian white supremacist's idea of what Christianity *is*, of what it enjoins upon those who embrace it, and thereby dislodge her cognitive, affective, and motivational commitments. In addition, I explore Du Bois's argument for the thesis that humanly crafted works of art—including dramatic actions, as well as works of art that rank with Dürer's artistic achievements—can speak with a moral authority unmoored from the sort of religious commitment that may seem essential to the purport of the short story. Specifically, I consider "Jesus Christ in Texas" in the perspective of Du Bois's writing about the dramatic, final days of the abolitionist John Brown.

A tall stranger overhears a negotiation between "the colonel," who needs laborers to build a railroad line, and a "promoter," who promises that leasing convicts will make the colonel a millionaire. After striking a bargain with the promoter, and after a short exchange with the stranger, the colonel, a white man who in the twilight takes the stranger to be white, invites him to ride to town with him, his wife, and his little girl. During the trip, the stranger's "long cloak-like coat" gives the colonel and other members of his family the impression that he is a foreigner. Anticipating the arrival of the guests she has asked to dinner—including the judge, the judge's wife and daughter, and a rector—the colonel's wife wonders whether she should invite their apparently "cultured" companion to join them. Upon arriving home, she decides, finally, to ask him in, but when she rings for the butler to bring tea and switches on "a blaze of light" to illuminate the dark parlor she is stunned.¹⁰ In Du Bois's words,

> With one accord they all looked at the stranger, for they had hardly seem [*sic*] him well in the glooming twilight. The woman started in amazement and the colonel half rose in anger. Why, the man was a mulatto, surely; even if he did not know the Negro blood, their practiced eyes knew it. He was tall and straight and the coat looked like a Jewish gabardine. His hair hung in close curls far down the sides of his face and his face was olive, even yellow.¹¹

It is striking that, at this critical juncture of the story, Du Bois's description of the stranger, whom we eventually learn is Jesus Christ, highlights a discrepancy between his racially and ethnically ambiguous looks and the racial classification to which he is subject. As Edward Blum has noticed, Du Bois characterizes the stranger's dress and facial features in ways that could quite reasonably be taken to indicate "a Middle-Eastern or Mediterranean ethnic background."¹² In the eyes of Du Bois's Texas white Southerners, however, he is either white, black (Negro), or a "mulatto," which is to say, *partially black*. From these southerners' perspective, racial identity is always determinable with reference to the simple opposition between white and not white, and if one is not white, which is to say, *not purely white*, then one's nonwhiteness is due to the fact that one is descended from blacks. In effect, observable ambiguity gives way to the "practiced" imposition of a conceptual frame of reference that provides for the possibility of unambiguous, binomial classification: either one is white or not white, and if one is not white it is because one is either wholly or partially black—in other words, because whether one acknowledges it or not *some* quantity of "Negro blood" runs through one's veins.

The remainder of the story emphasizes a series recognitions and misrecognitions of Du Bois's nonwhite Jesus Christ.[13] Neither the rector; nor the colonel and his wife; nor the judge and his wife; nor the judge's daughter and the navel officer accompanying her—all of which characters are white—recognize that the stranger is Jesus Christ. In contrast, the black nurse sees that the stranger is Jesus and kneels before him "in the dust."[14] So too does the black butler apprehend the stranger's divinity when, falling to his knees, he lets drop to the floor the china tea service he has been carrying. The black convict seems also to recognize that the stranger is Jesus Christ when, after looking into his eyes, he drops the hammer he has been using to pound stones, and when later, after running away, he looks into the stranger's face and enjoys the same gladness the butler and the nurse experience in their encounters with the stranger.

Only two white characters appear to recognize that the stranger is Jesus Christ. One is the little girl who converses with him "in low tones" and who later, "with a glad cry," nestles in his arms. The other is the farmer's wife, who appears near the end of the story. There is innocence about the girl, as Du Bois depicts her, which implies that she has yet to yield, or fully to yield, to the character-forming heritage that Du Bois associates with the modern discovery of personal whiteness. Put otherwise, she has yet to acquire the vicious cognitive, affective, and motivational dispositions that mark the character of the white supremacist. But the farmer's wife is a different story altogether, for like the colonel and the other white adults appearing in Du Bois's story, she exemplifies that character and personifies its entrenchment. In his depiction of the farmer's wife, Du Bois draws the portrait of someone whose white supremacist commitments abide peaceably with Christian doctrine. That portrait, I suggest, serves Du Bois as a case study for examining the possibility that beauty can unsettle such commitments. In the story, the farmer's wife is transformed through her beautiful vision of the black stranger as Jesus Christ.

The farmer's wife begins to converse with the stranger, thinking from his voice that he is white. After recounting something of her life, and of her and husband's ambition to buy a "new farm," she notes that it is "hard to get niggers to work," adding that "they ought all to be in a chain-gain and made to work."[15] After the stranger asks her if she likes all her neighbors, Du Bois writes the following:

> She hesitated.
> "Most of them," she said, and then, looking up into his face and putting her hand into his as though he were her father, she said:
> "There are none I hate; no none at all."
> He looked away, holding her hand in his, and said dreamily:
> "You love your neighbor as yourself?"
> She hesitated.
> "I try—" she began, and she looked the way he was looking; down under the hill where lay a little half-ruined cabin.
> "They are niggers," she said briefly.
> He looked at her. Suddenly a confusion came over her and she insisted, she knew not why.
> "But they are niggers!
>
> With a sudden impulse she arose and hurriedly lighted the lamp that stood just within the door, and held it above her head. She saw his dark face and curly hair. She shrieked in angry terror and rushed down the path, and just as she rushed down, the black convict came running up with his hands outstretched. They met in midpath, and before he could stop he had run against her and she fell heavily to earth and lay white and still. Her husband came rushing around the house with a cry and an oath.[16]

While the farmer's wife hates blacks, despises them, and believes, apparently, that they should be forced to labor for the Earth's rightful owners, like her and her husband, she demonstrates confidence in the paternal, moral authority she attributes to the stranger. Reciprocating her trusting and intimate hand gesture, the stranger exploits that confidence by reasoning with her, by adducing an argument: namely, that she should revise her behavior toward blacks because the Christian moral imperative she endorses—that one should love one's neighbor as oneself—requires that she do so. But the farmer's wife resists the stranger's charge of hypocrisy and his attempt at an internal critique of her golden rule–flouting, hostile behavior—rather she insists on it, repeating that the neighbors residing in the half-ruined cabin down under the hill "are niggers!" In the eyes of the farmer's wife, there is no contradiction between her avowed white supremacy and her Christian commitment to the golden rule. The stranger's protestations to the contrary confuse her, for by questioning her white supremacist commitments they disturb her confidence in his moral authority. Indeed, the farmer's wife's confidence is so deeply disturbed that she abruptly withdraws her hand from the stranger's hand, arises, and hurries to light a lamp in order to see just whom she is dealing with.

What she sees is curly hair and a dark face—certainly a nonwhite face and a face that, like the colonel and his wife, she doubtlessly identifies as belonging to someone black, if not wholly then partially. Believing, then, that she has just been clasping hands with a black man, the farmer's wife shrieks in "angry terror" and rushes down a path where the now escaped black convict collides with her. The collision seals the convict's fate, for the farmer then accuses him of attacking his wife and rallies a lynch mob to murder him.

"Jesus Christ in Texas" ends with Du Bois's descriptions of the vision the farmer's wife sees and of her responses to what she sees after she hears "the creaking of the limb where the body hung."[17]

But resolutely she crawled to the window and peered out into the moonlight; she saw the dead man writhe. He stretched his arms out like a cross, looking upward. She gasped and clung to the window sill. Behind the swaying body, and down where the little, half-ruined cabin lay, a single flame flashed up amid the far-off shout and cry of the mob. A fierce joy sobbed up through the terror in her soul and then sank abashed as she watched the flame rise. Suddenly whirling into one great crimson column it shot to the top of the sky and threw great arms athwart the gloom until above the world and behind the roped and swaying form hung quivering and burning a great crimson cross.

She hid her dizzy aching head in an agony of tears, and dared not look, for she knew. Her dry lips moved:

"Despised and rejected of men."

She knew and the very horror of it lifted her dull and shrinking eyelids. There heaven-tall, earth-wide, hung the stranger on a crimson cross, riven and bloodstained, with thorn-crowned head and pierced hands. She stretched her arms and shrieked.

He did not hear. He did not see. His calm dark eyes, all sorrowful, were fastened on the writhing, twisting body of the thief, and a voice out of the winds of the night, saying—

"This day thou shalt be with me in Paradise."[18]

The farmer's wife is undone, but what devastates her? Du Bois's answer to this question, I believe, is that the farmer's wife is undone by the beauty of the vision she sees when she peers out her bedroom window in the direction of the half-ruined cabin. But what about that vision makes it beautiful?[19]

When she looks out her window, the vision the farmer's wife sees reveals itself through several episodes. The first image she sees is of the convict swaying and stretching his arms out like a cross. Then a second image, a flashing flame forming itself into a cross behind the mob's victim, immediately supplements the first. The farmer's wife's sight of the second image prompts her to hide her head in an agony of tears, for her abashment, her sense of shame, stifles her courage openly to face what she has seen and now knows (she "dared not look"): namely, that the sequence of images unfolding before her is a dramatization of the crucifixion of a black man who is Jesus Christ. Mouthing the words of the prophet, Isaiah—"despised and rejected of men"[20]—she finally regains her courage, lifting her eyelids and candidly observing that the black stranger is Jesus Christ as she follows her vision to its end. But is the end apt? Is it suited to the completion of her vision? Because the farmer's wife knows the Bible, she knows the story of self-sacrifice that her vision expresses and she perceives that her vision has come to a fitting end—more precisely, to an end that builds upon and coheres with the episodes through which it unfolded, showing Christ accepting death on the cross and confirming the redemption of a convicted thief. The farmer's wife's vision satisfies the first criterion of beauty, for it comes to a suitable conclusion. It also satisfies the second criterion, for it shows Christ's death to have been the self-sacrifice not of a white Jesus, but of a black, suffering servant demonstrating solidarity with the suffering of other despised and rejected black people.[21] Put differently, the image of "the cross and the lynching tree" that concludes the farmer's wife's vision casts the vision's presentation of the stranger's self-sacrifice in a light that is *unfamiliar* to her—namely, as the morally righteous sacrifice of a *black* Christ on behalf of the humanity of *black* people.[22]

Du Bois's description of the farmer's wife's vision is carefully wrought. To appreciate its specificity, we need only contrast that description and the picture that foreshadows it (noted above) to the Dürer artwork to which the picture alludes. The picture foreshadows the ending of the story, for it depicts the apex and crossbar of Christ's crucifix as flames shooting above and to the sides of his head, and because it portrays Jesus's eyes as "fastened . . . on the body" of the hanging man placed below him and to his left. And the picture alludes to the "Adoration of the Kings," the Dürer painting appearing on the cover of the "Christmas Crisis," for it depicts the tilt of Christ's head, as he peers down at the lynching victim beside him, as mirroring the tilt of Balthazar's head, Dürer's self-portrait in profile, as he peers at the late arriving black Magus, a figure set off from the other figures and dominating the right side of the painting.[23] Du Bois improvises on Dürer, I suggest, by replacing the image of Dürer/Balthazar's gesture of recognition, which bridges the divide between Dürer's Christian world and its black "others," with the image of Jesus Christ's gesture of recognition, which affirms a despised and rejected black man's humanity, yet without positing him as an "other" in whom the Christian self must learn to discover itself. For Du Bois, the juxtaposition of the cross and the lynching tree is paradigmatic of, not incidental to, the substance of Christianity.

But what *is* Christianity? For Du Bois's Christian white supremacist, I have argued, Christianity does not demand that a Christian demonstrate Christian virtue in her transactions with blacks. Thus, a putatively internal critique of the Christian white supremacist's behavior, such as the stranger attempts with the farmer's wife, is bound to fail. Yet the farmer's wife's vision unsettles her in a way that neither the charge of hypocrisy nor scientific inquiry ever could. And that, I suggest, is because it concludes with an image that casts Christ's self-sacrifice and the moral goodness it embodies in a new and unfamiliar light—in a black light, so to speak. Witness to an unfolding vision, the farmer's wife seems first to gasp in terror when she sees the lynched convict. But her terror is soon augmented by joy, as the flame she sees forms itself into a cross. As the flame rises, finally, and the farmer's wife sees the stranger hanging from the cross, a feeling of shame supplements her feelings of terror and joy. The sight of a black Christ affirming black people dramatically challenges the farmer's wife's understanding of what Christianity is, of what it requires of her, by asking her to emulate the moral goodness of the crucified stranger—thus, implicitly, to reform her behavior toward her black neighbors. If she feels shame, it is because a riveting re-visioning of the meaning of the cross has disturbed the white supremacist commitments behind that behavior.[24] In terms I introduced in chapter 2, the farmer's wife's vision of a black Christ challenges her guiding conception of Christian conduct. As a mode of second-person moral address, it appeals to her practically to reflect on and transform that conception—that is, to recognize that her guiding conception of Christian conduct is incorrect, and that a correct conception demands of her that she broaden the compass of her moral concern to include the lives and voices of black citizens.

Within the context of the story, Christ is the artist of the farmer's wife's vision. In that capacity, he brings her vision to an apt and definite end that represents his own moral goodness in terms unfamiliar to her, thus widening her ethical horizons and meeting Du Bois's two criteria of beauty. In keeping with Du Bois's analysis, her response to what she sees is temporally bipolar. By shaping an unfamiliar representation of his own moral goodness, the divine artist uses that goodness to elicit the farmer's wife's sympathy for black life—a sympathy she expresses when she stretches her arms toward the crucified Christ, shrieking a second time, not now because she is terrified by the stranger's blackness, but because she is horrified by the suffering she witnesses. Traumatically captivated by the sight of that suffering, she aspires now to live her life differently, to conjure a future less ugly than the past, by embracing a (by her lights) novel and unsettling conception of the requirements of Christian morality and hence the heretofore unforeseen possibility of forging a life that receptively hearkens to the insights of the black stranger. Paradoxically, however, the work of art that reveals and calls her to take up this unforeseen possibility likewise exhibits a self-contained perfection, a completeness expressing a tranquil indifference to her feelings characteristic of "utter music." For the divine artist portrays himself as neither seeing nor hearing the farmer's wife's expression of sympathy, but, to borrow Michael Fried's term, as calmly "absorbed" by the writhing, twisting body of the thief.[25] Du Bois captures the completeness of the farmer's wife's vision with the portrait of it that he appends to the beginning of the 1911 version of his short story. If the farmer's wife herself finds satisfaction in the vision, if it affords her a "fierce joy," it seems that that satisfaction is soon overwhelmed by her feelings of shame and dissatisfaction with the life she has heretofore lived.[26]

It would be a mistake to assume that the farmer's wife has put her white supremacist moral character behind her. Impervious to Christ's reasoning and argument, she is nonetheless gripped by his artwork, which invokes neither scientific inquiry nor a contradiction between principle and practice, but appeals to her sense of who she fundamentally is. In Du Bois's story, Christ's art demonstrates a power to upend the farmer's wife's self-understanding, to compel her to see that Christianity is not what she thought it was, and thus that the life she has been living is not a Christian life. Prior to envisioning the cross and the lynching tree she felt no ambivalence between living as a Christian and living as a white supremacist. But her vision creates ambivalence, an inner conflict of warring ideals that utterly disorients her. Christ's artwork expands the farmer's wife's ethical horizon, imbuing her with new sympathy and human interest, but she ultimately remains "dizzy" and in "agony," which suggests that she has lost without fully regaining a secure and confident moral bearing, not that she has completely shed the white supremacist beliefs, feelings, and motivational dispositions that Christ's artistically crafted vision has dislodged.[27]

In "Jesus Christ in Texas," propaganda in the mode of art leaves the farmer's wife discomposed and embattled by the competing claims of her white supremacist commitments and her newfound understanding of Christianity. Through his portrait of her transformation, Du Bois's proposes that artistic propaganda, through realizations of beauty that thrust moral goodness into unfamiliar and potentially unsettling lights, can combat white supremacy and help to dismantle racial hierarchy. The vision that shocks the farmer's wife is divinely crafted propaganda that functions less to promote faith than to transform it. In the idiom of analytical theology, it is a revelation at once manifestational *and* propositional; it is a visible appearance of a person, Jesus Christ, as well as a communication of a proposition, a message—namely, and most simply stated, that her Christianity requires the farmer's wife to endorse the golden rule in her dealings with blacks as well as whites. The farmer's wife takes the message to be true, and to be justifiably calling her to question her guiding conception of Christian conduct, for the revealed person of Jesus Christ, through his artistic crafting of her vision, attests to its truth.[28] A natural question to ask here, of course, is whether Du Bois maintained that the invocation of divine testimony is an essential feature of those beautiful acts, visions, lives, and artworks that we regard as justifiably calling us to question our ideal, guiding conceptions of ethical conduct.

"No," I think, is the accurate answer to this question, and my reason for this answer is Du Bois's account of the aesthetic and, specifically, dramatic power of the final forty days of the life of John Brown. Du Bois's biography of Brown appeared in 1909, the year before he first published "The Souls of White Folk," and in the book's final chapter he writes of the "wonderful message of his [Brown's] forty days in prison, which all in all made the mightiest Abolitionist document that America has known. . . . [S]poken in the shadow of death, its dramatic intensity after that wild and puzzling raid, its deep earnestness as embodied in the character of the man, *did more to shake the foundations of slavery than any single thing that ever happened in America.*"²⁹ This last remark—that Brown's last days did more to shake the foundations of slavery than any single thing that ever happened in America—should give us pause, for it suggests that during those last days at least some of Brown's fellow citizens came to regard him as making a valid claim on their consciences. How did this happen?

"How should we know [the right]?," Du Bois asks. "That is the Riddle of the Sphinx. We are but darkened groping souls, that know not light often because of its very blinding radiance. Only in time is truth revealed. To-day at last we know: John Brown was right." John Brown played a critical role in revealing that slavery is wrong. Expanding on this proposal, Du Bois further maintains that the revelation of moral truth that Brown embodied forcefully challenged his fellow Americans' "life morality," a morality of temporizing expediency, as when, Du Bois writes, "there shines a great white light . . . blinding by its all-seeing brilliance making a whole world simply a light and a darkness—a right and a wrong." Such a light can be blinding, and thus tend to hide the truth it reveals, but it need not obscure the truth to such a degree that keeps men from whispering, Du Bois writes, "'But—but—of course'; 'the thing is plain, but it is too plain to be true—it is true but truth is not the only thing in the world.'" Blinding, radiant light may conceal the truth it reveals, but when the truth still, somehow, shines through the light, men hide from it, "they burrow and grovel," even as in, through, and on them "blazes that mighty light with its horror of darkness . . . [while] behind it peals the voice—the Riddle of the Sphinx, that must be answered." Here, Du Bois's second reference to the riddle of the sphinx suggests that the question "How should we know [the right]?" has a twofold significance—that it asks not only how we can tell right from wrong, but, also, *how do we take up what we know to be right?*: do we avoid what we know, or do we acknowledge it, which would be to receive what we know in such a way that makes a difference to the way we live?³⁰

Du Bois believed that "the soul of John Brown" was a light that revealed the truth about slavery, thus helping his fellow citizens to tell right from wrong, and that the revelation of that truth led his fellow citizens, at least some of them, to regard him as authoritatively calling them, first, to question the compromised ideals animating their life morality and, second, to embrace the truth in such a way that changed their lives and shook the foundations of slavery. But, again, how did that happen? The essence of Du Bois's answer to this question, I propose, is his assertion that Brown "did not use argument, he was himself an argument."[31] Du Bois's clearest explanation of this assertion comes in the following passage:

> To be sure, the nation had long been thinking over the problem of the black man, but never before had its attention been held by such deep dramatic and personal interest as in the forty days from mid-October to December, 1859. This arresting of national attention was due to Virginia and to John Brown:—to Virginia by reason of its exaggerated plaint; to John Brown whose strength, simplicity, and acumen made his trial, incarceration and execution the most powerful Abolition argument yet offered. The very processes by which Virginia used John Brown to "fire the Southern heart" were used by John Brown to fire the Northern conscience.[32]

The nation's attention was arrested by its interest in the person of John Brown and the drama of his trial, incarceration, and execution. Du Bois describes the person, the character, of John Brown in terms of strength, simplicity, and acumen, and later, we have seen, in terms of his deep earnestness. Indeed, it is the character of John Brown—or, more exactly, the dramatization of his character over the course of his trial, incarceration, and execution—that initially attracts and then sustains the nation's attention, particularly Brown's "obedience to the highest call of self-sacrifice for the welfare of his fellow men" (here, as in "Jesus Christ in Texas," Du Bois glosses the theme of self-sacrifice with reference to the Isaiah 53).[33] For Du Bois, Brown's final forty days constituted an artwork, a theatrical performance of moral virtue embattled with a defense of slavery that, anticipating *Darkwater*'s explanation of the nature of beauty, triumphs in death. And it was precisely this dramatically intense display of embattled virtue that explains Brown's preeminent role in shaking the foundations of slavery, Du Bois proposes, for it revealed the truth about slavery and so gripped the nation's Northern citizens that they came to view John Brown's performance of virtue as *itself* an argument making a valid claim on their consciences, as justifiably calling them to reject their life morality.

When Du Bois completed *John Brown*, he had yet fully to articulate his analysis of the nature of beauty, or clearly to argue that beauty can help to undermine white supremacy. As I hope to have shown, however, there is much in his discussion of John Brown's final days that contains the seeds of that argument—including the idea that beautifully wrought lives, actions (we can think of John Brown's final days as an extended action), or works of art can reveal moral truths that challenge our guiding, prereflective understandings of what it is to live a moral life. In addition, I also hope to have shown that Du Bois rejected the view that a dramatic or otherwise artistic revelation of a moral truth could claim the conscience of a nation only if backed by divine testimony. In *John Brown*, Du Bois invokes the idea of a revealed moral truth—that slavery is wrong—but without suggesting, as he may seem to in "Jesus Christ in Texas," that the power of such a revelation to claim the conscience of its audience—that is, to be regarded by its audience as justifiably calling it to question its ideal conception of ethical conduct[34]—depends essentially on the attestation of a divine being to the truth in question. But even there, I think, we need not read Du Bois along these lines. Rather he might be read as suggesting that the vision of the cross and the lynching tree to which the farmer's wife was privy so powerfully, so insistently conveyed its moral message that even a nonbeliever could have experienced it as making a valid claim on her conscience. If this was Du Bois's position, then we can note his affinity to some other philosophers of art, including, for example, Iris Murdoch, who held that the "objective vision" afforded by good art carries us beyond "the selfish and obsessive limitations of our personalities," and so enlarges our sensibility. Good art "is not a diversion or a side-issue," she averred, but "a place where the nature of morality can be *seen*. . . . We surrender ourselves to its *authority* with a love which is unpossessive and unselfish."[35] Or, to take an example from a different philosophical tradition, Hans-Georg Gadamer, who highlights the second-personal, dialogical power of aesthetic world disclosure to pull us "up short," thus, persuasively to challenge our understanding of some subject matter—including the nature of morality—by surprising and shocking us.[36] It is likely, I believe, that Du Bois thought that "Jesus Christ in Texas," the short story itself, could also have this sort of effect. Beginning with the words "It was in Waco, Texas," it ends with words—"This day thou shalt be with me in Paradise"—that, by alluding to a world beyond the world of dehumanizing black lynchings, express a crucified Christ's acknowledgment of black humanity. Thus, like Du Bois's story of Alexander Crummell's life, "Jesus Christ in Texas," follows a narrative trajectory from tragedy to comedy, from an invocation of the site of Jesse Washington's murder to an anticipation of his otherworldly redemption. The story's power to pull the reader "up short" comes in its final paragraphs, which bring the story to an apt ending, and which invite the white Christian reader to adopt the farmer's wife's point of view—thus to render herself vulnerable to the shock of recognizing in the farmer's wife's transformation the revelation of a possibility that similarly exists for her and for white Christians like her.

Among contemporary critics, artists, and political theorists, finally, we need not look far to appreciate the analytical relevance of Du Bois's views. Let three examples suffice. One is Darryl Pinckney's reading of the movie *Moonlight*—specifically, his claim that the film "bestows the capability of feeling romantic love onto a figure that has long been a symbol of predatory sexuality: the big, bad black male."[37] Here, Pinckney views the film as exposing the immorality, the antiblack racism, that is implicit in the notion of romantic love that generally animates our fellow citizens' lives. On Pinckney's account, in other words, *Moonlight* prompts us to see, he hopes to our chagrin, that our operative idea of romantic love, our ordinary ways of talking and thinking about what it is, about who experiences it and how it appears in the world, typically exclude the possibility that big, bad black men enjoy tender, amorous feelings of affection. In terms that echo Du Bois, at least as I have interpreted him, the film questions our received and morally compromised ideal of romantic love, and so reveals the possibility of reorienting our thinking and lives around a more inclusive conception. A second example is Chris Ofili's painting *The Thinker*, the black British artist's portrait of a scantily clad black woman in the image of Rodin's famous sculpture. As I regard Ofili's painting, it suggests that the concept of intellectual virtue (of the qualities of character that make for intellectual flourishing) operative in our professional practices and in many citizens' daily lives is, like the operative concept of romantic love, morally compromised by the tendency to exclude the possibility that black women, forever sexualized by racial ideology, can truly thrive as thinkers. In Du Bois's terms, again, Ofili's painting reveals the possibility of culture shaped by a more inclusive, operative conception of intellectual virtue.[38]

My third example concerns the aesthetic dimensions of social movements. Echoing Du Bois's discussion of John Brown, Karuna Mantena has recently highlighted Martin Luther King Jr.'s 1963 staging of the dignity of civil rights protestors in Birmingham,

Alabama. King regarded protest as a theatrical affair, Mantena argues, and he staged the dignity of the civil rights protestors to make it public. In Birmingham, the effect of the protestors' dramatization of their dignity, when they "stopped and knelt in prayer," was to leave the policemen, who had been commanded to turn a high-pressure hose on them, shaken, undone, and so morally unbalanced that they were unable to do what they had been ordered to do.[39] On Mantena's view, the protestors' actions unexpectedly presented the protestors' dignity as making a claim on the policemen; that is, as holding them to account and implicating them in the perpetuation of injustice. The effect of this presentation, of this theatrical appeal to the policemen's conscience, she argues, was to shame them. Put in terms of Du Bois's political aesthetics, the protestors' public theater thrust their dignity into a new light, challenged the policemen's understanding of what respect for human dignity morally requires, and thus caused the policemen to regard their commitment to following orders as shameful.

A PROBLEM

At its best, Du Bois's account of art as propaganda helps us to see how political art and theater can challenge our received conceptions of what morality is, of what it requires of us, and, I have also suggested, how our ordinary manner of talking and thinking about our lives can be morally compromised. In these ways, moreover, political art and theater can expand the scope of our moral sympathy and interest. At its worst, however, Du Bois's understanding of art as propaganda invites a tendency to strictly discipline artists who fail to represent blacks as moral exemplars. Du Bois himself succumbs to this tendency when, in a 1928 book review, he compares Claude McKay's *Home to Harlem* to Nella Larsen's *Quicksand* and praises the latter at the expense of the former.

Du Bois castigates McKay's novel, writing that, "for the most part," it "nauseates me, and after the dirtier parts of its filth I feel distinctly like taking a bath." Du Bois's central complaint against *Home to Harlem* is that it caters to whites' demand for literature that depicts Negroes as licentious. Especially when contrasted to his praise for Nella Larsen's novel, whose heroine he lauds in the same review as "typical of the new, honest, young fighting Negro woman," it seems that Du Bois's assessment of McKay's fiction amounts to the proposition that, rather than portray moral virtue in a new light—as manifest, say, in the exemplary moral goodness of Larsen's *black* female protagonist—it mainly serves to reproduce familiar stereotypes of blacks behaving immorally.[40] Although such an aesthetic judgment is prima facie consistent with the aesthetics Du Bois outlines in "Criteria" and "Of Beauty and Death," it also highlights a problem with that aesthetics: namely, that it lends itself to a dogmatism, a moralism, that nowadays we tend to characterize as expressing a "respectability" ideology intended to sanction wayward black folk. To put the point a little differently, Du Boisian artistic propaganda, because it depends on moral strictures to expand our ethical horizons, is double-edged.

In Du Bois's view, I suggest, Larsen's portrait of her protagonist envisions a black woman as a responsible, morally virtuous person whose voice deserves to be heard by her white fellow citizens, and so, like Jesus Christ's self-portrait in the vision he creates for the farmer's wife, might well convince those citizens to reconsider their tendency to exclude blacks like her from their circle of concern. To the extent, however, that Du Bois wields Helga Crane's character as cudgel to lambast McKay's depiction of black life, he himself effectively insists on a narrow, exclusionary—perhaps Victorian—conception of the requirements of moral virtue. Du Bois endorses beautiful propaganda, because it can serve to contest and expand white supremacists' conceptions of what morality demands of them, yet he uncritically takes for granted that the idea of moral goodness that he himself avows is not subject to valid contestation by McKay's or any other work of art. Considered against the backdrop of the thesis that art is propaganda, Du Bois's review of Larsen's and McKay's novels suggests that whenever art serves the purposes of propaganda, its emancipatory invocation of moral considerations (in Du Bois's case, conceptions of moral virtue and moral goodness cast in a "black light") to challenge a narrow, exclusionary social morality (in Du Bois case, the social morality of the Christian white supremacist) cannot but risk the tendency to treat those considerations themselves, and the exclusions *they* entail, as morally incontestable—what I have called "moralism."[41]

It is obvious, perhaps, that Du Bois's sometimes disposition to discipline black artists, like McKay, is rooted in his sometimes disposition to discipline black life, a point with which I conclude the present chapter because it reminds us that the example of a beautiful life is paradigmatic for Du Bois's general account of the nature of beauty. In contrast to his gloss on McKay's protagonist, Jake, "who has something appealing,"[42] Du Bois's gloss on Larsen's protagonist is *prescriptive* for black life, and for black women's lives, in a way that resonates not only with "Of Beauty and Death" but with "The Damnation of Women," chapter 7 of *Darkwater*. As I shall argue, in chapter 7, this prescriptive tendency sometimes tends to prolepsis—Du Bois's move from recommending that we strive to live, or to have lived, complete and beautiful lives to envisioning current, ongoing black lives as beautiful, and thus complete—and so enables us to see that and how the moralism that haunts his aesthetics limits his commitment to democracy. Before further exploring that limitation, however, I turn in the next chapter to Du Bois's account of natural beauty.

6

PESSIMISM

I begin the present chapter by returning to the following passage.

> Here, then, is beauty and ugliness, a whole vision of the world-sacrifice, a fierce gleam of world-hate. Which is life and what is death and how shall we face so tantalizing a contradiction? Any explanation must necessarily be subtle and involved. No pert and easy word of encouragement, no merely dark despair, can lay hold of the roots of these things. And first and before all, we cannot forget that this world is beautiful. Grant all its ugliness and sin—the petty, horrible snarl of its putrid threads, which few have seen more near or more often than I—notwithstanding all this, the beauty of this world is not to be denied.[1]

In chapter 4, I quoted these remarks to establish that Du Bois investigates the nature of beauty in order to identify features of the phenomenon that contradict, limit, and reduce the ugliness of the world. Beauty and ugliness coexist and beauty contradicts ugliness. But what should we make of that contradiction, and of the relation of its terms to our understanding of life and death? To those who despair at the world's ugliness, Du Bois replies that no pert and easy word of encouragement will seem adequate to answering these questions. And yet, in the same breath, he criticizes persons who despair for failing to fathom, for failing to grasp, that despair itself is no answer. It appears, therefore, that when Du Bois protests "that the beauty of this world is not to be denied," he means in part to respond to the questions he has posed by, again, asserting that beauty can serve life by functioning as an antidote to ugliness—a thesis I examine at length in chapter 4. But that he remonstrates, that his response is likewise a complaint, an insistence that beauty *is not to be denied*, suggests that he additionally intends to answer persons disposed to despair with *more* than a pert and easy word of encouragement—in particular, that he intends to prevail upon such persons to see that an important part of beauty's antidotal function is to counteract despair.

Du Bois again protests the despairer's tendency to downplay, even to deny the world's beauty, when, several paragraphs later in "Of Beauty and Death," he proclaims,

> Pessimism is cowardice. The man who cannot frankly acknowledge the "Jim-Crow" car as a fact and yet live and hope is simply afraid either of himself or of the world. There is not in the world a more disgraceful denial of human brotherhood than the "Jim-Crow" car of the southern United States; but, too, just as true, there is nothing more beautiful in the universe than sunset and moonlight on Montego Bay in far Jamaica. And both things are true and both belong to this our world, and neither can be denied.[2]

Jim Crow is ugly to the point of being disgraceful, and the sunset and moonlight at Montego Bay are as beautiful as beautiful can be. Neither can be denied. Here, as before, Du Bois's primary preoccupation is the person who denies the latter: that is, the person who, having denied the world's beauty, has been driven to despair, to living without hope, by the disgraceful ugliness of Jim Crow. And, as before, he remonstrates with the despairer for denying the world's beauty. The despairer, whom he now describes as a pessimist, could be "saved" from her "pessimistic despair," Du Bois implies, were she to acknowledge the fact of the world's beauty even as she acknowledges the fact of the Jim Crow car.[3]

In what follows, I propose that Du Bois's claims relating beauty to pessimistic despair involve a moral psychology of the latter and the start of an argument regarding the antidotal power of the former. Du Bois held that, no less than artistic beauty, natural beauty had a role to play in the struggle against democratic despotism. As we saw in chapters 3 and 5, he believed that the Christian white supremacist's moral character and culture prop up democratic despotism (at home [e.g., in East St. Louis] as well as abroad [e.g., the domination and exploitation of black Africans]), and that artistic beauty can advance the fight against racial hierarchy by contesting the Christian white supremacist's self-understanding. As we shall presently see, he thought that natural beauty can advance the same fight by helping black citizens to cope with their despair at the possibility of undermining racial oppression that appears to be irrevocably entrenched. When, again (see chapter 1), deep-seated white supremacy appears to preclude the possibility of subverting racial oppression, resistant black citizens may *cease to see* that possibility as existing for them, *relinquish* their desire to answer to it, *and hopelessly quit* their efforts at subversion. Through the medium of natural beauty, the function of aesthetic education in this circumstance is to relieve blacks of their tendency to despair of and quit the struggle by disclosing to them that the causal regularities that structure their social world are susceptible to interruption and so do not rule out the prospect of action that subverts racial oppression. Du Bois's argument regarding the unsettling, devastating power of artistic beauty presupposes his account of the moral character of the Christian white supremacist (see chapter 2). In a similar vein, his argument regarding the antidotal power of natural beauty presupposes his account of the moral character of the despairer—in short, his moral psychology of pessimistic despair.

The present chapter divides into three parts. The first examines the moral psychological presuppositions of Du Bois's argument about natural beauty, while the second focuses on the argument itself. In part 3, I consider three objections to Du Bois's argument and Du Bois's replies to those objections.

MORAL PSYCHOLOGY OF PESSIMISTIC DESPAIR

Du Bois's moral psychology of pessimistic despair is less complicated than his moral psychology of white supremacy, and so I do not devote a full chapter to it. As a profile of the moral character of the despairer, the gist of Du Bois's depiction is the proposition that pessimism involves the vice of cowardice. Du Bois diagnoses pessimistic despair—the inability to acknowledge the 'Jim-Crow' car yet live and hope—as an effect of either fear of the world or fear of oneself. In a passage I briefly discussed in chapter 4—precisely the passage that led him to write of a "fierce gleam of world-hate" and that recounts his personal experience of the ugliness of racial oppression—he explains his diagnosis in some detail.

In answer to his pale friend's query as to whether he experiences racial insult "each day," Du Bois replies, "certainly not," but then admits that he fears the experience. Specifically, he acknowledges that he repeatedly falls victim to a "*craven* fear," to a panic that robs him of his wherewithal to "rise above" racial insult, "looking for insults or hiding places from them, shrinking . . . from blows that are not always, but ever; not each day, but each week, each month, each year." And, then, just as he has "choked back" his craven fear, and seemed to gather courage enough to assume a higher ground, to not let racial indignity get the best of him ("'I am and will be the master of my—'"), comes yet another slight ("No more tickets downstairs; here's one to the smoking gallery"), which deflates his resolve, and which causes him to hesitate and ask "What's the use? Why not always yield—always take what's offered,—always bow to force, whether of cannon or dislike?" The fear of the world Du Bois describes here involves the sense that there is no possibility of unsettling Jim Crow, that racial insult and discrimination are, if not always, then "ever"—which I gloss as "forever"—thus, that there is no use, no point, to fighting against Jim Crow, for subverting it is impossible. Fear of the world is fear that the world is closed to the possibility of undermining racial oppression; it is a fear that can move a person to relinquish her desire to realize that possibility and, ultimately, hopelessly to quit the fight altogether—thus to yield to racial oppression as something inevitable. For Du Bois, then, pessimistic despair is *ceasing to hope* to realize possibilities that, one fears, the world has ruled out (despair), as well as *resigning the struggle* to realize possibilities that one heretofore has hoped and struggled to realize (pessimism). Pessimistic despair is a moral failing, a form of cowardice, because it expresses a disposition to be cowed by fear into obeisance.[4]

More needs to be said here, however, because the fear that gives rise to pessimistic despair need not be a fear of the world, but the fear of the man who is "afraid of himself." The "great fear," the "real" fear, Du Bois explains, is "the fear lest right there and then you are losing your own soul; that you are losing your own soul and the soul of a people; that millions of unborn children. . . . are being there and then despoiled by you because you are a coward and dare not fight." With these words, Du Bois suggests that fear of oneself is fear of one's own fear—more exactly, a fear of one's own tendency to a craven fear of the world and to the cowardice, the pessimistic despair, that this tendency can engender. Put differently, he proposes that humiliation wrought by others can prompt the fear that, in responding to that humiliation, one will further humiliate oneself. In effect, Du Bois argues that the fear of succumbing to pessimistic despair can itself cause a "second-order" pessimistic despair, or, in other words, that the fear that the self itself is closed to the possibility of resisting pessimistic despair can prompt a person, ultimately, hopelessly to quit the effort to discover that possibility within herself. Thus, where first-order pessimistic despair is the cowardice involved in ceasing to hope to realize certain worldly possibilities and then resigning the struggle to realize them, second-order pessimistic despair is ceasing to hope that it is possible to find within oneself the ability to resist first-order pessimistic despair and resigning the effort to summon that resistance.[5]

Second-order pessimistic despair is parasitic on first-order pessimistic despair, in the sense that the former depends on the prospect of the latter. But the converse is not true. It stands to reason, then, that Du Bois's aesthetic engagement with pessimistic despair would focus on worldly, first-order pessimistic despair. Du Bois believes that artistic beauty can call the Christian white supremacist to moral self-reflection (see chapters 2 and 5). In addition, and as we shall see in the next section, he believes that natural beauty can call the cowardly black pessimist to moral self-reflection: specifically, that by challenging the black pessimist's fear of the world, natural beauty can move him to reevaluate, not his guiding, ideal conception of what he is doing, but his life and the choices that shape it, and through that reevaluation to substitute the virtue of courage for the vice of cowardice.

THE ARGUMENT: ABDUCTION AND JUSTIFICATION

But may we not compare the least of the world's beauty [the glory of "physical nature"] to the least of its ugliness—not murder, starvation, and rapine, with love and friendship and creation—but the glory of sea and sky and city with the little hatefulnesses and thoughtlessnesses of race prejudice, that out of this juxtaposition we may, perhaps, deduce some rule of beauty and life—or death?[6]

To make sense of the contradiction between beauty and ugliness, and of the relation of its terms to our understanding of life and death, Du Bois proposes to set aside the contrast between great ugliness and great beauty—e.g., between murder and friendship, or between rapine and creation—and to juxtapose instead the lesser beauty of physical nature and the "little hatefulness and thoughtlessness of race prejudice." From that juxtaposition, he tells us, we might "deduce some rule of beauty and life—or death."

The rule, the principle, that he ultimately endorses, I suggest, is that the beauty of physical nature—the glory of sea and sky and city—can serve black Americans as an antidote to the world's ugliness by counteracting the despair and pessimism that this ugliness engenders. Du Bois's principle of natural beauty is the proposition *that the perception of natural beauty can thwart the power of life's ugliness to engender (first-order) pessimistic despair.* His "deduction," I argue, is best read as an example of abduction as Charles Sanders Pierce understood the concept: in other words, as a process of reasoning toward and adopting an explanatory hypothesis.[7] Du Bois abduces, or adopts, the rule he advances—the principle of natural beauty—through the juxtaposition he advances. Only then does he proceed to justify that principle.

The least of the world's beauty, the glory of sea, sky, and city, is the spirit renewing natural beauty that Du Bois remembers from his visit to Maine's Mount Desert Island and the town of Bar Harbor. The little hatefulnesses and thoughtlessnesses of race prejudice are the dispiriting experiences of riding Jim Crow attested to by some black Americans Du Bois meets in a "Southern home" during the "spring of a Georgia February."[8] As we have seen, Du Bois himself has suffered the slights of racial prejudice, as recounted, for example, to his pale friend, but finds himself rejuvenated by his visit to a site of natural beauty. The black Americans he meets have likewise suffered the slights of racial prejudice, but they do not visit such sites. What matters to Du Bois, then, is the difference the experience of natural beauty makes to the sensibility of black persons who have been affected by the slights of Jim Crow. What interests him, in other words, is the juxtaposition of the experience of natural beauty with the felt slights of Jim Crow *within the life of the black traveler.*

In Du Bois's description of Mount Desert Island the beauty of the place is manifest in its physical dynamism: e.g., in the water that flames and sparkles; in the air that springs and sparkles; and in the mists that pile high in the evening. Of particular significance is the experience Du Bois describes as he departs the coast of Bar Harbor, sighting a "black mountain . . . [that] rises suddenly, threateningly, until far away on Frenchman's Bay it looms above the town in withering vastness," for it is precisely this sighting—of a looming mass of rock ascending unexpectedly off Maine's coast—that so rejuvenates Du Bois that "turning" he goes to work again. "God molded his world largely and mightily off this marvelous coast," he writes, "and meant that in the tired days of life men should come and worship here and renew their spirit."[9]

Sitting in a Southern home, Du Bois queries the other guests: "Why do not those who are scarred in the world's battle and hurt by its hardness travel to these places of beauty [like Mount Desert

Island] and drown themselves in the utter joy of life?" Du Bois's question meets with no response until one of his interlocutors, "the "white one," says, "I should think you would like to travel." One (or more?) of the other guests of color ("brown," "soft-yellow," "cream-like duskiness") then answers the white guest with a detailed account of the experience of riding the Jim Crow railway car. Riding Jim Crow is cold (in the winter), stifling (in the summer), hurried, dirty, and, of course, always an insult to the dignity black people. In sharp contrast to the withering vastness of the Maine mountain Du Bois takes in, it is also small and cramped. It is typically a "smoker cut in two" and "[y]our compartment is a half or a quarter or an eighth of the oldest car in service on the road." A white newsboy "occupies two seats," we are told, and the white crew uses the car "to lounge and perform their toilet." In addition, "dirty colored section hands will pour in at night and drive you to the smallest corner." Hearing this last comment and concluding the exchange, one of the black interlocutors, "the little lady in the corner," finally responds to the white guest's conjecture that blacks "should like to travel." "No," she tells him, "we don't travel much."[10]

Echoing *Darkwater*'s "Postscript," Du Bois's recollection of his "Southern Home" conversation suggests that riding Jim Crow is but one, representative part of a widespread practice of racial oppression that quite generally drives black Americans into a corner. But while it is one thing to be driven into a corner, it is something else altogether to acquiesce to life in the corner into which one has been driven, like the little lady and the other black interlocutors whom "the thought of a journey" seems "to depress," Du Bois tell us.[11] Du Bois notices, then, that in contrast to the black Americans who don't travel and who acquiesce to life in the corner of American life to which the practice of racial oppression has consigned them, he, himself, while also compelled to inhabit the perspective of the veiled nook, has traveled to places of beauty—like Mount Desert

Island—and then *not* acquiesced. From this contrastive observation, I propose, he reasons abductively to the principle of natural beauty, his response to the remark, "No . . . we don't travel much." Again,

> Pessimism is cowardice. The man who cannot frankly acknowledge the "Jim-Crow" car as a fact and yet live and hope is simply afraid either of himself or of the world. There is not in the world a more disgraceful denial of human brotherhood than the "Jim-Crow" car of the southern United States; but, too, just as true, there is nothing more beautiful in the universe than sunset and moonlight on Montego Bay in far Jamaica. And both things are true and both belong to this our world, and neither can be denied.[12]

The principle of natural beauty is implicit in Du Bois's thinking, here, for the idea he indirectly conveys is that the perception of natural beauty can offset blacks' despair at the prospect of subverting Jim Crow and counter their pessimistic tendency to acquiesce to the frankly acknowledged fact of its existence. Du Bois implies, in other words, *that the perception of natural beauty can thwart the power of life's ugliness and, specifically, of the ugliness embodied in Jim Crow to engender despair and pessimism (at the prospect of subverting Jim Crow).*[13]

Consider Pierce's schema for abductive reasoning:

The surprising fact, C, is observed,
But if A were true, C would be a matter of course;
Hence, there is reason to suspect that A is true.[14]

Now for Du Bois, I suggest, C is the observation that a black person who has been driven to a corner of American life by Jim Crow, yet has also traveled to and been rejuvenated by places of beauty (e.g., by sea, sky, and city), in contrast to a black person who has been driven to the same corner of American life by Jim Crow, yet has *not* also traveled to and been rejuvenated by places of beauty, is not prone or is significantly less prone to acquiesce to the power of life's ugliness and, specifically, the ugliness of Jim Crow to engender despair and pessimism. A, the principle of natural beauty, is the hypothesis Du Bois adopts by abduction, reasoning that were A true, then C, his contrastive observation, would be a matter of course. So Du Bois has reason to suspect that A is true and, therefore, that the beauty of the Montego Bay sunset and moonlight can thwart the power of life's ugliness to engender despair and pessimism.

Du Bois reasons by abduction toward a hypothesis he has yet to justify. The justification he presents for the natural beauty principle is a phenomenological argument that appeals to his own subjective experience. Consider, then, Du Bois's description of his perception of the Montego Bay sunset.

> The sun, prepared to cross that awful border which men call Night and Death, marshals his hosts. I seem to see the spears of mighty horsemen flash golden in the light; empurpled banners flame afar, and the low thunder of marching hosts thrills with the thunder of the sea. Athwart his own path, screening a face of fire, he throws cloud masses, masking his trained guns. And then the miracle is done. The host passes with roar too vast for human ear and the sun is set, leaving the frightened moon and blinded stars.
>
> In the dusk the green-gold palms turn their star-like faces and stretch their fan-like fingers, lifting themselves proudly, lest any lordly leaf should know the taint of earth.
>
> Out from the isle the serpent hill thrusts its great length around the bay, shouldering back the waters and the shadows. Ghost rains sweep down, smearing his rugged sides, yet on he writhes, undulant with pine and palm, gleaming until his low, sharp head and lambent tongue, grown gray and pale and silver in the dying day, kisses the molten gold of the golden sea.

Then comes the moon. Like fireflies nesting in the hand of God gleams the city, dim-swathed by fairy palms. A long, thin thumb, mist-mighty, points shadowy to the Spanish Main, while through the fingers foam the Seven Seas. Above the calm and gold-green moon, beneath the wind-wet earth; and here, alone, my soul enchained, enchanted![15]

In chapter 4, I characterized an apt end as comparable to the conclusion of a good story, and I interpreted Du Bois's notion of beauty to imply that a beautiful life must come to an apt end. Does a similar implication hold with regard to a beautiful, *natural* event, like the setting of the sun? In proposing that we think of the end of a good story as cohering with what came before, I followed the lead of the philosopher W. B. Gallie, who believed that the conclusion of a good story, while it cannot be deduced or predicted on the basis of what has come before, has to be congruous with earlier episodes. Samuel Coleridge-Taylor's death failed to cohere with what preceded it, for his life up to his death prefigured a long career of accomplishment, well beyond his thirty-seventh year. In contrast, Alexander Crummell's life (as Du Bois represents it), followed the traditional, Christian plotting of human existence, coming to an end that lets us see it as a unified enterprise that triumphed over tragedy and ugliness. Could something similar be said about the sunset? Is it possible to see the sunset as coming to an appropriate end, an end that coheres with what has come before?

Du Bois's depiction of the sunset suggests that his answer to this question is "yes," for it vividly describes the sun's disappearance below the horizon as the apt conclusion of a story recounting a brief episode in the life of the sun—a story of the sun standing prepared for decisive action; of the sun preparing further by gathering his hosts, including cavalry and marching foot soldiers; and then, finally, after concealing his face with fire, and concealing his guns with clouds, of the sun leading his men across the awful border that men call "Night and Death." As Du Bois recounts the tale of the sunset, the completion of the event—the host passing "with roar too vast for human ears"—coheres with what has come before: it brings to dramatic fruition the preparation and the action that have preceded it. In effect, Du Bois depicts the sunset as coming to an apt end through its completion, and thus as satisfying his first criterion of beauty: that an event counts as beautiful only if it comes to apt end.

When he writes that with the setting of the sun "the miracle is done," Du Bois likewise depicts the sunset as satisfying his second criterion of beauty. In *Darkwater*, the term "miracle" functions as a term of art—a thesis I elaborate below. Let it suffice here to emphasize Du Bois's use of the term to designate events that escape causal explanation in terms of laws of nature and, with regard to human actions, laws discovered by sociology—put otherwise, events not determined by causal regularities that alter those regularities.[16] For Du Bois, the setting of the sun, through its completion, presents the setting of the sun in a new light—specifically, as something miraculous, and so as satisfying his second criterion of beauty: that an event counts as beautiful only if, through its completion, it presents itself in a new light. By coming to an appropriate end, in other words, the sunset presents itself, a natural event *presumptively* subject to the laws of nature, as *not* subject to them—thus, in the view of science, as something supernatural—or, again, as something miraculous. Whereas the deaths of Keith Lehrer's Glorya and Alexander Crummell cast their lives in a new light that enriches our conception of life to include heretofore unfamiliar possibilities, the completion of the sunset casts that event in a new light that enriches our conception of natural events to include the unfamiliar possibility of world-altering actions and other events not determined by causal law.

Du Bois's perception of the sunset's beauty lingers in its backward-looking contemplation of the afterglow of the orb's disappearance, a completed event that remains present to him *as* a completed event (the miracle "*is* done," the sun "*is* set"), even as the dusk and the moonlight unfold about him. Notice, however, that Du Bois's experience is temporally bipolar—that his soul is not only contemplative, but enchanted. As we saw in chapters 4 and 5, the Du Boisian experience of beauty involves a captivated, forward-looking sense of being called to conjure a future less ugly and more beautiful than the past. That sense of promise is also evident here, and bears directly on the despair and the pessimism that threaten the fight against Jim Crow, for it is the basis of Du Bois's argument for the principle of natural beauty. In the paragraph that follows his phenomenological description of his perception of the sunset's beauty, Du Bois implicitly says as much:

> From such heights of holiness men turn to master the world. All the pettiness of life drops away and it becomes a great battle before the Lord. His trumpet,—where does it sound and whither? I go. I saw Montego Bay at the beginning of the World War. The cry for service as high as heaven, as wide as human feeling, seemed filling the earth. What were petty slights, silly insults, paltry problems, beside this call to do and dare and die? We black folk offered our services to fight.[17]

Du Bois's perception of natural beauty prompts a radical shift in sensibility, in mood[18]—indeed, so arresting is his vision that he finds himself moved to a new view of his life, to seeing it as belonging to a magnificent, morally compelling drama, "a great battle before the Lord." Considered in *that* light, the petty slights he has suffered under Jim Crow disappear from view—they "drop away"—and his disposition to be cowed by fear evaporates. Du Bois's mood shift discloses the world, not as a vise that has squeezed him into a tiny corner, but as an open field calling for action—for commanding warriors to perform righteous deeds that "master the world" and challenge injustice. More precisely, and in keeping with his moral psychology, the sunset nullifies Du Bois's cowardice: it allays his fear that the world is closed to the possibility of subverting racial oppression; it renews his aspiration to realize that possibility; and, contra his despair and his pessimism, it restores both his hope and his agency—his striving to serve and thus to realize that possibility. Rather than despair at the possibility of subverting Jim Crow and resign the struggle to realize that possibility, Du Bois now summons the courage to rise above racial insult, to answer the "cry for service" from the "the heights of holiness," because the captivating miracle of the sun's disappearance embodies the promise of a future different from the past, reminding him that, in fact, the world *allows* for miracles, that it is open to action, undetermined by causal law, that undermines racial oppression and transforms the world. At the beginning of the war, when he visited Montego Bay, Du Bois seemed to have believed that the courageous service most urgently needed from black Americans who aspired eventually to undermine Jim Crow was to close ranks and join the war effort (see chapter 4).

Du Bois's justification of the principle of natural beauty is essentially phenomenological because it appeals to the quality of his own subjective experience to show that natural beauty can thwart the power of life's ugliness to engender despair and pessimism. In perceiving the sunset as beautiful, Du Bois sees it as something that is scientifically inexplicable. His sight of the sunset, in recalling him to the possibility of miraculous action, enchants his soul and prompts him to do and dare. In the life of a black traveler like Du Bois, in contrast to the lives of blacks who have declined to travel and acquiesced to the corner of life to which racial prejudice has consigned them, the perception of natural beauty functions to frustrate despair and pessimism. The principle of natural beauty explains this difference in experience. Du Bois vindicates the principle through phenomenological description that presents *his* perception of natural beauty as a testament to its truth.

I conclude this section by noting the perhaps obvious: namely, that Du Bois's description of the psychological transformation from feelings of fear to a sense of superiority, of rising above the causes of those feelings, echoes Kant's psychological account of the dynamical sublime. For Kant, the experience of the dynamical sublime is a movement through which a person comes to discover that, as a suprasensible, moral subject, she enjoys a superiority to whatever natural forces (a volcano, for example) she regards as fearful—that is, as impossible to resist were one to be threatened by it. In Du Bois's case, a like movement is responsive to real fear, not to the prospect of fear and futile resistance, but the upshot is similar: an ability to regard as small, by comparison to our sense of moral vocation, other concerns: Kant writes of property, health, and life; Du Bois of slights, insults, and other paltry problems. Importantly, Du Bois revises, or improvises, on Kant in that he situates his renewed sense of moral vocation, of being called to "service," within the phenomenal world—not as involving the revelation of some suprasensible moral propensity, but as a response to the perception of the beauty of a manifestly sensible event, the setting of the sun.[19]

OBJECTIONS AND REPLIES

Keith Lehrer writes that it "is not an accident that a sunset, the end of days and a symbol of endings is a natural source of beauty."[20] Lehrer's point is well taken, but Du Bois's thought that we can see the sunset as following a narrative arc to an acceptable conclusion should give us pause. It is reasonable to maintain that a beautiful *life* follows a narrative arc to a conclusion similar to the ending of a good story, for arguably, if not uncontroversially, human lives have the shape of narratives. In the slogan of one philosopher, "Stories are lived before they are told—except in the case of fiction."²¹ But even granting the truth of this slogan, it strains credulity to suppose that Du Bois's story of the sunset, a natural event, was lived before *it* was told. More sensibly, it will be argued, Du Bois's depiction of the sunset should be read as a fiction—not as the expression of what he in fact perceived, but as a projection, an exercise in poetic license. In a similar vein, a skeptic might well take issue with Du Bois's representation of his perception of natural beauty in terms of the concept of a miracle, for it is not clear what justifies his use of the concept, or that his use is anything but fanciful. In the present section, I draw on Du Bois himself to sketch some responses to these objections, starting with the worry about his use of the concept of a miracle and then proceeding to his narrative depiction of the sunset. I conclude by considering a third objection, invited by Du Bois's own remarks. In defending the principle of natural beauty, Du Bois sets aside great beauty and great ugliness, the latter of which he describes as "depths of degradation which it is not fair for us to probe."²² It may be argued, then, that he himself gives us reason to doubt that his principle of natural beauty applies to despair and pessimism stemming from such depths, from murder and rapine, for example.

Objection 1: That Invoking the Concept of a Miracle Is Not Justified

In the opening, autobiographical chapter of *Darkwater*—"The Shadow of Years"—Du Bois's uses the notion of a miracle to characterize the first and final phases of his life through age fifty: "I seem to view my life divided into four parts," he writes: "the Age of Miracles, the Days of Disillusion, the Discipline of Work and Play, and the Second Miracle Age."²³ In discussing objection 1, I focus on the shift in self-understanding that marks Du Bois's maturation from the first to the last of these phases. The central feature of this shift is Du Bois's changed conception of just what about his life's successes made them miraculous.

Du Bois writes that the first-age miracles "began with Fisk and ended with Germany. I was bursting with the joy of living. I seemed to ride in conquering might. I was captain of my soul and master of my fate! I *willed* to do! It was done. I *wished!* The wish came true." Remembering his years at Fisk, Du Bois entreats us to "consider, for a moment, how miraculous it all was for a boy of seventeen, just escaped from a narrow valley: I willed and lo! my people came dancing all around me." Recalling his arrival at Harvard, he reverberates his earlier exclamation: "I willed and lo!," remarking that "I was now walking beneath the elms of Harvard,—the name of allurement, the college of my youngest, wildest visions." After receiving his second BA from Harvard, Du Bois went on to do graduate work in Germany. The first age of miracles ends when he returns to the United States for want of funding to continue his graduate studies abroad: "after two long years, I dropped suddenly back into 'nigger' hating America!"[24]

During the first age of miracles Du Bois conceptualized himself as a self-sufficient, essentially sovereign subject—that is, as someone who relied on no one other than himself and nothing other than his independent will to achieve what he wanted in life. What was miraculous about his success during this first phase, he believed, was precisely the unbounded efficacy of his individual will. He willed that his people come dancing about him, and lo!, they came; he willed that he attend Harvard, and lo!, he attended Harvard. In Du Bois's youthful image of himself, his will, the captain of his soul, made him master of his fate. His return to America soon shattered that self-image: "For the first time in my life I realized that there were limits to my will to do. The Day of Miracles was past."[25]

During his "Days of Disillusion," Du Bois soon realizes that he had been wrong to attribute his successes to his ability to master his fate. His remarks to this effect deserve careful scrutiny:

> My Days of Disillusion were not disappointing enough to discourage me. I was still upheld by that fund of infinite faith, although dimly about me I saw the shadow of disaster. I began to realize how much of what I had called Will and Ability was sheer Luck! *Suppose* my good mother had preferred a steady income from my child labor rather than bank on the precarious dividend of my higher training? *Suppose* that pompous old village judge, whose dignity we often ruffled and whose apples we stole, had had his way and sent me while a child to a "reform" school to learn a "trade"? *Suppose* Principal Hosmer had been born with no faith in "darkies," and instead of giving me Greek and Latin had taught me carpentry and the making of tin pans? *Suppose* I had missed a Harvard scholarship? *Suppose* the Slater Board had then, as now, distinct ideas as to where the education of Negroes should stop? Suppose *and* suppose! As I sat down calmly on flat earth and looked at my life a certain great fear seized me. Was I the masterful captain or the pawn of laughing sprites? Who was I to fight a world of color prejudice?[26]

Suppose and suppose. Du Bois's retrospective recounting of a sequence of counterfactuals expresses his recognition, first, that his successes were due to the play of chance in his life—to what he calls "luck—and, second, that the chance events that made a difference to the course of his life were actions undertaken by other individuals. Having ceased to regard himself as a self-sufficient, sovereign subject, Du Bois now acknowledges that he has depended on others to achieve his aims.[27] It is striking, however, that through the second and third parts of his life, he remains profoundly self-absorbed, highlighting not his dependence on the human beings with whom he interacts, but the difficulty with which he found himself coping with the fact that racial oppression in "'nigger'-hating" America limited his will. Describing his self-understanding during the "Discipline of Work and Play," for example, he writes that "I was ready to admit that the best of men might fail. I meant still to be captain of my soul, but I realized that even captains are not omnipotent in uncharted and angry seas." During the third phase of his maturation, Du Bois clearly denies that he is a self-sufficient, sovereign subject, yet he still clings to the ideal of sovereignty, of perhaps finding a way to calm the seas, chart uncharted waters, and remain the captain of his soul.[28]

It is only with the advent of the "Second Miracle Age" that Du Bois fully embraces the insight that nonsovereignty and the chance actions of others have been critical to his success, and have a decisive role to play in the fight against color-prejudice:

> Away back in the little years of my boyhood I had sold the Springfield *Republican* and written for Mr. Fortune's *Globe*. I dreamed of being an editor myself some day. I am an editor. In the great, slashing days of college life I dreamed of a strong organization to fight the battles of the Negro race. The National Association for the Advancement of Colored People is such a body, and it grows daily. In the dark days at Wilberforce I planned a time when I could speak freely to my people and of them, interpreting between two worlds. I am speaking now. In the study at Atlanta I grew to fear lest my radical beliefs should so hurt the college that either my silence or the institution's ruin would result. Powers and principalities have not yet curbed my tongue and Atlanta still lives.
>
> It all came—this new Age of Miracles—because a few persons in 1909 determined to celebrate Lincoln's Birthday properly by calling for the final emancipation of the American Negro. I came at their call.... The result has been the National Association for the

Advancement of Colored People and *The Crisis* and this book, which I am finishing on my Fiftieth Birthday.[29]

With no pretension to self-sufficiency and no lurking aspiration to the ideal of sovereignty, Du Bois presents his involvement with the NAACP and his editorship of *The Crisis* as a response to a call. Du Bois calls the new age of miracles an age of *miracles*, not now because it seems to him to manifest the unbounded efficacy of his individual will, but because he presently sees what he did not see during the first age of miracles: namely, that the chance actions of just a few persons—not now his mother, the village judge, Principal Hosmer, or the members of the Slater Fund, but the men and women who collaborated to establish the NAACP—have combined to render his life a success. Where the mantra of the young man was "I willed and lo!," that of the mature and more modest editor of *The Crisis* is, in effect, "I dreamed and my dreams came true." Du Bois knows, of course, that his dreams and plans need not have come true, but he no longer suggests that his will brought them to fruition. Having taken to heart the truism that, had his luck been different (suppose and suppose), there would have been no call to answer, no editorship, and no involvement with the NAACP, he recognizes that the miracle of his later-in-life success was the favor bestowed by the adventitious actions and interactions that brought the NAACP into existence.

The political scientist Brian Barry has argued that success = luck + decisiveness.[30] Put in Barry's terms, the argument of the present section so far is that the youthful Du Bois, as the quinquagenarian Du Bois later describes him, largely but falsely attributes his success to the miracle of individual decisiveness, while the quinquagenarian Du Bois, as he describes himself, largely attributes it to the miracle of chance. Barry conceptualizes luck, or chance, in terms of probability estimates. How does Du Bois's conceptualize it? "In the Shadow of Years" explains why I have regarded Du Bois's perception of the sunset as *reminding him* that the world allows for miracles, for what he sees in the Montego Bay sunset—that the world is open to life and world-altering actions undetermined by causal law—coincides with what he had come to see in his life during the course of his maturation. Du Bois, in other words, by the time he visited Montego Bay, had already come to conceptualize and see the miracles, the chance actions that he believed shaped his life, as actions undetermined by causal law.

In "Sociology Hesitant" (ca. 1905), an early but unpublished essay, Du Bois sketches his philosophy of science, which is the source of his conception of chance actions.[31] Rejecting Comte's and Spencer's collectivist holism[32]—the thesis that society is a concrete whole (for Du Bois, a "mystical whole") formed of discrete units—Du Bois maintains that society comprises the "deeds of men," as well as the "law, rule, and rythm" [*sic*] governing those deeds. For Du Bois, sociology is the science of human action, not the science of society as such, or of society as a whole. But Comte's approach cannot easily be dismissed. Why did the French thinker "hesitate so strangely" before the prospect of treating human action as the object of sociological inquiry, Du Bois asks. Du Bois's answer is the "Great Assumption . . . that in the deeds of men there lies along with rhythm and rule . . . something incalculable"—an assumption in light of which the prospect of launching a science that "would discover and formulate the exact laws of human action . . . seemed to be and was preposterous." Comte wavered before a paradox: on one hand, "the evident rhythm of human action"; on the other, "the evident incalculability of human action." Where Comte wavered, however, Du Bois sallies forth, urging that we "flatly face the Paradox . . . frankly state the Hypothesis of Law and the Assumption of Chance and seek to determine by study and measurement the limits of each." According to Du Bois, physical (natural) laws and the laws sociology discovers limit the scope of incalculable chance; thus they limit the scope of "undetermined" choice—or, as he sometime writes, of "free" and "inexplicable" will. Sociology attempts to measure the limits of chance, by determining the degree to which physical and social regularities constrain human choice and action that is "undetermined by and independent of actions gone before."[33] What are we to make of these claims, and on what understanding of the relation between chance and free will do they depend?

Like Kant, to whose notion of an "Absolute and the Undetermined Ego" he explicitly alludes in "Sociology Hesitant," Du Bois understands determination by causal laws as determination by an antecedent event, or action, in accordance with the laws (for Kant, natural laws; for Du Bois, natural *or* sociological laws) governing the succession of events or actions.[34] For Du Bois, then, actions undetermined by causal law—actions undetermined by and independent of all actions gone before—can be explained neither by the laws of nature nor by the laws discovered by sociology. As a philosopher, Du Bois is metaphysically committed to the claim that such actions exist: specifically, that there are actions, undetermined by causal law, that can be attributed to agents as their authors—agents he describes as "human wills" and "indeterminate force."[35] Speaking strictly as a sociologist, however, he eschews the metaphysician's description of what is scientifically inexplicable, restricting himself, rather, to characterizing as chance actions that exceed the scope of scientific explanation. If, occasionally, Du Bois seems to conflate the two perspectives, connecting sociological inquiry to free will and indeterminate force, for example, it is because he regards them as correlative, as mutually implicative: "Chance," Du Bois writes, "[is] the scientific side of Inexplicable Will," adding that "Sociology ... is the Science that seeks the limits of Chance in human conduct."[36]

Crucially, Du Bois seems also to believe that actions stemming from "free" and "inexplicable" will, precisely because they are not determined by causal regularities, can intervene on the order of nature or the order of society in ways that remake and significantly alter those regularities. With regard to the order of nature, for example, he remarks that "today as strongly as, and even more strongly than ever, men after experiencing the facts of life have almost universally assumed that in among the physical forces stalk self-directing Wills, which modify, restrain, and re-direct the ordinary laws of nature. The assumption is tremendous in its import."[37] The assumption here, the "Great Assumption" mentioned above, "means that from the point of Science this is a world of Chance as well as Law; that the conservation of energy and the correlation of forces are not universally true, but that out of some unknown Nowhere burst *miraculously* now and then controlling Energy."[38] With regard to the order of society, he similarly suggests that the regularities (or rhythms) shaping social life, while arising in accordance with a prearranged plan, are "liable to stoppage and change according to similar plan."[39] When these passages are read in tandem, Du Bois's point seems to be that chance actions, miraculous actions (for the philosopher-metaphysician, actions attributable to the indeterminate force of human will), by initiating a new course of events that cannot be explained by past successions of events, "by beginning something new," in Hannah Arendt's felicitous phrasing, effectively reshape the world.[40] Put differently, he proposes that miraculous actions have an essentially emancipatory significance—that it is *in the nature of such events* to permute the natural and/or social landscape by subverting the regularities that otherwise govern it and by establishing new ones.[41]

What most engages Du Bois, of course, is the possibility of changing society, not physical nature. With regard to social change, Du Bois suggests that miraculous action ranges across the social world—as when his mother, Principal Hosmer, and the Slater Fund all broke with the racially oppressive rules and rhythms that generally governed and organized the upbringing and education of young black man, of "darkies" and "Negroes" (the mother choosing higher training rather than child labor for her son, the principal choosing to teach Greek and Latin rather than carpentry to his pupil, the Slater Fund choosing to send an unusually ambitious young black man to study in Germany); and as when a few persons, acting in concert, undertook properly to celebrate Lincoln's birthday. Yet his belief that physical nature admits of miraculous events (rooted in his skepticism regarding the putative universality of the law of the conservation of energy) remains pertinent here, for it lets us see why, again, his perception of the sunset, in recalling him to the prospect of miraculous and emancipatory social action, in reminding him that the world is open to causally undetermined action that remakes the world, enchants his soul and calls him to service.

Through my readings of "The Shadow of Years" and "Sociology Hesitant," I hope to have shown that Du Bois could have justified his use of the concept of a miracle by appeal to its applicability to his own life, and by appeal to his philosophy of science. But that said, it may still be objected that Du Bois's description of the Montego Bay sunset in terms of that concept, no less than his description of the sunset as a drama about preparing and going to battle, is nothing but fanciful projection. Du Bois would have denied this claim, for he believes that it is a truth about "our world" that there is nothing more beautiful in it (indeed, in the entire universe) than sunset and moonlight on Montego Bay. For Du Bois, the beauty of the sunset is a *fact* about the world that must be frankly acknowledged—like the Jim Crow car. When, then, he is perceiving the sunset as coming to a suitable end that casts it as something miraculous—when, in short, he is perceiving the beauty of the sunset—he thinks that he is perceiving a fact about the world and not that he is whimsically attributing to it properties it does not possess.[42] In explaining Du Bois's response to Objection 2, I shall argue that his philosophical romanticism best explains his realism about natural beauty.

Objection 2: That Du Bois's Depiction of the Sunset Is an Exercise in Poetic License

What is a dreamer? In considering his life from the perspective of his fiftieth year, Du Bois represents himself as a dreamer of ambitious dreams. Even before he left Great Barrington, he tells us, he "almost pitied . . . [his] pale companions, who were not of the Lord's anointed and who saw in their dreams no splendid quests of golden fleeces."[43] As we have seen, however, Du Bois also tells us that he came retrospectively to view himself as a dreamer, to write "I dreamed" rather than "I will, or "I willed," only after experience chastened his pretense to sovereign subjectivity and led him to view his life from the vantage of the second age of miracles. From this point of view, Du Bois now represents himself as ever a dreamer, although he is undecided, in the conclusion of his short autobiography, as to whether he will continue to dream after he dies: "in the fullness of days I shall die, quietly, I trust, with my face turned South and eastward; and, dreaming or dreamless, I shall, I am sure, enjoy death as I have enjoyed life."[44] But, again, what is a dreamer? And what is it to dream?

"The Shadow of Years" answers these questions, early on, with its striking and multiply allusive description of Du Bois's father:

> Alfred, my father, must have seemed a splendid vision in that little valley under the shelter of those mighty hills. He was small and beautiful of face and feature, just tinted with the sun, his curly hair chiefly revealing his kinship to Africa. In nature he was a dreamer,—romantic, indolent, kind, unreliable. He had in him the making of a poet, an adventurer, or a Beloved Vagabond, according to the life that closed round him; and that life gave him all too little. His father, Alexander Du Bois, cloaked under a stern, austere demeanor a passionate revolt against the world.[45]

Three allusions declare themselves here. One is to William Wordsworth's "Intimations" ode; another is to one of Du Bois's own, earlier allusions to the "Intimations" ode in *The Souls of Black Folk*; the third is to the "Postscript" with which *Darkwater* begins. As I have argued elsewhere, Du Bois's references to Wordsworth's poem can be traced at least as far back as his Fisk commencement address of 1898.[46] In describing his father, he alludes to the ode's fifth stanza:

> Our birth is but a sleep and a forgetting:
> The Soul that rises with us, our life's Star,
> Hath had elsewhere its setting,
> And cometh from afar:
> Not in entire forgetfulness,
> And not in utter nakedness,
> But trailing clouds of glory do we come
> From God, who is our home:
> Heaven lies about us in our infancy!
> Shades of the prison-house begin to close upon the growing Boy
> But he beholds the light, and whence it flows
> He sees it in his joy;
> The Youth, who daily farther from the east
> Must travel, still is Nature's Priest,
> And by the vision splendid
> Is on his way attended;
> At length the Man perceives it die away,
> And fade into the light of common day.[47]

"In the central stanzas of the Ode," says one critic, "the celestial infant descends from the imperial palace of 'God, who is our home,' to become the 'foster-child' of earth, to become finally imprisoned in the deterministic social world."[48] In stanza 5, Wordsworth tells a part of this story, emphasizing the gradual demise of the glorious vision that derives from the infant's heavenly origin. In passing from childhood to youth, and then from youth to adulthood, the growing boy continues to apprehend the sublime "vision splendid"—the darkening of the prison-house earthly life has become notwithstanding—but the man will see it "die away / And fade into the light of common day." When Du Bois describes Alfred's appearance under the shelter of mighty hills, he invokes the ode's fifth stanza to suggest that his father once embodied the vision splendid. And when he writes that Alfred had the makings of a poet, an adventurer, or a beloved vagabond, depending on the life that "closed round him," he echoes the ode's reference to the imprisoning power of the deterministic social world, as well as his own ode-echoing remark in the first chapter of *Souls*—"the shades of the prison-house closed round about us all"—describing the power of racial prejudice to obscure the vision splendid.[49] When, finally, Du Bois compares Alfred's dreaming and poetic nature to his grandfather's "stern, austere demeanor," he evokes his reflections in the "Postscript" contrasting "Fancy" and "poetry" to "Thought" and the "sterner flights of logic." Fancy, through poetry, he tells us, offers "tributes to Beauty."[50]

The upshot of all this, I suggest, is that when Du Bois presents his authorial perspective as (at least in part) the perspective of a dreamer, he acknowledges that he is his father's heir. In addition, he affirms that to see the world as his father, the dreamer, saw it is, in effect, to see it as a poet still attended by the vision splendid might well see it, despite his subjection to surrounding racial prejudice. For Du Bois, poetic imagination, fancy, is a mode of perception that pays tribute to beauty by restoring to sight a vision of the world—the vision splendid—that is unavailable to logical, rigorous thought and, perhaps, to severe personalities like those of Du Bois's grandfather. Against the claim that poetic imagination is *merely* fanciful, the critical point here is that poetic, imaginative perception discloses aspects of reality—in Du Bois's terms, facts and truths about the world—that rigorous thought and inquiry cannot get into view. Sociology measures the limits of chance in human conduct, but to perceive the beauty of the sunset we must exchange the point of view of the sociologist, and of science more generally, for that of the poet. This, arguably, is part of the purpose of traveling—for Du Bois, not simply an escapist enterprise, but a practically engaged undertaking the aim of which is to "renew" the spirit by revisiting the vision splendid that nature affords, even in a world of Jim Crow.

In Du Bois's view, his description of the Montego Bay sunset as miraculous and as following a narrative arc to an acceptable conclusion is at once creative *and* disclosive: it is an expression of imaginative perception that reveals a fact about the world.[51] Time and again, the beauty of the Montego Bay sunset lingers in the moonlight for anyone to see—that is, for anyone disposed to exercise her power of creative imaginative perception to see. When we exercise that power, Du Bois suggests, we can recover the vision splendid that the shades of the racial prison-house perpetually dim and that an insistently scientific approach to the race problem can never restore to sight. To the objection that his descriptions of the sunset are little more than whimsical projections and expressions of poetic license, Du Bois's implicit answer is that the objection relies on too narrow a conception of reality and too stilted a conception of perception, insisting that there is no more to reality than the reality thought can measure and denying that fancy is sometimes required for accuracy of perception. To state these claims just a little differently, and in terms familiar to philosophical aesthetics, Du Bois thinks that judgment of natural beauty demands agreement, and that it is objective as well as subjective. It demands agreement, because anyone disposed to exercise her powers of imaginative perception can be expected to perceive the sunset as beautiful.[52] It is subjective, because the proper basis of the judgment, say, that the Montego Bay sunset is beautiful, is the experience of the particular individual (thus the need to travel)—here, her exercise of her power of imaginative perception to restore the vision splendid to sight.[53] It is also objective, however, for Du Bois believes that imaginative perception discloses aspects of the world that we cannot see without it.

I can summarize the argument of this section by saying that Du Bois belongs to what the philosopher Akeel Bilgrami has called "the long Romantic philosophical tradition." Central to Bilgrami's interpretation of Romanticism is his account of what he calls "natural supernaturalism," a phrase he takes from the literary critic M. H. Abrams. If the "natural" is what the natural sciences study and the "supernatural" is what falls outside the coverage of the natural sciences, then properties that make "normative demands" on us—"properties of value and meaning"—count as supernatural, for "science has nothing to say about them." By an alternative criterion of the natural, however, where the natural is the perceptible, perceptible properties of value and meaning belong to nature *just in virtue of being perceptible*. Natural supernaturalism, then, is the idea that, by this alternative criterion of the natural, nature has (nonsacralized) perceptible properties that in the view of the natural sciences nature does not have. It is "the most central idea in Romantic metaphysics," Bilgrami writes, "that . . . objects and things in the world, including nature, are filled with properties of value and meaning." Bilgrami defends and further clarifies the metaphysics of natural supernaturalism by distinguishing between two points of view on the world—the one "detached" and the other "practically engaged." From the detached point of view, a mode of perception of which natural science is the "most regimented and systematic" version, we see the world as an object of study, but not as making claims on us. When, however, we adopt a practically engaged perspective, we perceive the world as having properties of value. To elaborate on one of his examples, a fisherman considering the sea from a detached point of view might describe a storm brewing offshore as a *meteorological perturbation*. But the fisherman might also see the storm as a *threat* to his livelihood, which would be to perceive it in light of his practical desire to secure his livelihood, and as calling on him to act to protect his boats from possible damage. Nature really exhibits value properties, it really makes normative demands on us, natural supernaturalism avers, but we perceive those demands only if we switch from a detached perspective to one that considers nature in light of our own desires and concerns.[54]

Despite the brevity of my summary of Bilgrami's discussion of the long Romantic philosophical tradition, I hope that my reasons for placing Du Bois within that tradition are already evident. To be sure, few events are more predictable than the sunset, even for the denizens of Montego Bay. But when Du Bois travels to Jamaica, to enlist his powers of imagination to revive his spirit, he sees the sunset as following a narrative arc to an apt conclusion that reveals it as something miraculous. Viewing the sunset from a scientific point of view, Du Bois regards it as conforming to natural law. When, however, he views it from a different vantage point—from the point of view of his practically engaged powers of poetic imagination—he sees in it an enchanting interruption of causal law that makes a claim on him, thus enabling him to answer a call to service. Like other Romantics, Du Bois suggests that nature makes normative demands on us—not only instrumental demands, say, to preserve our property from damage, as in the fisherman example, but demands of moral import as well.[55] In particular, he suggests that the property of natural beauty demands that we reevaluate our lives and our choices in light of the revelation that the world is not closed to the possibility of undermining racial oppression. Du Bois's realism about natural beauty makes him a natural supernaturalist in Bilgrami's sense, for it asserts that, by the criterion of perceptibility, nature harbors events the significance of which science cannot bring to light.

Objection 3: That the Principle of Natural Beauty Does Not Apply to Great Ugliness

In "Of Beauty and Death" Du Bois applies his philosophical method to add a distinctively black point of view to a received Euro-American conversation about universal themes—beauty, as I emphasized in chapter 4, but also death, war, and, as his discussion of natural beauty makes clear, pessimism. As I have argued elsewhere, Du Bois gestures in a similar direction in "Of the Coming of John," the short story that is the penultimate chapter of *Souls*. In the story's final scene, Du Bois depicts its protagonist, black John, in the image of one of Schopenhauer's saints—pessimists who recognize that life is everywhere blind, frustrated desire, offering no lasting satisfaction, and who resign all willing and striving for the tranquility of a will-less nothingness.[56] Schopenhauer's urging that resignation is the singularly proper response to human life is rooted in his metaphysics of the will. Du Bois's short story improvises on Schopenhauer, suggesting that, even if his metaphysics of the will is false, it captures the recurrent plight of black desire and the possible suitability of black resignation under conditions of antiblack racial oppression. In the chapter of *Souls* that follows "Of the Coming of John," Du Bois adduces the beauty of the sorrow songs to counter the temptation of pessimism. In "Of Beauty and Death," he invokes natural rather artistic beauty to the same end. With these gestures, Du Bois resonates with Nietzsche as much as with Schopenhauer—in particular with Nietzsche's arguments that beautiful art and beautiful willing can counter the spirit of Schopenhauer's pessimism.[57]

During the decade of World War I, Nietzsche, Schopenhauer, and the themes of pessimism, beauty, and war belonged to what Kwame Anthony Appiah has called "the intellectual milieu" of Du Bois's thinking.[58] Put differently, these thinkers and their preoccupations belonged to the "matrix" of figures and ideas that shaped the philosophizing of Du Bois and his Euro-American contemporaries.[59] Before the war, for example, Thomas Mann entered into dialogue with Schopenhauer and Nietzsche in his novella of 1912, *Death in Venice* (*Der Tod in Venedig*), developing his own distinctive treatment of the notions of pessimism and beauty.[60] And shortly after the war began (1915), in an essay that eerily resonates with "Of Beauty and Death"—"On Transience" ("Vergänglichkeit")— Sigmund Freud recounted his conversation with Rainer Maria Rilke in the company of Lou Andreas-Salomé (who also knew Nietzsche), the summer before the war. During a walk in the countryside, Freud tells us, Rilke felt "no joy" in the "beauty of the scene" around them, for he was "disturbed" by the thought that it was "fated to extinction." But Freud took issue with this suggestion that beauty's transience diminishes its worth. To the contrary, he insisted, the transience of beautiful things enhances their worth: "transience value is scarcity value in time." When the war broke out "it robbed the world of its beauties," Freud admits, but with greater affinity to Du Bois than to Rilke, he ties the value of these beauties to their demise.[61] Close to the end of the war, finally, Max Weber worried, in the vocation lecture I discussed in chapter 4, that modern science had so disenchanted a world that Du Bois thought imaginative perception could reenchant that it was no longer possible for human lives to come to an apt and meaningful ending.[62]

Mann, Rilke, Freud, and Weber—and Du Bois. Du Bois mentions none of the other thinkers, but he understands himself to be contributing to a broader conversation that they and others helped to shape. For Du Bois, if not for his white European contemporaries, the temptation of pessimism is part of the race problem, and the need to cope with that temptation persists with the perpetuation of the race problem.[63] In "Of Beauty and Death," for example, it persists well beyond Du Bois's visit to Montego Bay. Du Bois felt called to serve by his perception of natural beauty, but he soon learned that blacks' efforts to serve were not welcome. Detailing the hostility with which "Negro volunteers" were met, he affirms blacks' successful struggle to secure their eligibility for the draft and establish a training camp for black officers. In a less encouraging vein, he also mentions the Army's refusal to promote Charles Young, its highest black officer, to the rank of general, as well as the injustices suffered by black soldiers in Houston, Texas: "At Houston black soldiers, goaded and insulted, suddenly went wild and 'shot up' the town. At East St. Louis white strikers on war work killed and mobbed Negro workingmen, and as a result 19 colored soldiers were hanged and 51 imprisoned for life for killing 17 whites at Houston, while for killing 125 Negroes in East St. Louis, 20 white men were imprisoned, none for more than 15 years, and 10 colored men with them." In contrast to the *least of* uglinesses that Du Bois's juxtaposes to the least of beauties to abduce the principle of natural beauty, the events of Houston and East St. Louis exemplify the *great* ugliness of murder, rapine, and unjust execution. One may wonder, then, whether the principle applies equally well to the pessimistic despair prompted by events like these—horrors that overwhelm any sense of progress that the drafting of black men and the organization of a black training camp may have encouraged. Du Bois addresses this question, I propose, through another juxtaposition: specifically, of his references to the terrifying, violent ugliness that transpired in Houston and East St. Louis to his description of his visit to and descent into the Grand Canyon, which immediately follows those references.

Du Bois characterizes the canyon as "the awful . . . it is the earth and sky gone stark and raving mad." Indeed, he initially describes it in terms that depict it not as beautiful, but as a symbol of the hurtful violence he associates with great ugliness: the Grand Canyon is a "sudden void in the bosom of the earth down to its entrails—a wound where the dull titanic knife has turned and twisted in the hole, leaving its edges livid, scarred, jagged, and pulsing over the white, and red, and purple of its mighty flesh." Du Bois's descent into the chasm is, figuratively, his descent into the hell of a "wounded world"—a world rent by world war and the murder of black folk.⁶⁴ That natural beauty of a sort could allay his terror of that world, thus calming him and mitigating the prospect of a pessimistic response to that terror, he suggests with his description of his "dreamed" perception of the canyon, yielded by the sunrise, from the vantage point of the canyon's floor—an enchanting, intensely sexualized vision that recalls his perception of the Montego Bay sunset: "the canon,—the awful, it depths called; it heights shuddered. Then suddenly I arose and looked. Her robes were falling. At dim-dawn they hung purplish-green and black. Slowly she stripped them from her gaunt and shapely limbs—her cold, gray garments shot with shadows stood revealed. Down dropped the black-blue robes, gray-pearled and slipped, leaving a filmy, silken, misty thing, and underneath I glimpsed her limbs of utter light." Like the miracle of the sunset, the miracle of the sunrise occasions a saving grace—here, a mode of imaginative perception that relieves Du Bois of the fear, the awful terror, that the worst kinds of ugliness engender. Notice, however, that it is not the sunrise itself that relieves Du Bois of his terror, but the vision of the canyon, which, again, the sunrise occasions. Still, as with his vision of the Montego Bay sunset, the psychological movement Du Bois outlines here—from his experience of awful and shuddering depths and heights to a revelation of utter light, of light that bears no reference to and transcends those depths and heights—resonates with Kant's account of the dynamical sublime.⁶⁵

As we have seen, Du Bois calls "optimists" those who hold "that all is beauty." But optimists lie, for "all is not beauty." Ugliness, hate, and ill "will always be here," he claims, though "perhaps God send, with lessened volume and force."⁶⁶ Du Bois's "perhaps God send," I believe, is the crux of his response to pessimism. For while entrenched antiblack prejudice and hatred persistently claw at black life, Du Bois insists that the possibility of action that interrupts their perpetuation, thus reducing their force and volume, can never be foreclosed. Against the optimist, Du Bois argues that the struggle against white supremacy, like the struggle against ugliness more generally, may ever fail wholly to destroy it. But against the pessimist, he denies that white supremacy is so totalizing and indivisible a force that it is impossible to check it without ending the world.[67] If Schopenhauer and Nietzsche belong to the milieu shaping Du Bois's distinctively black response to the thematics of pessimism, then certainly Du Bois belongs to the milieu shaping contemporary responses to a totalizing Afropessimism. And if Du Bois's response to pessimism echoes Nietzsche, it should come as no surprise that contemporary Afropessimisn echoes Schopenhauer. In the final chapter of this book I return to these thoughts, considering Du Bois as a bridge between the European pessimism of his era and the Afropessimism of ours.

7

DU BOIS'S PLURALISM

Unfinished Lives, Unfinished Societies

In *Darkwater*, Du Bois's political aesthetics involves two fundamental claims. One is that artistic beauty can further the fight against democratic despotism, whether in the form of imperialism abroad, or race riots, lynching, and Jim Crow at home, by appealing to the Christian white supremacist to reconsider her conception of what Christianity requires of her (chapter 5). The other is that natural beauty can contribute to the same fight, by persuading the pessimist who would resign her struggle against racial hierarchy that the world is open to action that interrupts its perpetuation (chapter 6). By advancing the fight against democratic despotism, both modes of aesthetic education also advance the democratic development of the world's darker peoples, which is to say that both do battle for the democratic culture of the crowd at the expense of the tyrannical culture of the mob: in the first case, by enhancing the Christian white supremacist's receptivity to the unfamiliar possibilities black and other dark strangers voice; in the second, by enhancing the black pessimist's receptivity to the seemingly remote possibility of subverting institutions that embody the culture of the mob.

In this final chapter I turn from Du Bois's accounts of artistic and natural beauty, and I return to his thinking about the idea of a beautiful life, the paradigm case for his analysis of the nature of beauty (see chapter 4). Specifically, I return to the theme of Du Bois's moralism, which is apparent when his endorsement of the propagandistic power of artistic beauty expresses a dogmatic understanding of the requirements of moral virtue. When Du Bois depicts current, ongoing black women's lives as if they satisfied his notion of beauty—thus, as if they had come to an apt end—his moralism, in conjunction with his aesthetics, compromises his commitment to the promotion of a democratic culture. In part 1 of this chapter I argue that Du Bois's conceptualization of a democratic culture cuts against his prescriptive and proleptic aesthetic moralism as it applies to black life. In part 2, I argue that his hope to promote a democratic culture cuts against present-day Afropessimism for reasons tied to his belief that natural beauty can counteract pessimism. Broadly speaking, what unites these arguments is the thought that, with regard to both individual lives and the character of human society, Du Bois is a pluralist—that, like William James, his teacher, he regards the "universe" as fundamentally "unfinished, with doors and windows open to possibilities uncontrollable in advance."[1] If we embrace Du Bois's democratic and pluralist commitments, then we should beware not only of the moralizing potential of his aesthetics, but of social theories of black life that rule out the prospect of transformative social change highlighted by his aesthetics.

THE BLACK FEMALE IDOL

Given Du Bois's democratic commitments, is his praise of *Quicksand* felicitous? At issue here is not *that* Du Bois praises Nella Larsen's novel, but *how* he praises it.

A commitment to epistemic humility is implicit in Du Bois's understanding of the normative demands of democratic citizenship. We should universalize the franchise, he argues, for only the sufferer knows his suffers. Thus, "no state can be strong which excludes from its expressed wisdom the knowledge possessed by mothers, wives, and daughters."² (See chapter 1, for my extended analysis of this argument.) Husbands, fathers, and brothers may profess to look after women's needs, but democratic citizenship requires them to acknowledge that they lack the insight necessary to do so, and that they listen to women's voices in considering what laws to enact. A closely related commitment, likewise implicit in Du Bois's understanding of democracy, is husbands', fathers', and brothers' openness, their receptivity, to women's voices. It is not enough that male citizens simply listen to women, to female strangers of whose wisdom about the world they know next to nothing, but that the novelty and unfamiliarity of these strangers' thoughts and ideas notwithstanding male citizens must also answer to them, giving these considerations their due. Rather than make infinite human nature finite by "choking back" women's voices, thus treating women as "potential criminal[s]" or "certain inferiors," and rather than "speak . . . interpret and act" for women, male citizens hoping to promote a democratic culture, having acknowledged the limited range of their familiar reservoir of experience, must continuously seek out and weigh the importance women's insights.³

Consider, now, Du Bois's praise of *Quicksand*. Larsen, he says,

> has seized an interesting character and fitted her into a close yet delicately woven plot. There is no "happy ending" and yet the theme is not defeatist. . . . Helga Crane sinks at last still master of her whimsical, unsatisfied soul. In the end she will be beaten down, even to death but she will never utterly surrender to hypocrisy and convention. Helga is typical of the new, honest, young fighting Negro woman—the one on whom "race" sits negligibly and Life is always first and its wandering path is but darkened, not obliterated by the Shadow of the Veil.⁴

Larsen's plotting of her protagonist's trajectory appeals to Du Bois, I suggest, because it satisfies his criteria of beauty, and so approximates his conception of a beautiful life. Readers of her novel know that it concludes with Helga Crane about to give birth, but Du Bois imagines Crane's life beyond that ending, "even to death." In effect he imagines Crane's life as a whole, as if it had come to an apt and triumphant end, the ugliness that had otherwise afflicted her life notwithstanding, including the shadow of the veil and the hypocrisy of convention. In addition, Du Bois reads Larsen as casting moral virtue (honesty, autonomy) in a new light, as the virtue of black women, a reading meant to drive home his moralistic condemnation of Claude McKay's *Home to Harlem*. Du Bois sarcastically writes that whites will not like the novel (it is not nasty enough for New Yorkers yet too sincere for denizens of the South and Midwest), but he cannot but hope that Larsen's depiction of her heroine will move her fellow white citizens to expand the scope of their moral concern, and, as I have previously suggested (see chapter 5), to take Helga Crane's voice to heart.

But not only *her* voice, for Helga Crane is a fictional instance of a sociological type. Reading Larsen's novel as, in Henry Louis Gates Jr.'s words, a social "document," Du Bois presents Crane as "typical," as exemplifying a type of women—"the new, honest, young fighting Negro woman"—*of whom he already knows*.[5] Differently put, Du Bois's praise of the novel is rooted not in epistemic humility, but in the presumption to know and know well the moral character exhibited by an entire class of actually existing black women. From reading *Quicksand* whites may learn that, contrary to their biased expectations, moral virtue is evident in the lives of black women: thus, that not all black women resemble the characters of McKay's novel. But Du Bois, it seems, has nothing to learn. If there are strangers among his fellow citizens to whose unfamiliar voices he must hearken to promote a democratic culture, they do not appear to be black women of the sort Helga Crane exemplifies. As a democratic citizen who holds to the view that men may no more presume to speak for women than whites for blacks, Du Bois is committed to approaching his fellow black female citizens as conversation partners to whose strange ideas he must be prepared to listen receptively. As a literary critic, however, he seems to set aside that commitment and to regard at least some of these same women as irrevocably fixed in their identity—as icons of a strict moral probity who, in addressing him as a conversation partner, could not possibly confront him with original insights that, for example, put into question the moral principles he regards as incontestable. When Du Bois praises Larsen and castigates McKay we often respond as McKay himself responded—that is, by taking Du Bois to task for wanting to exclude "the doings of the common Negroes" from literature and art.[6] Less frequently do we express the related worry that Du Bois's treatment of Larsen assumes the form of a sort of false praise that transforms highly regarded fellow citizens—in this case, highly regarded black female citizens—into tokens of well-defined types about whose views and sensibilities there is nothing unfamiliar, and to whose voices, therefore, one need no longer listen.

Stanley Cavell writes "that false praise kills what we have to be grateful for." "A traditional concept of this false praise," he adds, "is idolatry, freezing allegiance into superstition."[7] Put in Cavell's terms, I have been arguing that Du Bois's false praise works to "kill" black women as fellow citizens, only to resurrect them as idols. Du Bois's allegiance to the voices of his black sister citizens is important, for it involves a gratitude for, and a willingness to take account of, these women's unfamiliar insights. But when Du Bois projects his sister citizens as monuments of moral rectitude, defined in essence by a purity that excludes from their lives the "dirtier parts of... filth" that make him "feel... like taking a bath" when he reads *Home to Harlem*, he betrays that allegiance: in effect, he remakes his female conversation partners into objects of worship, while remaking himself from a conversation partner into a votary—not, strictly speaking, of black women, but of false representations of black women.[8] When Du Bois depicts Helga Crane as a type, he conceptualizes the women belonging to that type as he conceptualizes Helga Crane—again, *as if* their lives had come to apt and triumphant ends, leaving them not "open to possibilities" in view of which strange new ideas could continue to occur to them, but closed in on themselves, forever reduced to the moral outlook that, for Du Bois, is the sign of their triumph. In short, when Du Bois pictures his black female contemporaries as untainted icons of moral integrity, embodying complete and beautiful lives, he effectively washes his hands of them, denying that what they have to offer can be anything other than what they have already offered, hence *finishing them off.* Thus precluding the possibility of lending his ear to new insights that his contemporaries may have yet to offer, he proleptically idolizes them.

If the antidemocratic tendency to idolize black female fellow citizens is largely implicit in Du Bois's review of Nella Larsen's and Claude McKay's novels, it is difficult to miss in "The Damnation of Women," the chapter of *Darkwater* that immediately succeeds his defense of democracy in "Of the Ruling of Men." Among political-theoretical readings of "The Damnation of Women," I situate my own remarks with reference to the essays of Lawrie Balfour and Shatema Threadcraft, both of which evaluate Du Bois's contribution to a feminist theory of citizenship. Very briefly, Balfour argues that that contribution interweaves three themes: an expansive notion of black women's sexual freedom; a celebration of their economic independence; and advocacy for "the full inclusion of African-American women as full citizens," though not without acknowledging "their historical importance as political actors, even in the absence of recognition by the polity."[9] Threadcraft, however, while sympathetic to Balfour's argument, stresses nonetheless that Du Bois's inclusion of black women as citizens is conditional: that it is qualified by his belief that, to enter "the struggle for citizenship," women must "become men," and that, "to participate . . . as citizens," women must "behave like men."[10] Following in the spirit of Threadcraft's remarks, I shall be arguing, here, that Du Bois's endorsement of black women's democratic citizenship is further qualified by a tendency to adulation that excludes black women even as it includes them, damning them, so to speak, with high praise. More specifically, I shall be arguing, first, that Du Bois improvises on a received, conventional conversation about human beauty as the beauty of human beings' physical appearance, a conversation he himself often echoes, by adding to that conversation an understanding of human beauty as a feature of a properly shaped and inspiring life—in short, to an understanding of human beauty such as he expounds from the perspective of the veiled corner (see chapter 4); but, second, and more importantly for the argument of the present chapter, that Du Bois applies that understanding to the lives of his contemporaries, thus, and again, finishing them off.

The story "Damnation" tells is not difficult to summarize, and falls, roughly, into four parts: an introduction, a narrative of the history of black women; a moral and economic analysis of the standing of the modern black American woman; and a conclusion. Demonstrating his familiar bent for typologies, Du Bois's begins by identifying four women from his "boyhood" who exemplify "the problem of the widow, the wife, the maiden, and the outcast." Reflecting on these women's fates, he adds that "all womanhood is hampered today because the world on which it is emerging is a world that tries to worship both virgins and mothers and in the end despises motherhood and despoils virgins." Quite quickly, however, he comes to his central theme: "All this of women,—" he remarks, "but what of black women? The world that wills to worship womankind studiously forgets its darker sisters."[11]

Du Bois's narrative of black women's history stretches from the "the primal, black All-Mother" through "dusky Cleopatras, dark Candaces, and darker, fiercer Zinghas, to our own day and our own land." In the extended story Du Bois tells, the "African mother-idea" initially looms large, but it eventually falls prey to the "the westward slave trade and American slavery," which "struck like doom." The result of that catastrophe is a "history of insult and degradation," which, when it brought "bits of stern, dark womanhood" to North American shores, yielded a "panoply of the ancient African mother of men, strong and black, whose very nature beat back the wilderness of oppression and contempt." A cousin of one of Du Bois's grandmothers, "Mum Bett," was among that panoply, and its spiritual descendants included Mary Still, a mother of the "Negro church," as well as a host of individuals exemplifying, again, a set of types: "strong primitive types," like Harriet Tubman and Sojourner Truth; a "finer" artistic "type," exemplified by Phyllis Wheatley; and a sympathetic and self-sacrificing type, represented by Kate Ferguson, Mary Shadd, and Louise de Mortie.[12]

It is in the context of his discussion of the modern black American woman that Du Bois explicitly reflects on the nature of beauty. Earlier in the chapter, he writes of "the beauty of creating life"; of "all religion, from beauty to beast" that lies on the primal mother's breast; of "*the Ethiop queen who strove to set her beauty's praise above the sea-nymphs*"; of Phyllis Wheatley's "delicate sense of beauty"; of Mary Shadd as a "dream-born beauty"; and of black women "showing forth . . . our [black people's] strength and beauty." But it is only when he asks, "What is today the message of these [modern] black women to America and the world," famously adding that "The uplift of women is, next to the problem of the color-line and the peace movement, our greatest modern cause," that Du Bois begins to reflect on what he later calls "the nature of Beauty." Indeed it is precisely through his reflection on the nature of beauty that Du Bois, in "Damnation," explains that message.[13]

Echoing Mary Wollstonecraft's descriptions of the "specious homage," the "adoration" that men pay beautiful and alluring women, Du Bois begins his reflections by remarking that "the white world has lavished on its womankind,—its chivalry and bows, its uncoverings and courtesies—all the accumulated homage disused for courts and kings and craving exercise." That homage, an "almost mocking homage," Du Bois writes, is the "partial compensation" that white men pay white women for confining them to a narrow, "preordained destiny," which is "to be beautiful, to be petted, and to bear children." But black women have not benefitted from this homage, he reminds us, for they have not been judged to be beautiful in "face and form," and "they have been frankly trodden under the feet of men." Expanding his argument, Du Bois further remarks that when "a man comes forth with a thought, a deed, a vision, we ask not, how does he look,—but what is his message? . . . the *message* is the thing." But when a woman comes forth with the same, the message only partially matters, for "the world still wants to ask that a woman primarily be pretty and if she is not, the mob pouts and asks querulously 'What else are women for?' Beauty 'is its own excuse for being.'" When a man is ugly, his message gets through. And while an ugly white woman will have trouble getting her message through, a beautiful white woman will have a much less difficult time of it. But black women's efforts to get their message through are consistently hindered, Du Bois suggests, because the white world universally judges them to be wanting in beauty. Faced with this judgment, the black world poses two questions: one, about the nature of beauty, "What is beauty?," and the other, about the implications of the white world's answer to that question, "Suppose you think them ugly, what then?" Du Bois answers the second question by explicating and vindicating the message of the modern black American women, her failure to satisfy the white world's concept of beauty notwithstanding. He answers the first in the conclusion of "Damnation," by gesturing toward a notion of the nature of beauty that he explains in detail in "Of Beauty and Death": that is, toward a conceptualization of beauty as a function not of physical appearance, of face and form, but, again, of the shape of a life.[14]

Black women are not beautiful by the "present standards" of the white world, yet they are not subject to the "devilish decree" that any woman failing to meet those standards is not a woman, for black women are not "expected to be merely ornamental." Still, Du Bois takes issue with the white world's standards, insisting that by *his* standards a woman "crowned in curly mists" who is also black or brown "is the most beautiful thing in the world." In other words, he implies that judgments of the beauty of women's appearance are relative to the eye, the standards, of the (black or white male) beholder. The eye of the white beholder is "defective," Du Bois claims, but he does not press the point. Rather he attempts to move the discussion *away* from a dispute over the aesthetic merit of black women's physical appearance *to* the aesthetic merit of their actions. For "black women alone," he writes, "'handsome is as handsome does' and they are asked to be no more beautiful than God made them, but they are asked to be efficient, to be strong, fertile, muscled, and able to work. If they marry they must as independent workers be able to support their children, for their men are paid on a scale which makes sole support of the family often impossible." Du Bois suggests that, for the white world, there must be an aesthetic reason to accept black women (rather than consign them to "spiritual incarceration and banishment"). That black women are beautiful cannot be such a reason, for by hypothesis the white world rejects "black women as beauties." But that black women's actions are *handsome* can serve as such a reason, especially because the measure of handsomeness is efficiency, not physical appearance. In short, Du Bois encourages the white world to discover in black women's actions—*in their deeds and in the message their deeds manifest, rather than in the way they look*—a typically masculine form of aesthetic merit that justifies accepting them. That message, Du Bois suggests, is that efficient womanhood, as enacted by the economically independent black working mother, is a viable human ideal.[15]

Because black women have been "objected to" on aesthetic grounds—for "reasons peculiarly exasperating to reasoning human beings," Du Bois writes—he presumes that, to defeat the objection against them, he must adduce one or more aesthetic reasons to warrant their acceptance. The reason he adduces, the handsomeness of black women's actions, is his answer to the question "Suppose you think them ugly, what then?," for to those actions and the message they manifest it ascribes an aesthetic value that the white world can endorse even though black women fall short of white world standards for evaluating women's physical appearance. Du Bois's turn to handsomeness, to treating efficiency as an aesthetic value, is strategic. In part, it provides the white male reader a view of the modern black woman that, rather than highlighting her (in his eyes) ugly physical appearance, depicts her as embodying, through her actions, an attractive form of human agency (efficiency). But it also offsets the threat of aesthetic relativism evident in his account of conflicting black and white standards for judging women's physical appearance. For while black and white disagree about modern black women's physical beauty, they can agree about the handsomeness of her deeds.[16]

In the concluding paragraphs of "Damnation," Du Bois similarly offsets the threat of aesthetic relativism by gesturing toward and applying to his contemporaries a conception of human worth that prefigures the conception of a beautiful life that he only explicitly articulates in "Of Beauty and Death," and that provides the paradigm for his general account of the nature of beauty.

"Wait till the lady passes," said a Nashville white boy.

"She's no lady; she's a nigger," answered another.

So some few women are born free, and some amid insult and scarlet letters achieve freedom; but our women in black had freedom thrust contemptuously upon them. With that freedom they are buying an untrammeled independence and dear as is the price they pay for it, it will in the end be worth every taunt and groan. Today the dreams of the mothers are coming true. We have still our poverty and degradation, our lewdness and our cruel toil; but we have, too, a vast group of women of Negro blood who for strength of character, cleanness of soul, and unselfish devotion of purpose, is today easily the peer of any group of women in the civilized world. And more than that, in the great rank and file of our five million women we have the up-working of new revolutionary ideals, which must in time have vast influence on the thought and action of this land.

For this, their promise, and for their hard past, I honor the women of my race. Their beauty,—their dark and mysterious beauty of midnight eyes, crumpled hair, and soft, full-featured faces—is perhaps more to me than to you, because I was born to its warm and subtle spell; but their worth is yours as well as mine. No other women on earth could have emerged from the hell of force and temptation which once engulfed and still surrounds black women in America with half the modesty and womanliness that they retain. I have always felt like bowing myself before them in all abasement, searching to bring some tribute to these long-suffering victims, these burdened sisters of mine, whom the world, the wise, white world, loves to affront and ridicule and wantonly to insult. I have known the women of many lands and nations,—I have known and seen and lived beside them, but none have I known more sweetly feminine, more unswervingly loyal, more desperately earnest, and more instinctively pure in body and in soul than the daughters of my black mothers. This, then,—a little thing—to their memory and inspiration.[17]

Addressing himself, again, to the white world and, specifically, to the white male gaze as figured by "a Nashville white boy," Du Bois again acknowledges the relativism of aesthetic judgments regarding black women's physical appearance, allowing that if white men fail see beauty in midnight eyes, crumpled hair, and the like it is because their background, their birth and upbringing, has been different than his. And while there may be no background-independent basis for deciding questions of black women's physical beauty, black and white men can certainly agree on questions of black women's "worth"—or so Du Bois seems to propose. But what does worth amount to here? Du Bois's invocation of the concept echoes his famously uncredited quotation of Anna Julia Cooper's declaration of black women's "undisputed dignity," a citation of Cooper's words that represents them as paraphrasing *his* thought.[18] To vindicate black women's worth, I suggest, Du Bois paints a portrait of them as due the homage traditionally due "ladies," a portrait that shows them to have forged lives that triumphed over ugliness, over the hell of force and temptation, and as expressing the revolutionary promise of a future different than the past. Put otherwise, I read Du Bois's depiction of the black women he would praise as imaginatively outlining and, perhaps, as a possible source of the temporally bipolar notion of beauty that is central to his political aesthetics.[19] Here, then, Du Bois's turn from aesthetic relativism no longer yields a celebration of handsome efficiency, but an image of virtuous womanhood, prefiguring his later description of Helga Crane.

Where Shakespeare's Malvolio is flattered to think that greatness will be thrust upon him, Du Bois's modern black heroines have actually achieved greatness by exercising the freedom that has contemptuously been thrust upon them.[20] Indeed, through the exercise of that freedom, they have contended with the insults they have suffered and the evil with which they have been burdened, thus transforming themselves into paragons of moral excellence. Anticipating his review of Nella Larsen's novel, Du Bois represents the virtue of these women—their strong characters, clean souls, and unselfish devotion, not to mention their modesty and womanliness—as manifest signs of their triumph over the unlovely ill and hurt to which their lives have fallen prey. Forming a vision of his heroines as having defeated the ugliness that has otherwise beset them, Du Bois bows down before the image he has crafted, just as the white world bows down before the image of white womankind that it has crafted and "wills to worship." Next to the problem of the color-line he advances the cause of women's uplift by rhetorically uplifting black women, placing them on a pedestal as idols to be revered.[21]

Du Bois's idolization of his modern black "sisters" reaches its culmination with his final paean to their perfection, insisting with no epistemic humility that he knows his mothers' daughters; that he has known no women "more sweetly feminine, more unswervingly loyal, more desperately earnest, and more instinctively pure in body and in soul" than them; and then adding, as sort of offering, an afterthought: "This, then,—a little thing—to their memory and inspiration." Du Bois's commemoration of Alexander Crummell's life, his "little tribute" to his "dear memory" of Crummell, involves a backward-looking account of his mentor's life as something finished, but also the forward-looking suggestion that his life revealed inspiring new possibilities that Du Bois as well as his contemporaries might take up. In a similar vein, Du Bois's "little thing," his tribute to the idol he depicts here, involves a backward-looking account of modern black women's lives, highlighting the past, redemptive triumphs he presents as objects of "memory"—hence, as belonging to a past he himself has surpassed—but also a forward-looking emphasis on the inspirational significance these lives will have for the future. A difference, of course, is that Du Bois's tribute to Crummell is a tribute to a life *which is* finished and past, whereas his tribute to his black female fellow citizens is a tribute to lives *which are not* finished and past. If we read "Damnation" as I have here, then we should interpret Du Bois's tribute to modern black women as what *Darkwater*'s "Postscript" describes as a tribute to beauty, where, again, Du Bois begins to reimagine beauty neither as handsomeness nor as pertaining to face and form, but in terms he later conceptualizes as defining its nature from within the perspective of the veiled corner. As we have seen, however, the application of Du Bois's reimagined concept of beauty to one's fellow citizens is a form of false praise that sees them not as still alive to possibilities in view of which strange, new ideas could continue to occur to them, ideas from which one might yet learn something, but, again, as closed in on themselves, reduced to the past triumphs Du Bois celebrates. "Comrade" is the final word of "Of the Ruling of Men," because it expresses Du Bois's belief that modern socialism at its best is modern democracy at its best. But Du Boisian comrades we approach as conversation partners to whom we are prepared receptively to listen, not as idols before which we are prepared to abase ourselves. And when we approach our comrades as idols, Du Bois's democratic commitments imply, we treat them not as our fellow citizens, but as gods or goddesses.

I conclude part 1 of the present chapter by briefly recalling Saidiya Hartman's critique of Du Bois close to the conclusion of *Wayward Lives, Beautiful Experiments*—not, then, her critique of Du Bois's sociology, earlier in the book, but her later allusion, near the end, to the final paragraphs of "Damnation." Invoking the figure of a chorus comprising singing and dancing wayward women and girls, Hartman writes that "to fall in step with the chorus is to do more than shake your ass and hum the melody, or repeat, the few lines of the bit part handed over like a gift from the historian . . . or to be grateful that the sociologist has taken a second look and recognizes the working out of 'revolutionary ideals' in an ordinary black woman's life. Guessing at the world and seizing chance, she eludes the law and transforms the terms of the possible.... the matter of life returns as an open question." What Hartman quite rightly sees here, I suggest, is that the sociological Du Bois's celebration of black women as agents of revolutionary ideals in "Damnation" is no less worrisome than his blaming black women in *The Philadelphia Negro* for their moral failings, for it treats living black women's lives *not* as questions open to decision, but as fixed in their significance for the future. For a similar reason, she might also have noted that the literary critical Du Bois's false praise of Helga Crane is no less worrisome than his moralistic condemnation of Claude McKay's characters. What I hope here to have added to Hartman's insight, to her vision of her chorines asking *"How can I live?,"* is simply the proposition that Du Bois's normative notions of democracy and democratic culture and, more generally, his Jamesian pluralism insist on the same insight.[22]

AGAINST AFROPESSIMISM

In the remainder of this chapter I defend my claim that, for reasons tied to his belief that natural beauty can counteract pessimism, Du Bois's hope to promote a democratic culture cuts against contemporary Afropessimism; or, to be precise, against a prominent and influential strand of Afropessimism evident in the work of Frank B. Wilderson III, what I call "apocalyptic Afropessimism."[23] I begin by considering Wilderson's book, *Afropessimism*, as both philosophy of history and social theory. I do not do justice to the book's anecdotes; rather I highlight its central theoretical claims.[24] I finally recur to Du Bois's hope to promote a democratic culture by way of an interpretation of his short story "The Comet," which I read as a critique of apocalyptic Afropessimism, *avant la lettre*.

As philosophy of history, Wilderson's *Afropessimism* is a critique of the application of emancipatory narratives of redemption—narratives that Wilderson associates with Marxist accounts of workers' struggles, feminist accounts of struggles against patriarchy, and postcolonial accounts of the struggles of the subaltern—to Blacks. Wilderson begins by seeming to presume that, necessarily, these narratives have a general form—from a past plenitude, to the loss of plenitude, to a restoration of plenitude that these narratives envision as liberation.[25] In short, Wilderson generally conceptualizes contemporary emancipation narratives as so many instances of a secularized Neoplatonic narrative trajectory, familiar from the writings of European philosophers and poets in the Romantic tradition (including Hegel and Wordsworth, for example), from a primal fullness and unity, through a consequent differentiation and loss of said fullness and unity, to a restoration of the same.[26] Presenting Afropessimism as metatheory of theories of liberation that, in order to tell a "story of Black liberation" or "Black political redemption," apply the standard emancipatory narrative to Blacks, Wilderson insists that these theories make a category mistake: specifically, that they apply to Blacks a narrative form that properly applies only to non-Blacks.[27] Put differently, he insists that they conceptualize Black life in terms that no more apply to Blacks than the predicate "blue" applies to the number two.[28] Blacks are not beings of the sort to which emancipatory narratives apply, Wilderson maintains, for the narrative arc of Black life "is *not an arc at all*, but a flat line, what Hortense Spillers calls 'historical stillness': a flat line that moves from disequilibrium, to a moment in the narrative of faux-equilibrium, to disequilibrium restored and/or rearticulated."[29]

To see why Wilderson thinks that it is a mistake to apply narratives of liberation to black life, we need to turn from his philosophy of history to his social theory. That Wilderson's philosophy of history presupposes his social theory he suggests in an autobiographical aside, claiming that if "my upstairs neighbor is my master and I am her slave . . . There's no hope for a redemptive narrative."[30] Further developing the same point, he contends that "Afropessimism is premised on an iconoclastic claim: that Blackness is coterminous with Slaveness. Blackness *is* social death, which is to say that there never was a prior moment of plenitude, never a moment of equilibrium, never a moment of social life."[31] Wilderson's thesis that Black life is historically still is predicated on his social-theoretical proposal that social death is constitutive of Black life. Following Orlando Patterson, he conceptualizes Slaveness as social death, but further claims that there is no Blackness without Slaveness, thus understood, and hence no Blackness not characterized by an *absence* of "plenitude" or "equilibrium."[32] What this last claim amounts to is the proposition that Blacks have never not been socially dead, which is to say, in part, that Blacks have never not lacked the moral, political, or, more generally, social standing that could come only through being recognized by non-Blacks as enjoying "rights and claims" that could in principle be "violated."[33] Emancipation narratives don't apply to Blacks, Wilderson argues, because Blacks, as such, have never known social life: that is, they have never been recognized as having rights and claims, from which it follows that they have never suffered a loss of social standing that they could then strive to regain by returning Black life to its former equilibrium.[34] Because Blacks have lost nothing, he implies, it is a mistake narratively to represent them as struggling to restore what they have lost. If Black life has been and can only be historically still, it is because it is not possible for Blacks to progress from the condition of social death—to improve their condition, in other words—when "the antagonism between Blacks and the world" is the "*essential* antagonism."[35] Blacks may fall prey to the illusion of historical progress, to mistaking merely apparent, faux-equilibria for real ones, Wilderson seems to suggest, but, strictly speaking, Black reality is the endless, flat line of persistent disequilibrium.[36]

In claiming that the antagonism between Blacks and the world is *the* essential antagonism, Wilderson means to distinguish Afropessimism from Marxist social theories that treat class conflict, the "dustups between the worker and the capitalist," as the defining, essential antagonism structuring modern societies.[37] Contra Marxism, Wilderson's social theory proposes that the world (the modern world) is essentially structured not only by the historical stillness of the slave who is Black, but, in addition, by a "relational dynamic," an unrelenting, antagonistic "violence" that pervades Black life.[38] Indeed, it is precisely this violence that explains the historical stillness of Black life: "the violence that both elaborates and saturates black 'life' is totalizing, so much so as to make narrative inaccessible to Blacks."[39] Even if Black life, as such, has always been historically still, one could plausibly conjecture that it need not be so in the future—thus, that Blacks might improve their condition through struggles for recognition that persuaded some whites and other non-Blacks, in some social contexts, to extend to Blacks the recognition and the social standing that they have never heretofore enjoyed. But Wilderson denies this possibility, insisting, again, that "violence saturates Black life . . . [that] for Black people . . . there is no relative respite from force and coercion; violence spreads its tendrils across the body, chokes the community, and expands, intensifies, and mutates into new and ever more grotesque forms in the collective unconscious."[40] In short, Wilderson rules out the possibility of progress from the condition of social death, arguing that the violent, totalizing structure of modern societies precludes Blacks from undertaking actions or political mobilizations that could, at least partially, undermine that structure, constrain the scope and intensity of its violence, and thus overcome historical stillness. To the extent that the modern world is structurally defined by its violent antagonism toward Black life, progress within that world is impossible. Piecemeal, within-the-world "reformist" efforts are ultimately beside the point, for where *"Anti-Black violence is a paradigm of oppression . . . there is no coherent form of redress, other than Frantz Fanon's 'the end of the world.'"*[41] Wilderson's Afropessimism is an "apocalyptic Afropessimism" because it leads to this conclusion, implying that the amelioration of Black life demands a total reconstitution of the world, the replacement of the violent structure that essentially defines modern societies by a fundamentally different social system.

Let me turn now to "The Comet," the *Darkwater* short story wherewith Du Bois himself entertains the idea of the world's coming to an end. A "new comet" strikes the Earth, killing millions, it seems, in part through the release of "deadly gases." In New York, the only two people left alive are Jim, a black man who works as a "messenger" for a New York bank, and Julia, a beautiful and well-to-do white woman. Jim "rescue[s]" Julia from her apartment, near 5th Avenue and 72nd Street, and together they drive around the city, first stopping in Harlem, where Jim finds neither his wife nor their baby, but retrieves the baby's "filmy cap." Subsequently they head to the Metropolitan Tower in search of Julia's father, and find a note indicating that he has gone for a drive with her boyfriend, Fred. Eventually Jim and Julia return to the Tower, after driving all around the city, and they ascend by elevator to the Tower's roof platform. There they are discovered by Julia's father, by Fred, and by a crowd of onlookers. Jim's black wife, cradling their dead baby in one of her arms, also appears.[42]

For most of the story Jim and Julia are alone, and during that time they come to imagine themselves as the sole human survivors of the comet catastrophe, and as the soon-to-be progenitors of a new race and a new world. Allusions to the biblical apocalypse, to the Book of Revelations, abound in Du Bois's short story, as Jim and Julia anticipate the prospect of wholly replacing a now dead world, wherein differences of class and race structured social life and working-class black men like Jim did not count as human, with a world within which "distinctions of race and wealth . . . mean nothing."[43] Enchanted by this utopian vision, Julia sees Jim as "Humanity incarnate, Son of God, and great All-Father of the race to be," while regarding herself as "no mere woman," as "neither high nor low, white nor black, rich nor poor," but, now visited by the hovering "Angel of Annunciation," as the "mighty mother of all men to come." Jim, for his part, sees himself uplifted from "the crass and crushing and cringing of his caste," as if "some might Pharoah lived again, or curled Assyrian lord." Together, in spiritual communion, they share a vision of "a mighty beauty," as well as a "divine" and "splendid" thought that animates their gazing into each other's eyes. Just as Jim and Julia are about to consummate their marriage, but with neither "lust" nor "love," Fred, Julia's father, and the crowd of onlookers appears. This is how the short story ends:

> "Julia," he whispered; "my darling, I thought you were gone forever."
>
> She looked up at him with strange, searching eyes.
>
> "Fred," she murmured, almost vaguely, "is the world—gone?"
>
> "Only New York," he answered; "it is terrible—awful! You know,—but you, how did you escape—how have you endured this horror? Are you well? Unharmed?"
>
> "Unharmed!" she said.
>
> "And this man here?" he asked, encircling her drooping form with one arm and turning toward the Negro. Suddenly he stiffened and his hand flew to his hip. "Why!" he snarled. "It's—a—nigger—Julia! Has he—has he dared———"
>
> She lifted her head and looked at her late companion curiously and then dropped her eyes with a sigh.
>
> "He has dared—all, to rescue me," she said quietly, "and I—thank him—much." But she did not look at him again. As the couple turned away, the father drew a roll of bills from his pockets.

"Here, my good fellow," he said, thrusting the money into the man's hands, "take that,—what's your name?"

"Jim Davis," came the answer, hollow-voiced.

"Well, Jim, I thank you. I've always liked your people. If you ever want a job, call on me." And they were gone.

The crowd poured up and out of the elevators, talking and whispering.

"Who was it?"

"Are they alive?"

"How many?"

"Two!"

"Who was saved?"

"A white girl and a nigger—there she goes."

"A nigger? Where is he? Let's lynch the damned———"

"Shut up—he's all right—he saved her."

"Saved hell! He had no business———"

"Here he comes."

Into the glare of the electric lights the colored man moved slowly, with the eyes of those that walk and sleep.

"Well, what do you think of that?" cried a bystander; "of all New York, just a white girl and a nigger!"

The colored man heard nothing. He stood silently beneath the glare of the light, gazing at the money in his hand and shrinking as he gazed; slowly he put his other hand into his pocket and brought out a baby's filmy cap, and gazed again. A woman mounted to the platform and looked about, shading her eyes. She was brown, small, and toil-worn, and in one arm lay the corpse of a dark baby. The crowd parted and her eyes fell on the colored man; with a cry she tottered toward him.

"Jim!"

He whirled and, with a sob of joy, caught her in his arms.

In Jim and Julia's utopian vision, in their thought and imagination of the divinely splendid and mighty beauty of the new world they aspire to beget, there appears to be no ugliness. As in Revelations 21, where the advent of "a new heaven and a new earth" is said to entail that "there shall be no more death, neither sorrow, nor crying, neither shall there be any more pain: for the former things are passed away," Jim and Julia's vision of a new earth—or, at least, of the old earth blessed with a new world[44]—seems similarly to lack anything of the ill and hate and hurt that "Of Beauty and Death" tells us will always be there. Put differently and in Du Bois's words, Jim and Julia have for a few moments become optimists who, with the apparent demise of the old world and its ugliness, imaginatively fantasize a world in which "all is beauty." But their fantasy is short lived, for with the "Honk! Honk!" of the car that announces the arrival of Julia's father and Fred they are forced to acknowledge that the future before them will not be a future where the descendants of a new, Pharaonic son of man and his "Bride of Life" know nothing of ugliness. Through their interaction, which has in fact set aside distinctions of race and wealth, Jim and Julia have interrupted the endless recurrence of ugliness, but they have been deluded in believing that they could put it behind them.

Before the comet strikes, the president of the bank where Jim works contrasts the oncoming cosmic snowball to Halley's comet, which is well known, noting that "this is a new comet, quite a stranger." Refusing to be treated as a "potential criminal and certain inferior,"[45] which is how the culture of the mob treats Du Bois's paradigmatic stranger, the "American Negro" (see chapter 1), his fictional "comet-stranger" appears to be a figure for the dark-skinned revolutionary who would destroy and remake the world in order to rid it of racial oppression. But the attempt at total revolution is destined to fail, Du Bois believes, for in its wake, and in the wake of the indulgence of the utopian fantasy with which he associates it—here, Jim and Julia's fantasy—ugliness will persist.[46] During the course of their time together, Julia ceases to see Jim as a stranger and comes to regard him, again, as "Humanity incarnate." But with the return of

Fred and her father it seems clear that Jim will resume his status as stranger in her eyes, and that the rest of the white world will continue to see him as a stranger. Still, Jim's plight is not hopeless, and it does not warrant pessimism, at least in Du Bois's eyes. Indeed, I read the ending of "The Comet" as expressing Du Bois's rejection of the belief that, without an apocalyptic destruction of our white supremacist world, and the replacement of that world by a fundamentally different one, progress that improves black life is impossible.

I highlight two features of the ending to support my reading. One is Du Bois's reengagement with the distinction between a crowd and a mob. As in "The Second Coming," a chapter of *Darkwater* I considered in chapter 1, Du Bois stresses the fragility of America's normatively distinctive project, its commitment to make known to the world a polity organized around the concept of the crowd. Noting, again, that an episodic crowd can quite easily mutate into an episodic mob—"A nigger? Where is he? Let's lynch the damned—"—the crowd's receptivity to the stranger prevails nonetheless. As Du Bois dramatically, perhaps cinematically, scripts the closing scene of the story, the crowd parts to provide a harbor for Jim to reunite with his wife. Although the culture of the mob has always to be combatted, and although America still fails fully to honor its commitment to creating a polity organized around the concept of the crowd, the culture of the crowd is sufficiently strong to provide Jim and his wife a safe space to begin their lives anew. And begin again, they do. Imagining the scene as shot from behind Jim's wife, the concluding action sequence, the second feature of the ending I highlight, gradually unfolds: the crowd parts, letting Jim's wife see Jim, his back to her. Holding their dead baby in one arm, she then totters toward him with a cry; and he, hearing her, and still gripping his dead baby's filmy cap, as well as the money given him by Julia's father, whirls toward her, now catching her in his arms with a sob of joy. As

Du Bois depicts this final sequence, it culminates in Jim's joyful embrace of his wife against a backdrop of persistent ugliness: on one hand, the death of his infant child; on the other, the reestablishment of his subordinate position as a worker dependent for his well-being on the wages paid him for his service—on the wages Julia's father pays him for rescuing her, and which he will continue to pay him if he accepts the job her father has offered him. With his story's patiently awaited ending, its image of a "tardy triumph of [black] joy," as *Darkwater*'s "Credo" puts it, of a moment of fulfillment that anticipates a future Jim and his wife will undertake together, all too aware of ongoing racial domination and of the corpse his wife cradles at her side, Du Bois sketches a clear picture of a beautiful action that, against the odds, succeeds in interrupting all that ugliness.[47]

Absent an apocalypse, progress that improves black life is possible, Du Bois believes, because the social world blacks inhabit is unfinished. To emphasize this point, I have through several chapters relied on the language of "subversion" and "interruption" to characterize Du Bois's understanding of social change, and I have similarly stressed that beauty's power to constrain and curtail the sway of ugliness, to lessen its volume and force, explains his interest in the phenomenon. Just as it is an error to think of ongoing human lives as fixed and finished in their significance, an error to which Du Bois succumbs, his democratic commitments notwithstanding I have argued, it is similarly a mistake to think of the social world as having a fixed and finished shape, or character, that is impervious to transformative agency that would revamp it. Even where capitalist self-interest, racial hierarchy, and the culture of the mob conspire to dominate and exploit black life, Du Bois believes, the astonishingly ugly social landscape is susceptible to amelioration through permutation— again, through interruption and subversion—sometimes, though hardly all or even most of the time, through the efficacy of beautiful works of art, as in the impact of a divinely crafted vision on Du

Bois's fictional farmer's wife (see chapter 5); through the shaping of beautiful lives, as in Alexander Crummell's fashioning of his life; and through the performance of beautiful actions, as in Jim's joyful embrace of his wife.[48] In "Sociology Hesitant," I have argued (see chapter 6), Du Bois proposes that the social world is open to actions that, by beginning something new, rearrange it, thus echoing William James's pluralist supposition that "some things at least are decided here and now, that the passing moment may contain some novelty, be an original starting point of events, and not merely transmit a push from elsewhere."[49] Du Bois's hope to promote a democratic culture of the crowd, which is apparent in his depiction of a crowd that resists the lyncher's impulse and parts to provide Jim and his wife a haven to begin their lives anew, is premised on his belief that the social world is open to action that, short of total revolution, transforms and improves it, step by step.

As a social theorist, then, Du Bois's thinking cuts against Wilderson's, for Wilderson is committed to the view that stepwise actions geared to partial reform cannot but "transmit a push from elsewhere," that while they might appear to make a difference, they at best create the illusion of progress—again, what Wilderson calls faux-equilibria—for the push of the violent, totalizing, antiblack structure of modern social life inevitably constrains blacks to historical stillness. In more general terms, Du Bois's thinking cuts against Wilderson's, because Wilderson endorses a social-theoretical version of the monism that Du Boisian and Jamesian pluralism rejects: specifically, it endorses an idea about the social world that the contemporary, avowedly pragmatist social theorist Roberto Unger calls "the thesis of indivisibility." According, again, to James, the monist claims that "the universe is *tight* . . . not loose; . . . [that] you must take the irreducible whole of it just as it is offered, or have no part or lot in it at all."[50] The "thesis of indivisibility" is the social-theoretical correlate of monism, I suggest, for it amounts to the claim that each and every social structure—"for example, the feudal or capitalist modes of production in Marxist theory—is an indivisible system. Its different parts stand or fall together. A practical consequence is that politics must consist either in temporizing reforms or in revolutionary transformation, replacing one such system by another."[51] Wilderson's endorsement of the thesis of indivisibility is evident in his view that there is a single, "essential antagonism" structuring the whole of modern social life, such that no reformist tinkering with the parts of the world, short of ending it through the apocalypse of total revolution, could coherently make a difference to the quality of black life. While Wilderson takes issue with Marxist theory on the question of *what* indivisible antagonism fundamentally structures modern social life, he assumes with it *that some such indivisible antagonism does so.*[52] The Du Boisian pluralist rejects that assumption and, practically speaking, adopts the meliorist position that modern social life, because it is not a tightly organized indivisible system, invites step-by-step "piecemeal reconstruction"—"revolutionary reform," in Unger's words, not total revolution.[53]

It is beyond the scope of the present chapter systematically to spell out the consequences of a Du Bois–inspired rejection of Wilderson's apocalyptic Afropessimism for a political aesthetic. I conclude, however, by noting two recent contributions to black aesthetics that, with an eye to Du Bois's "Sociology Hesitant," implicitly embrace the pluralist view that human societies are "open to possibilities uncontrollable in advance." One is an essay by Fred Moten that describes "Hesitant Sociology" as "an attempt to think the imbrication of blackness and poetry in the ongoing moment and irreducible materiality of their conception, as social life in the making." Without presuming to do justice to Moten's complex engagement with Du Bois, I note first that he understands Du Bois's attunement to miraculous phenomena that escape explanation in terms of scientific law to entail a *more general attunement* to phenomena that exceed traditional understandings of meaning and being; second, that he takes blackness to be one of these phenomena; and third, that he interprets blackness as an aesthetic practice, as a form of social life that is animated by a lawlessly dispersive and disbursive imagination—which is to say, for Moten, by poetry.[54] For the second contribution, I return to the concluding reflections of Saidiya Hartman's *Wayward Lives*. Hartman casts a skeptical eye on the Du Bois of "Damnation," no less than on the Du Bois of *The Philadelphia Negro*, I've argued. But the Du Bois of "Sociology Hesitant" she vindicates when, again, envisioning one of her chorines, she writes, "Guessing at the world and seizing chance, she eludes the law and transforms the terms of the possible." Taking up Du Bois's distinction between law and chance, the latter of which she, like Du Bois, ties to human action, Hartman also echoes her earlier "Short Entry on the Possible," in which she characterizes waywardness as a "*beautiful experiment*. . . . a practice of possibility at a time when all roads except the ones created by *smashing out*, are foreclosed."[55] Du Bois need not have looked to natural beauty to disclose the social world's vulnerability to action intended to interrupt it, she implies, for closer to home were beautiful, unfinished lives, whose transformative agency revealed the same vulnerability.

ACKNOWLEDGMENTS

In the fall of 2018, at the invitation of Lawrie Balfour and Stephen White, I presented a paper on Du Bois's Darkwater to the Political Theory Colloquium at the University of Virginia. Afterward, Lawrie and I went for a drink, and the invigorating conversation that followed inspired the idea for Democracy and Beauty. In many ways, the book is my attempt to answer the provocative and insightful questions Lawrie posed regarding my treatment of Du Bois's World War I–era philosophical thought.

I wrote the first few chapters of *Democracy and Beauty* with the support of a John Simon Guggenheim Fellowship, which I was enormously honored to receive. In 2022 I completed a first draft, when I was privileged to deliver the Leonard Hastings Schoff Memorial Lectures at Columbia University

I especially want to thank Martha Nussbaum, Tommie Shelby, Sally Haslanger, and Alice Crary for their early, unstinting support for my study of Du Bois's political aesthetics. For constructive criticism, when I was first forming my arguments and while I was rethinking the structure of the book as a whole, I am particularly indebted to my partner, Sara Gooding-Williams, and to my Columbia University colleague and friend Philip Kitcher. I am similarly indebted to my colleague and friend Saidiya Hartman for hours of conversation that helped me to think more clearly about Du Bois's aesthetics in relation to contemporary Black aesthetics and Afropessimism.

I am immensely grateful to a large community of brilliant scholars for pointed feedback on one or another particular chapter. Regarding chapter 1, I profited from insights offered by Linda Zerilli, Cristina Beltrán, and Axel Honneth; and regarding chapter 2, I sharpened the analysis with the help of Alice Crary, Matthew Congdon, Nancy Bauer, Karen Ng, Tamar Schapiro, and Steve Darwall. Chapter 3 and its discussion of democratic despotism would have been impossible to write without the guidance of Jennifer Pitts and Adom Getachew. Chapter 4 benefited from Lydia Goehr's and Ed Casey's astute commentary, and would not have been written at all absent Philip Kitcher's encouragement. With respect to chapter 5 I received helpful feedback from numerous interlocutors, including Justin Clark-Doane, Christopher Peacocke, Akeel Bilgrami, Michele Moody-Adams, Gayatri Spivak, Lorenzo Simpson, Ross Posnock, Julie Cooper, Jason Frank, Lori Marso, Melvin Rogers, Meena Krishnnamurty, Joshua Cohen, Desmond Jagmohan, Sarah Song, Shalini Satkunanandan, Stephen White, Dan Henry, Karuna Mantena, Brandon Terry, Skip Gates, Sarah Lewis, Christia Mercer, and Jill Frank. Susanna Siegel's, Patchen Markell's, and Francey Russell's responses to chapter 6 led me to revise key parts of its argument, and exchanges with Saidiya Hartman and Fred Moten helped me to strengthen the argument of chapter 7.

Thanks, finally, to my Columbia University Press editor, Wendy Lochner, who patiently waited for me to complete the book manuscript after I delivered the Schoff lectures; to two anonymous readers for the Press for their valuable comments; and to Robert Demke for his assiduous copyediting.

Some of the material appearing in *Democracy and Beauty* previously appeared in print. In that connection, I wish to thank *The*

Monist, published by Oxford University Press, for permission to reprint, with revisions, parts of "Democratic Despotism, Democratic Culture, and the Democratic Ideal" (see *The Monist* 107, no. 1 [January 2024]: 26–38). And I wish to thank *WestEnd* for permitting me to reprint as chapter 1 of *Democracy and Beauty* a revised, English-language version of an essay that it previously published (see "Demokratie und aesthetische Erziehung: Du Bois' Politik des Schönen," in *WestEnd: Neue Zeitschrift für Sozialforschung* 20, no. 1:113–137). Thanks too to Columbia University Press for permission to reprint, as chapter 3, an expanded version of "Freedom Through Unfreedom: Du Bois's Theory of Democratic Despotism," an essay I originally wrote for *Unfreedom in Liberal Democracies*, edited by Akeel Bilgrami and Jonathan Cole. Finally, I am grateful to Princeton University Press for permitting me to reprint a few pages of revised material from a chapter that was originally written for *The Princeton History of American Political Thought*, edited by Nicholas Buccola, Susan McWilliams, and Roosevelt Montas (Princeton University Press, 2025).

NOTES

1. *DARKWATER*, DEMOCRACY, AND AESTHETIC EDUCATION

1. See W. E. B. Du Bois, *Darkwater: Voices from Within the Veil* (1920; New York: Washington Square Press, 2004). Hereafter cited as *Darkwater*.
2. For all the material quoted in the paragraph, see *Darkwater*, 105–106.
3. Eric Hobsbawm, *The Age of Revolution, 1789–1848* (1962; New York: Vintage, 1996), 53.
4. *Darkwater*, 107.
5. In characterizing industrial capitalism as a form of tyrannical rule and "Captains of Industry" as "tyrants of the industrial age" (*Darkwater*, 106), Du Bois's criticism of modern capitalism and his defense of democracy echo motifs that would have been familiar to him from the nineteenth-century labor republican tradition. For an insightful political theoretical reconstruction of that tradition, see Alex Gourevitch, *From Slavery to the Cooperative Commonwealth: Labor and Republican Liberty in the Nineteenth Century* (Cambridge: Cambridge University Press, 2015).
6. In "The Present Outlook for the Darker Races of Mankind" (W. E. B. Du Bois, "The Present Outlook for the Darker Races of Mankind," in *The Problem of the Color Line at the Turn of the Twentieth Century: Essential Early Essays*, ed. Nahum Dimitri Chandler [New York: Fordham University Press, 2015], 111–137), Du Bois explicitly ties the French Revolution to the idea of universal suffrage and to the democratic political philosophy of the eighteenth century. He mentions Jean-Jacques Rousseau in particular.

In the opening pages of "Of the Ruling of Men" (chapter 6 of *Darkwater*), however, Du Bois omits to mention the French Revolution. That said, he does refer to it implicitly, for his allusions to democratic struggles to restrict menial service, to secure the right of property in handiwork, to regulate public taxes, to redistribute land ownership, and to free trade and barter all point to key moments in the history of the Revolution: e.g., to the abolition of serfdom and personal obligations; to the elimination of the guild system; to the incorporation of a "no taxation without representation" principle into "The Declaration of the Rights of Man and Citizen"; to the redistribution of lands owned by the Church; and to the implementation of free market principles. For overviews of the French Revolution that touch on all of these themes, see Peter Gay and R. K. Webb, *Modern Europe* (New York: Harper and Row, 1973), chap. 11; and Jeremy Popkin, *A New World Begins: The History of the French Revolution* (New York: Basic, 2019), passim. For a summary of most of the same themes, see Hobsbawm, *The Age of Revolution, 1789–1848*, 64–65. For a more recent work that, like Du Bois's World War I–era essay, interprets progressive European political movements of the late eighteenth century as *democratic* movements, see R. R. Palmer, *The Age of Democratic Revolutions: A Political History of Europe and American. 1760–1800* (1959, 1964; Princeton: Princeton University Press, 2014). In their conceptualizations of the ideological orientation animating these movements, Du Bois and Palmer overlap, although it is clear that Du Bois places greater emphasis on the theme of universal suffrage. In a related vein, Axel Honneth has recently argued that, after the French Revolution, "'early socialist groups'" (the followers of Robert Owen in England and the Saint-Simonists and Fouierists in France) derived "their rejection of the post-revolutionary social order . . . from their outrage at how the expansion of the capitalist market prevented a large portion of the population from taking advantage of the principles of freedom and equality proclaimed by the French Revolution." Du Bois, I think, would have characterized these groups as advocates for his broadly conceived "philosophy of democracy." Honneth takes the early socialists to task, however, for their "economic fundamentalism" and for not giving sufficient attention to the idea of a specifically "political democracy." See Axel Honneth, *The Idea of Socialism: Towards a Renewal*, trans. Joseph Ganahl (Cambridge: Polity, 2018), 8, 9, 26, 32–37, 76ff., and passim.

7. *Darkwater*, 106.
8. *Darkwater*, 106–107.
9. *Darkwater*, 107.
10. *Darkwater*, 107.
11. *Darkwater*, 107.
12. *Darkwater*, 107–108.
13. *Darkwater*, 108.
14. See W. E. B. Du Bois, "The African Roots of War," in *W. E. B. Du Bois: International Thought*, ed. Adom Getachew and Jennifer Pitts (Cambridge: Cambridge University Press, 2022), 25. Sir Henry Morton Stanley [1841–1904] was a Welsh-born journalist who explored the Congo river from the central African town of Nyangwe to the Atlantic mouth of the Congo in 1876–1877. Under the auspices of Leopold II of Belgium, Stanley returned to the lower Congo in 1879, where, through the exploitative and inhumane use of forced labor for commercial purposes, he helped Leopold to establish the Congo Free State (see Du Bois, "The African Roots of War," 25n6).
15. It is striking that Du Bois's sense of the nature and importance of this historical juncture persists in *Black Reconstruction* (1935). See, e.g., the penultimate paragraph of chapter 14, titled "The Counter-Revolution of Property," where he writes that "God wept; but that mattered little to an unbelieving age; what mattered most was that the world wept and still is weeping and blind with tears and blood. For there began to rise in America in 1876 a new capitalism and a new enslavement of labor. Home labor in cultured lands, appeased and misled by a ballot whose power the dictatorship of vast capital strictly curtailed, was bribed by high wage and political office to unite in an exploitation of white, yellow, brown, and black labor, in lesser lands and 'breeds without the law.'" W. E. B. Du Bois, *Black Reconstruction* (1935; New York: Free Press, 1998), 634. Du Bois's reference here, to "breeds without the law," alludes to Rudyard Kipling's poem "Recessional" (1897). I note, finally, that Du Bois quoted the same line from Kipling's poem in the context of his discussion of the theory of benevolent guardianship in *Darkwater*. See *Darkwater*, 109.
16. I analyze Du Bois's notion of democratic despotism elsewhere.
17. For Du Bois, artistic beauty attacks racial oppression directly. Natural beauty attacks it indirectly by attacking the dispositions to despair and pessimism it generates, dispositions that, to the extent to which they take hold among black opponents to racial oppression, effectively strength it.

18. For all the material quoted in this paragraph, see *Darkwater*, 109–110.
19. For all the material quoted in the paragraph, see *Darkwater*, 111, 113–114.
20. *Darkwater*, 113–114.
21. *Darkwater*, 114.
22. Elizabeth Anderson, "The Epistemology of Democracy" *Episteme* (2006): 14.
23. *Darkwater*, 112.
24. Du Bois's idea that democracy is a process through which citizens learn from one another's viewpoints has some affinities with John Dewey's epistemic defense of democracy, which emphasizes "the free exchange of varying modes of life-experience," as well as citizens' capacities "to learn from one another, and thereby to expand their horizons." See John Dewey, *The Middle Works, 1899–1924*, vol. 9, *1916 Democracy and Education*, ed. Jo Ann Boydston (Carbondale: Southern Illinois University Press, 1980), 90, 92. See also Dewey's defense of the "socialism of knowledge" in *John Dewey: Lectures in China, 1919–1920*, trans. Robert W. Clopton and Tsuin-Chen OU (Honolulu: University Press of Hawaii, 1973), 178–180. For helpful discussion of Dewey's views, see, especially, Anderson, "The Epistemology of Democracy"; and Hilary Putnam "A Reconsideration of Deweyan Democracy," *Southern California Law Review* 63 (1990): 1671–1697. For insightful discussion of Du Bois's epistemic defense of democracy from which I have also benefited, see Harriet Fertik, "Hell to Pay: Aristotle and W. E. B. Du Bois's Vision of Democracy in 'Of the Ruling of Men,'" *International Journal of the Classical Tradition* 26 (2019): 72–85; Liam Kofi Bright, "Du Bois' Democratic Defense of the Value Free Ideal," *Synthese* 195 (2018): 2227–2245; and Derrick Darby, "Du Bois's Defense of Democracy," *Democratic Failure: NOMOS LXIII*, ed. Melissa Schwartzberg and Daniel Viehoff, https://nyu.universitypressscholarship.com/view/10.18574/nyu/9781479804788.001.0001/upso-9781479804788-chapter-009?print=pdf.
25. Alexis de Tocqueville, *Democracy in America*, ed. J. P. Mayer, trans. George Lawrence (1835; New York: HarperCollins, 1969), vol. 1, pt. 2, chap. 7, "The Omnipotence of the Majority in the United States and Its Effects." For J. S. Mill's discussion of tyranny of the majority in *On Liberty*, see John Stuart Mill, *On Liberty*, in *John Stuart Mill: On Liberty and Other Essays* (1859; Oxford: Oxford University Press, 1991), 5–19. It is well known that Mill reviewed volume 1 of *Democracy in America* in 1836.
26. *Darkwater*, 119.

27. *Darkwater*, 118.
28. For all the material quoted in this passage, besides *Darkwater*'s subtitle, see *Darkwater*, xxiii. For the conceptualization of improvisation as performance involving the transformation of old models and the creation of new ideas, see Paul F. Berliner, *Thinking in Jazz: The Infinite Art of Improvisation* (Chicago: University of Chicago Press, 1994), 221–222. Implicit in the "performance," the application, of Du Bois's philosophical method is a commitment to what the philosopher Lorenzo Simpson calls "semantic democracy." "I would . . . deem ideological," says Simpson, "any self-interpretation that is promulgated by a society that arbitrarily restricts the interpretive agency of its members and that thus undermines its semantic democratic character. Semantic democracy, in which competing social interpretations can be granted public recognition, is a prerequisite of generalized social agency. The requisite reflexivity of a binding social interpretation, the first condition on social legitimacy alluded to previously, is facilitated by such a democratization of interpretive agency in which there are no arbitrary restrictions to participation in the interpretive practices that generate collectively binding and enabling social meanings. In this way, social legitimacy can be seen to require interpretive democracy. Thus my plea for hermeneutic democracy, for the democratization of social disclosure, and for the institutions that would enable and sustain it." See Lorenzo C. Simpson, *Hermeneutics as Critique: Science, Politics, Race, and Culture* (New York: Columbia University Press, 2021), 152.
29. Tocqueville, *Democracy in America*, 1:316.
30. That said, Du Bois has been rightly criticized for *not* giving due attention, in *Darkwater* and elsewhere, to issues raised by the history of settler colonialism.
31. Du Bois's concept of democratic despotism, which I explicate in detail in chapter 1, should not be confused with the notion that Tocqueville elaborates in volume 2 of *Democracy in America*.
32. *Darkwater*, 78, 109–110.
33. Were this Du Bois's aim, he would be echoing Tocqueville's interest in determining "the first causes" of Americans' "prejudices, habits, [and] dominating passions." See Tocqueville, *Democracy in America*, 1:32.
34. In distinguishing, here, between a causal, third-person point of view on "acts of beginning" and a normative, first-person point of view on such acts, I am indebted to Akeel Bilgrami's discussion of that distinction in his

remarks on Edward Said's *Beginnings: Intention and Method* (New York: Basic, 1975). Du Bois, I am suggesting, conceptualizes the beginning of the discovery of the crowd as if from a first-person point of view: that is, as if it could be regarded from the point of view of an unnamed agent who, through their founding (beginning) commitment to discovering to the world a polity organized around the concept of the crowd, defined the meaning of America. See Akeel Bilgrami, *Secularism, Identity, and Enchantment* (Cambridge, MA: Harvard University Press, 2014), 328–338.

35. Jacques Barzun, *From Dawn to Decadence: 500 Years of Western Cultural Life* (New York: HarperCollins, 2000), 285ff.

36. For wonderfully detailed discussion of the operation of ceremony and etiquette in the court of Louis XIV, see Norbert Elias, *The Court Society: The Collected Works of Norbert Elias*, vol. 2, trans. Edmund Jephcott (1969; Dublin: University College Dublin Press, 2006). According to Elias, etiquette and ceremony under Louis's reign "increasingly became . . . a ghostly *perpetuum mobile* that continued to operate regardless of any direct use-value. . . . Every slightest attempt to reform . . . inevitably entailed an upheaval, a reduction or even abolition of the rights of certain individuals and families. To jeopardize such privileges was, to the ruling class of this society, a kind of taboo" (95).

37. Here, I am struck by the affinity between Du Bois's conception of the crowd and the tendency of philosophers inspired by Stanley Cavell's interpretation of Wittgenstein to conceptualize "forms of life" as "dynamic and open rather than (ethnographically) static and closed." See Linda M. G. Zerilli, *A Democratic Theory of Judgment* (Chicago: University of Chicago Press, 2016), 24–25. Considered from the perspective of this affinity, I am tempted to read Du Bois as arguing that maintaining a genuinely democratic way of life—a way of life shaped by the culture of the crowd—requires that citizens recognize that "mutual intelligibility" is a fluid but fragile enterprise not reducible to the mutual mastery of a determinate set of rules. "It is not rules that guarantee our mutual intelligibility as democratic citizens," Zerilli writes, "but rather our mastery of speaking in particular public contexts" (Zerilli, *A Democratic Theory of Judgment*, 25). In this connection, it is also worth noting that Du Bois, like Cavell, gives pride of place "to voice rather than rules" (Zerilli, *A Democratic Theory of Judgment*, 26).

1. *DARKWATER*, DEMOCRACY, AND AESTHETIC EDUCATION ⚭ 207

38. America has not fulfilled its founding commitment, and Europe, Du Bois suggests, has outstripped America in fulfilling it. Thus, recalling his visit to France after World War I, Du Bois writes, "My God! For what am I thankful this night? For nothing. For nothing but the most commonplace of commonplaces; a table of gentlewomen and gentlemen—soft-spoken, sweet-tempered, full of human sympathy, who made me, *a stranger* [emphasis mine], one of them. Ours was a fellowship of common books, common knowledge, mighty aims. We could laugh and joke and think as friends—and the Thing—the hateful, murderous, dirty Thing which in American we call 'Nigger-hatred' was not only not there—it could not even be understood. It was a curious monstrosity at which civilized folk laughed or looked puzzled. . . . God! It was simply human decency and I had to be thankful for it because I am an American Negro, and white America, with saving exceptions, is cruel to everything that has black blood—and this was Paris, in the years of salvation, 1919. Fellow blacks, we must join the democracy of Europe." *Darkwater*, 184–185.

39. See Edgar Allen Poe, "The Man in the Crowd," in *Edgar Allen Poe: Selected Poems, Tales and Essays*, ed. Jared Gardner and Elizabeth Hewitt (New York: Bedford/St. Martin's Press, 2016), 120–128; and Georg Simmel, "The Stranger," trans. Donald N. Levine, in *Georg Simmel On Individuality and Social Forms*, ed. Donald N. Levine (Chicago: University of Chicago Press, 1971), 143–149. For the German original, see "Exkurs über den Fremden," in *Soziologie: Untersuchungen über die Formen der Vergesellschaftung* (Berlin: Duncker und Humblot, 1908), 509–512. Simmel was teaching philosophy at the University of Berlin when Du Bois was a student there, so it is likely that Du Bois was aware of him and his work. I do not know, however, that Du Bois read Simmel's 1908 essay. But whether or not he read it, I find it useful to interpret Du Bois with reference to "Exkurs über den Fremden," for doing so helpfully clarifies Du Bois's notion of the stranger.

40. See Poe, "The Man of the Crowd," 128. Walter Benjamin famously described Poe's tale as "something like the X-ray picture of a detective story. . . . [in which] the drapery represented by the crime has disappeared." See Walter Benjamin, *Charles Baudelaire: A Lyric Poet in the Era of High Capitalism*, trans. Harry Zohn (New York: Verso, 1997), 48. For a reading of the story that regards the crime not as a "refusal to be alone" (Poe's words), but as refusal of legibility, see R. A. Judy, *Sentient Flesh: Thinking in Disorder, Poēsis*

in Black (Durham: Duke University Press, 2020), 59–65. Judy's reading of "The Man of the Crowd" is part of a brilliant interpretation of Du Bois's short story "Of the Coming of John" (the penultimate chapter of *The Souls of Black Folk*). For an equally insightful reading of "Of the Coming of John" in terms of a conception of the crowd as embodying an apolitical, asocial mode of being that is "self-absent" and "identity-neutral," see Mary Esteve, *The Aesthetics and Politics of the Crowd in American Literature* (Cambridge: Cambridge University Press, 2003), 141–151. Neither Judy nor Esteve considers Du Bois's development of a democratic conception of the crowd in *Darkwater*, and neither scholar attends to the distinction Du Bois draws in that text between the crowd and the mob. My own appreciation of the importance of that distinction derives from a paper written by a graduate student, Jalen Coats, for a political theory seminar I taught several years ago at the University of Chicago.

41. Simmel, "The Stranger," 148.
42. Simmel, 143.
43. Simmel, 143, 145, 148. See, too, "Exkurs über den Fremden," 510.
44. *Darkwater*, 155. In contrast to the present discussion, Aldon Morris's recent consideration of Du Bois with reference to Simmel is a polemic against Robert Park that takes Park to task for crediting Simmel's notion of the stranger, rather than Du Bois's concept of double-consciousness, as an important influence on Park's development of his idea of "the marginal man." Park had taken courses with Simmel in Berlin, but Morris is doubtlessly right to insist that he was familiar with Du Bois's concept. See Aldon Morris, *W. E. B. Du Bois and the Birth of Modern Sociology* (Oakland: University of California Press, 2015), 144–148. The title of Park's doctoral dissertation, *Masse und Publikum*, has been translated into English as *The Crowd and the Public*, but Park's notion of the "Masse/Crowd" has little if anything in common with Du Bois's notion of the crowd as I have analyzed it here. See Robert E. Park, *The Crowd and the Public, and Other Essays*, trans. Charlotte Elsner (1904; Chicago: University of Chicago Press, 1972).
45. Only superficially does Du Bois's distinction between crowds and mobs resemble Elias Canetti's distinction between open and closed crowds. More apt, as a characterization of the lynch mob, is Canetti's description of the "hunting pack" as distributing its kill to spectators, just as antiblack lynch mobs sometimes distributed their kill—the body parts of their lynching victims—to spectators (Thanks to Axel Honneth for alerting me to the

I. *DARKWATER*, DEMOCRACY, AND AESTHETIC EDUCATION ○℞ 209

relevance, here, of Canetti's discussion of the "hunting pack"). In the tradition of American political thought, the thinker who comes closest to and may indeed have inspired Du Bois's normatively inflected understanding of American democracy in terms of the figure of the crowd, and the crowd in terms of the figure of the stranger, is Walt Whitman. As Williams James, Du Bois's teacher, famously wrote, Whitman "felt the human crowd as rapturously as Wordsworth felt the mountains." And as the political theorist Jason Frank has shown, Whitman celebrates the crowd (as in the lines: "Manhattan crowds, with their turbulent musical chorus! / Manhattan faces and eyes forever for me," from the second part of his poem "Give Me the Splendid Silent Sun") as the site of "promiscuous encounters with numberless strangers." See Elias Canetti, *Crowds and Power*, trans. Carol Stewart (New York: Farrar, Straus, and Giroux, 1962), 16–17, 97–98; William James, "On a Certain Blindness in Human Beings," in *Pragmatism, and Other Writings* (New York: Penguin, 2000), 277; and Jason Frank "Promiscuous Citizenship," in *A Political Companion to Walt Whitman*, ed. John Seery (Lexington: University Press of Kentucky), 171.

46. *Darkwater*, 4.
47. For detailed discussion of Louis XIV's persecution of the Huguenots, see Shelby T. McCloy, *Church History* 20, no. 3 (September 1951): 56–79. On the sans culottes' use of violence in their struggle against the aristocracy, see Albert Soboul, *The Sans-Culottes*, trans. Rémy Inglis Hall (1968; Princeton: Princeton University Press, 1980), 158–162. Soboul notes that sans culottes violence was not limited to aristocrats but also extended to moderates who opposed the establishment of an egalitarian Republic.
48. In an earlier essay, "On the Present Outlook of the Darker Races" (1900), Du Bois appears to describe the sans culottes when he refers to "the orgies of the French mob," yet clearly distances himself from the critics of the French mob and their distrust of the working class. Regarding Louis XIV, he writes that his reign represented "the problem of the privileged class—the question as to whether or not the state existed for the sole privilege of the King and the King's friends." See Du Bois, "The Present Outlook of the Darker Races," 120–121.
49. Susanna Siegel, "The Phenomenal Public" (forthcoming). For an argument that Hannah Arendt conceptualizes "the mob" in dispositional terms in *The Origins of Totalitarianism*, see Casper Verstegen, "Rethinking the Mob: An Analysis of Hannah Arendt's Concept of the Mob," *Arendt Studies*

ISSN 2474-2406 (online, February 19, 2022). According to Verstegen, "Arendt's mob . . . can subsist if all its elements are isolated." For a discussion of "city life" as a "being together of strangers" that has affinity to Du Bois's dispositional conception of the crowd, see Iris Young, *Justice and the Politics of Difference* (Princeton: Princeton University Press, 1990), 237–241. For a related account of the centrality of the idea of the stranger to the democratic political theory, see Danielle Allen, *Talking to Strangers* (Chicago: University of Chicago Press, 2004).

50. In Du Bois's story, the letter says: "And thou, Valdosta, in the land of Georgia, art not least among the princes of America, for out of thee shall come a governor who shall rule my people." Cf. Matthew 2:6: "And thou Bethlehem, in the land of Juda, art not the least among the princes of Juda: for out of thee shall come a Governor, that shall rule my people Israel."

51. For all the material quoted in this paragraph, see *Darkwater*, 81–83.

52. *Darkwater*, 83.

53. See Julie Buckner Armstrong, *Mary Turner and the Memory of Lynching* (Athens: University of Georgia Press, 2011), appendix 2. Armstrong's volume offers a detailed account of the events leading up to the murder of Mary Turner, as well as an excellent discussion of newspaper accounts of the murder.

54. Du Bois's insight that a crowd can easily become a mob may well have been rooted in his reading of Mark's Gospel, where the crowd, after having been called by and followed Jesus, abandons him and joins Judas in turning against him. On this point, see Elizabeth Struthers Malbon, *In the Company of Jesus: Characters in Mark's Gospel* (Louisville: Westminster John Know Press, 2000), 70–99.

55. See *Darkwater*, 83. "Massacre of the innocents" refers to the events described in Matthew 2:16–18.

56. For all the material quoted in the paragraph, see *Darkwater*, 161–165. Although I cannot explore the connection here, I note that there are important affinities between Du Bois's and Hannah Arendt's uses of the figure of the child (and the related idea of natality) to conceptualize the possibility of a politics that would counter despair and pessimism—an insight that I owe to the political theorist Brandon Terry. For Arendt's engagement with these matters, see Hannah Arendt, *The Human Condition* (Chicago: University of Chicago Press, 1958), chap. 5.

57. See Friedrich Schiller, *On the Aesthetic Education of Man in a Series of Letters. English and German Facing*, ed. and trans. Elizabeth Wilkinson and L. A. Willoughby (Oxford: Clarendon, 1982). It would be a mistake to suppose that the philosophical defense of aesthetic education as an instrument that can serve the aim of cultivating civic virtue begins with Schiller. Indeed, it may have begun with Plato, who, although he banishes the poets and repudiates aesthetic education in his *Republic*, defends it in the *Laws*. On this last point, see Marcus Folch, *The City and the Stage: Performance, Genre, and Gender in Plato's Laws* (Oxford: Oxford University Press, 2015).
58. Friedrick Beiser, *Schiller as Philosopher: A Re-Examination* (Oxford: Clarendon, 2005), 131.
59. Frederick Beiser, *Enlightenment, Revolution, and Romanticism: The Genesis of Modern German Political Thought, 1790–1800* (Cambridge, MA: Harvard University Press, 1992), 107. The account of the argument of Schiller's *Letters* and its relation to his political thought that I have sketched here follows Beiser's analysis—both his reconstruction of Schiller's political thought in the book cited in the present note and the analysis of the *Letters* set forth in chapter 4 of *Schiller as Philosopher* (see note 58).
60. For earlier, insightful analysis that highlights affinities between Schiller and Du Bois, see Ross Posnock, *Color and Culture: Black Writers and the Making of the Modern Intellectual* (Cambridge, MA: Harvard University Press, 1998), chap. 5. My own analysis, in arguing that there is a sense in which Du Bois inverts Schiller, suggests an affinity between my political positioning of his aesthetics and Gayatri Spivak's effort to "sabotage" and "re-territorialize" Schiller by invoking the figure of the "double-bind," thus "court[ing]" schizophrenia as a figure, and by "plumb[ing] . . . the social destructiveness of capital and capitalism . . . by way of deep language learning." Significantly, Spivak herself suggests a connection between her methodology and lines of thinking she associates with Du Bois and Gramsci. See Gayatri Spivak, *An Aesthetic Education in the Era of Globalization* (Cambridge, MA: Harvard University Press, 2012), 1–34, 517–518. Morton Schoolman has recently defended Schiller against Spivak's critique, but his reading of Schiller—an extended attempt to represent Schiller's *Letters* as prefiguring Walt Whitman's concept of reconciliation—I find unconvincing. That said, and as I note in note 45, I do think that there are important affinities between Whitman's and Du Bois's conceptions of democratic

culture. See Morton Schoolman, *A Democratic Enlightenment: The Reconciliation Image, Aesthetic Education, Possible Politics* (Durham: Duke University Press, 2020), 1–43.

61. For an analysis of the concept of receptivity to which my discussion here is indebted, see Nikolas Kompridis, "Receptivity, Possibility, and Democratic Politics," *Ethics and Global Politics* 4, no. 4 (2011): 255–272. I also owe a debt to Shalini Satkinanandan's insightful account of constitutive responsibility in her *Extraordinary Responsibility: Politics Beyond Moral Calculus* (Cambridge: Cambridge University Press, 2015). For related, political theoretical discussions of the concept of receptivity, see the essays by Nikolas Kompridis, Melissa Orlie, and Aletta Norval in *The Aesthetic Turn in Political Thought*, ed. Nikolas Kompridia (New York: Bloomsbury, 2014).

62. See Kompridis, "Receptivity, Possibility, and Democratic Politics," 256.

63. Martha C. Nussbaum, *Political Emotions: Why Love Matters* (Cambridge, MA: Harvard University Press, 2013), 11, 145.

64. For Keats's "negative capability letter," see www.poetryfoundation.org/articles/69384/selections-from-keatss-letters. For Unger on negative capability, see Roberto Mangabeira Unger, *Politics: The Central Texts* (New York: Verso, 1997), passim.

2. MORAL PSYCHOLOGY OF WHITE SUPREMACY

1. For all the material quoted in this paragraph, see W. E. B. Du Bois, *Dusk of Dawn: An Essay Toward an Autobiography of a Race Concept* (1940: New Brunswick, NJ: Transaction, 1984), 3–7. By "racial oppression" I have in mind what Du Bois describes as a "social condition" of unfreedom characterized by the "color bar": that is, by whites' domination and exploitation of blacks or, more generally, of the world's "darker races" (see Du Bois, *Dusk of Dawn*, 5–6).

2. Du Bois, *Dusk of Dawn*, xxix; See also Du Bois's discussion of his break from a "purely scientific program" and his corresponding decision to join the NAACP's "fight" for social progress in his "My Evolving Program for Negro Freedom," *Clinical Sociology Review* 8, no. 1:44–48; reprinted from Rayford Logan, *What the Negro Really Wants* (Chapel Hill: University of North Carolina Press, 1944).

3. When here and throughout this chapter I write of the "vice" of white supremacy, or of white supremacist "habits" of mind, I mean to refer to Du

Bois's moral psychological diagnosis of the psyches, the souls, of white folk. In his dissertation, *The Problem of Unfreedom* (PhD diss. [philosophy], Columbia University, 2021), Yarran Hominh develops an insightful but different approach to Du Bois's moral psychology of white supremacy from which I have learned a good deal.

4. Du Bois, *Dusk of Dawn*, 6.
5. Many thanks to Jennifer Pitts for pushing me to appreciate the complex chronology of Du Bois's intellectual development during this period.
6. Liam Kofi Bright has argued that Du Bois did not carefully distinguish between knowledge and true belief. See Liam Kofi Bright, "Du Bois' Democratic Defence of the Value Free Ideal," *Synthese* 195, no. 5 (2018): 2231–2232.
7. In several places in *Darkwater*, Du Bois quotes uses of or himself uses the term "appeal" to indicate a moral plea—or, at least, a plea with clearly moral resonance. In "The Hands of Ethiopia," for example, he quotes an Englishman, "familiar with the problems of Africa," as saying, "There does not exist any real international conscience to which you can appeal" (45). And in "The Princess of the Hither Isles," he portrays the Princess's response to the King's tyrannical claim that "the Sun belongs to us" as a cry of moral outrage that she directs at the face of the sun, writing that "[w]ith sudden, wild abandon she [the Princess] stretched her arms toward it [the sun] appealing, beseeching, entreating, and lo!" (58). Finally, in "Of Work and Wealth," Du Bois somewhat sarcastically notes that the South, in response to the northward migration of black laborers, "appealed frantically to the United States Government" by shedding "wild tears at the 'suffering' of their poor misguided black friends" (69). For Du Bois on the distinction between reason and appeal, and between appeal and argument in *Dusk of Dawn*, see *Dusk of Dawn*, 6, 172. In the first instance (6), I take Du Bois to be expressing the thought that a plea for moral self-reflection is called for when racial oppression is a function of "evil" and "ill-will." If I am right about this, then Du Bois's use of the idea of an appeal is in keeping with David Walker's use of the idea to honor his ("colored," not white) audience's capacity for "reflective agency." Regarding this last point, and for an insightful and historically informed analysis of Walker's use of the idea of an appeal in his *Appeal to the Colored Citizens of the World* (1829), see Melvin Rogers, "David Walker and the Political Power of the Appeal," *Political Theory* 43, no. 2 (2015): 208–233. For a related and insightful discussion,

which likewise associates the notion of an appeal with what I have called "practical deliberation," see Nahum Dimitri Chandler, *"Beyond this Narrow Now," Or, Delimitations of W. E. B. Du Bois* (Durham: Duke University Press, 2022), 183–185.

8. W. E. B Du Bois, *Black Reconstruction in American* (1935; New York: Free Press, 1998), 714–715.
9. See Max Weber, "Basic Sociological Concepts," in *Understanding and Social Inquiry*, ed. Fred R. Dallmayr and Thomas A. McCarthy (Notre Dame: Notre Dame University Press, 1977), 42. My remarks on Du Bois and Weber in this paragraph draw on my *Stanford Encyclopedia of Philosophy* essay on Du Bois: Robert Gooding-Williams, "W. E. B. Du Bois," *The Stanford Encyclopedia of Philosophy* (Spring 2020 Edition), ed. Edward N. Zalta, https://plato.stanford.edu/archives/spr2020/entries/dubois/. For a persuasive argument that Du Bois, in *The Souls of Black Folk*, owes a methodological debt to Wilhelm Dilthey's notion of *Verstehen*, see Kwame Anthony Appiah, *Lines of Descent: W. E. B. Du Bois and the Emergence of Identity* (Cambridge, MA: Harvard University Press, 2014), 78–82. When Du Bois studied in Germany, we know, one of the two books he checked out from the university library was the first volume of Dilthey's *Einleitung in die Geisteswissenschaften: Versuch einer Grundlegung für das Studium der Gesellschaft und der Geschichte* (Leipzig, 1883); on this point, see Harriet Fertik, "Hell to Pay: Aristotle and W. E. B. Du Bois's Vision of Democracy in 'Of the Ruling of Men,'" *International Journal of the Classical Tradition* 26 (2019): 74n11. For discussions of both Dilthey's and Weber's very different notions of *Verstehen*, see Michael Martin, *The Uses of Understanding in Social Science: Verstehen* (New York: Routledge, 2000), chap. 1.
10. For a recent defense of a similar attempt to understand domination and oppression with reference to both moral vice and "structural and material" conditions, see Robin Dillon, "Critical Character Theory: Towards a Feminist Perspective on 'Vice' (and 'Virtue')," in *Out of the Shadows: Analytical Feminist Contributions to Traditional Philosophy*, ed. Sharon L. Crasnow and Anita M. Superson (Oxford: Oxford University Press, 2012), 83–114.
11. See Du Bois, *Dusk of Dawn*, 138–139, for the all the material quoted in this paragraph.
12. For the material quoted in this paragraph, see Tamar Schapiro, "Kant's Approach to the Theory of Human Agency," in *The Routledge Handbook of Practical Reason*, ed. Ruth Chang and Kurt Sylvan (New York: Routledge,

2. MORAL PSYCHOLOGY OF WHITE SUPREMACY ∝ 215

2020), 164–165; and Tamar Schapiro, *Feeling Like: A Theory of Inclination and Will* (Oxford: Oxford University Press, 2021), 21.

13. W. E. B. Du Bois, "The African Roots of War," *Atlantic Monthly* 115 (May 1915): 709. I discuss this essay at greater length below. For an extended overview of Du Bois's research and reflections regarding the significance of World War I for African Americans, see Jennifer Keene, "W. E. B. Du Bois and the Wounded World: Seeking Meaning in the First World War for African-Americans," *Peace & Change* 26, no. 2 (April 2001): 135–152. In emphasizing that Du Bois regards white supremacy as serving a stabilizing function, I follow a line of argument that Yarran Hominh develops in his dissertation, *The Problem of Unfreedom* (see note 3 above).
14. W. E. B. Du Bois, "The Souls of White Folk," *The Independent* 69 (August 18, 1910): 339–342.
15. W. E. B. Du Bois, "Of the Culture of White Folk," *The Journal of Race Development* 7, no. 4 (1917): 434–447.
16. Among earlier scholarly treatments of the *Darkwater* version of "The Souls of White Folk," I am especially indebted to Lawrie Balfour's "*Darkwater's* Democratic Vision," *Political Theory* 38, no. 4 (2010): 537–563—really, the first detailed treatment of *Darkwater* by a political theorist—and, more recently, to Ella Myers, "Beyond the Psychological Wage: Du Bois on White Dominion," *Political Theory* 47, no. 1 (2019): 6–31.
17. Du Bois, "Of the Culture of White Folk," 434; *Darkwater*, 26.
18. Du Bois, "Of the Culture of White Folk," 434; *Darkwater*, 26.
19. Du Bois, "Of the Culture of White Folk," 437, 439; *Darkwater*, 28, 30.
20. Du Bois, "The Souls of White Folk," *The Independent*, 339; *Darkwater*, 22.
21. For all the material quoted in this paragraph, see Du Bois, "The Souls of White Folk," *The Independent*, 342.
22. Du Bois, 432.
23. Peter Brian Barry, *Evil and Moral Psychology* (London: Routledge, 2013), 57. For a similar view, see Rosalind Hursthouse, *On Virtue Ethics* (Oxford: Oxford University Press, 1999), 10–12.
24. Barry, *Evil and Moral Psychology*, 57.
25. *Darkwater*, 54.
26. *Darkwater*, 54–55.
27. When Du Bois discusses his "middle period" emphasis on the role ill-will plays in explaining racial oppression, he repeatedly speaks of evil or moral vice (e.g., of "deliberate deviltry"). See, for example, Du Bois, *Dusk of*

Dawn, 5, 194, and 221–222. His suggestion in the last of these passages (221–222) that, during the period between the time he left Atlanta University (1910) and "the time of reconstruction after World War I," he attributed "evil machinations" only to "a small minority of the nation and of all civilized peoples" is belied by the picture of the souls of white folk he depicts in 1910 as well as in 1920. Indeed, Du Bois's writings during this decade largely support the view that through much of his "middle period" he believed his moral psychological "ill-will" diagnosis to be far reaching, and to apply to white souls, white Christianity, and white culture in general. In the *Darkwater* version of "The Souls of White Folk," for example, Du Bois writes, "This theory of human culture and its aims has worked itself through warp and woof of our daily thought with a thoroughness that few realize. Everything great, good, efficient, fair, and honorable is 'white'; everything mean, bad, blundering, cheating, and dishonorable is 'yellow'; a bad taste is 'brown'; and the devil is 'black.' The changes of this theme are continually rung in picture and story, in newspaper heading and moving-picture, in sermon and school book, until, of course, the King can do no wrong,—a White Man is always right and a Black Man has no rights which a white man is bound to respect" (Du Bois, *Darkwater*, 31; see, too, Du Bois, "Of the Culture of White Folk," 439–440). Du Bois's allusion here to Judge Roger Taney's opinion in the Dred Scott decision ("a Black man has no rights which a white man is bound to respect") implies that Taney's view of black people has become culturally pervasive.

28. When Du Bois refers to "unconscious training," I take him to mean that the training occurred, over time, without any individual or group consciously intending to effect it. In *Darkwater*, moreover, there is no evidence of the richer Freudian conception of the unconscious that Du Bois endorses in *Dusk of Dawn* (see, e.g., *Dusk of Dawn*, 296). Du Bois sometimes suggests that his use of the concept of habit to explain racial oppression had to await the third phase of his intellectual development. But, in line with the scholarship of Shannon Sullivan and Terrance Macmullan, I believe that this suggestion is false. More to the point, I agree with Sullivan and Macmullan that the notion is already evident in *Darkwater*. Sullivan, however, holds that conception of habit that Du Bois endorses in *Darkwater* is a "thin" one in which habit is not difficult to change, although she seems also to acknowledge that there is evidence in the text of Du Bois's shift from a thin to a thicker, Freudian conception. My own view is that a thicker conception

(where habit is difficult if not always slow to change) is central to the argument of *Darkwater*. See Shannon Sullivan, *Revealing Whiteness: The Unconscious Habits of Racial Privilege* (Bloomington: Indiana University Press 2006), 20–22, 201n16; and Terrance Macmullan, *Habits of Whiteness: A Pragmatist Reconstruction* (Bloomington: Indiana University Press, 2009), 114–116.

29. Du Bois, *Darkwater*, 21–22. See also "The Souls of White Folk," *The Independent*, 339.
30. Rosalind Hursthouse's excellent discussion of the role of *training* in inculcating and entrenching racist feelings and of the recalcitrance of such inculcated and entrenched feelings to reason echoes Du Bois's views regarding the inculcation of white supremacist habits. On Hursthouse's account, extirpating such habits seems sometimes to involve the sort of change that we associate with "religious conversion." See Hursthouse, *On Virtue Ethics*, 12, 113–119. In chapter 5 below, in a discussion of Du Bois's short story "Jesus Christ in Texas," I suggest that Du Bois holds a similar view—namely, that the extirpation of such habits may require a transformation of faith.
31. In a valuable overview of the social psychological literature on prejudice, stereotyping, and discrimination, John Dovidio and his colleagues echo Du Bois when they begin their discussion of prejudice with the remark that "Prejudice is typically conceptualized as an attitude that, like other attitudes, has a cognitive component (e.g., beliefs about a target group), an affective component (e.g., dislike), and a conative component (e.g., a behavioral predisposition to behave negatively toward the target group)." See John Dovidio et al. "Prejudice, Stereotyping and Discrimination," in *SAGE Handbook of Prejudice, Stereotyping and Discrimination* (London: Sage, 2010), 5.
32. Du Bois, *Darkwater*, 22. See also "The Souls of White Folk," *The Independent*, 339.
33. See Jeremy Waldron, "Dignity, Rights, and Responsibilities," *Arizona State Law Journal* 43 (2011): 1107.
34. Du Bois, *Darkwater*, 23, 29; See also Du Bois, "The Souls of White Folk," *The Independent*, 340, and Du Bois, "Of the Culture of White Folk," 439.
35. Du Bois, *Darkwater*, 35.
36. Du Bois, 23–24. See, also Du Bois, "The Souls of White Folk," *The Independent*, 340.
37. Like Charles Mills, some philosophers sharply distinguish between hatred and ill-will. Hatred, Mills says, is an emotion, whereas ill-will is the desire

that bad things happen to someone. Like Macalester Bell, other philosophers distinguish between different kinds of hatred, e.g., between simple hatred (intense dislike for or strong aversion to an object perceived as unpleasant) and malicious hatred, which is "partially constituted by a desire to *harm* the target." Du Bois uses the term "hatred" to refer to both simple and malicious hatred. Indeed, as I read him, he tends to conceptualize white supremacist hatred, in its typical manifestations, as at once simple and malicious, as constituted by intense dislike *and* ill-will. On these points, see Charles Mills, "'Heart' Attack: A Critique of Jorge Garcia's Volitional Conception of Racism, *Journal of Ethics* 7, no. 1 (2003): 35–37; and Macalester Bell, *The Moral Psychology of Contempt* (Oxford: Oxford University Press, 2013), 55–56.

38. W. E. B. Du Bois, *The Souls of Black Folk*, ed. David Blight and Robert Gooding-Williams (Boston: Bedford, 1997), 38.

39. I do not mean to deny here that Du Bois rejects the possibility of applying figures of doubleness or twoness to white individuals. For a thoughtful defense of the view that Du Bois saw John Brown as an individual to whom such figures apply (Du Bois published his biography of John Brown in 1909, it should be noted, just a year before "The Souls of White Folk"), see Nahum Dimitri Chandler, *X—The Problem of the Negro as a Problem for Thought* (New York: Fordham University Press, 2014), 112–128.

40. See Melville's chapter on the "Metaphysics of Indian-Hating" in Herman Melville, *The Confidence Man: His Masquerade*, ed. Herschel Parker and Mark Niemeyer (New York: W. W. Norton, 2006), 151.

41. Matthew Frye Jacobson, *Whiteness of a Different Color* (Cambridge, MA: Harvard University Press, 1998), 42–43.

42. For the argument that, as early as 1898, Du Bois acknowledged that the white race comprised both English and Teutonic races, see Robert Gooding-Williams, *In the Shadow of Du Bois* (Cambridge, MA: Harvard University Press, 2009), 46–47.

43. Jacobson, *Whiteness of a Different Color*, 57.

44. Orlando Patterson, *Rituals of Blood: Consequences of Slavery in Two American Centuries* (New York: Basic, 1998), 222.

45. Quoted in Patterson, 223.

46. Du Bois, *Darkwater*, 19.

47. On the concept of internal critique, and the distinction between internal and immanent critique, see See Rahel Jaeggi, *Critique of Forms of Life*,

trans. Ciarin Cronin (Cambridge, MA: Harvard University Press, 2018), chaps. 5 and 6.
48. My understanding of "how possibly" explanations derives from Robert Nozick, *Philosophical Explanations* (Cambridge, MA: Harvard University Press, 1981).
49. Du Bois, *Darkwater*, 26.
50. On this point, see Anthea Butler, *White Evangelical Racism: The Politics of Morality in America* (Chapel Hill: University of North Carolina Press, 2021), 26–32.
51. See Philip S. Gorski and Samuel L Perry, *The Flag and the Cross: White Christian Nationalism and the Threat to American Democracy* (Oxford: Oxford University Press, 2022); and Kristin Kobes Du Mez, *Jesus and John Wayne: How White Evangelicals Corrupted a Faith and Fractured a Nation* (New York: Liveright, 2021).
52. See Gorski and Perry, *The Flag and the Cross*.
53. Gorski and Perry, 22, 27.
54. Gorski and Perry, 22, 27.
55. Gorski and Perry, 37, 101, 116.
56. Gorski and Perry, 128.
57. David Hollinger, *Christianity's American Fate: How Religion Became More Conservative and Society More Secular* (Princeton: Princeton University Press, 2022), 161.
58. Hollinger, 5.
59. Hollinger, 164.
60. Du Mez, *Jesus and John Wayne*, xvii.
61. For a recent and powerful example of such a challenge, see Obery M. Hendricks, *Christians Against Christianity: How Right-Wing Evangelicals Are Destroying Our Nation and Our Faith* (Boston: Beacon, 2021).

3. DEMOCRATIC DESPOTISM

1. For all the material quoted in this paragraph, see W. E. B. Du Bois, "The African Roots of War," *Atlantic Monthly* 115 (May 1915): 707–708.
2. For all the material quoted in this paragraph, see J. A. Hobson, *Imperialism: A Study* (New York: James Pott, 1902), 6–7, 11, 26, 42.
3. For the material quoted in this paragraph, see Du Bois, "The African Roots of War," 708. For evidence regarding Pliny's career in Africa, see Ronald

Syme, "Pliny the Procurator," *Harvard Studies in Classical Philology* 73 (1969): 201–236. For recent discussion of Pliny as a political theorist, and a defense of the thesis that his *Natural History* can be read as a defense of empire, see Thomas R. Laehn, *Pliny's Defense of Empire* (New York: Routledge, 2013). As for as I know, there is no evidence that Du Bois read Pliny in a similar light, but one wonders. In the introduction to his magisterial 1991 volume, *The Scramble for Africa: White Man's Conquest of the Dark Continent from 1876–1912* (New York: Avon, 1991), the historian Thomas Packenham wrote that there is still no "*general* explanation" of the scramble for Africa "acceptable to historians" (xxii).

4. For the translation and analysis of Weber's famous remarks I am wholly indebted to Fritz Ringer; see Fritz Ringer, *Max Weber's Methodology: The Unification of the Cultural and Social Sciences* (Cambridge, MA: Harvard University Press, 1997), 153–154, but also his discussion of singular causal analysis in chapter 3. The essay in which these remarks appear ("Die Wirtshaftethik der Welt religion. Vergleichende religionssoziologische Versuche. Einleitung") Weber read to friends in 1913; it was first published in 1915, the same year that "The African Roots of War" appeared (see Ringer, *Max Weber's Methodology*, 179). I am not arguing that Du Bois's essay was written under the influence of Weber—only that Du Bois seems to have relied on an analytical schema similar to one that Weber explicitly articulates.

5. In interpreting Weber's "switches" metaphor in terms of the central role that counterfactual reasoning plays in his approach to "singular causal analysis," I follow Fritz Ringer's reconstruction of Weber's arguments, which he nicely relates to some of the Anglo-American philosophical literature on causal explanation, including the writings of Donald Davidson (it is striking, however, that Ringer gives no attention to David Lewis's counterfactual analysis of causation). In emphasizing that, for Weber, world views must acquire efficacy (through, presumably, institutions and practices) in order to be causally significant, I am indebted to Wolfgang Schluchter's reading of Weber, as well as to conversation with my colleague Axel Honneth. See Ringer, *Max Weber's Methodology*, chap. 3, pp. 153–154. See also Wolfgang Schluchter, *The Rise of Western Rationalism: Max Weber's Developmental History*, trans. Guenter Roth (Berkeley: University of California Press, 1981), 25–27.

6. At this stage of his intellectual career, Du Bois leaves open the possibility of a moral, nonexploitative expansion of European capital into Africa. Thus,

3. DEMOCRATIC DESPOTISM ᛞ 221

in the context of envisioning a future, independent African state, he writes that "Capital could not only be accumulated in Africa, but attracted from the white world, with one great difference from present usage: no return so fabulous would be offered that civilized lands would be tempted to divert to colonial trade and invest materials and labor needed by the masses at home, but rather would receive the same modest profits as legitimate home industry offers" (see Du Bois, *Darkwater*, 54). Thanks to Yarran Hominh for drawing my attention to this passage, and for pointing out to me that Du Bois later grows skeptical of the vision of a humane capitalism that he embraces in the 1920s and 1930s.

7. For the material quoted in this paragraph, see Hobson, *Imperialism*, 86, 224, 91, 96.
8. Du Bois, "The African Roots of War," 709.
9. For all the material quoted in this paragraph, see Du Bois, 709.
10. Du Bois, *Darkwater*, 105.
11. Du Bois, "The African Roots of War," 709.
12. Du Bois, "African Roots of War," 709; *Darkwater*, 31, emphasis mine.
13. Du Bois, "African Roots of War," 711.
14. For my appreciation of the differences between Du Bois and Hobson, and of the importance of Du Bois's "The African Roots of War" in regard to our understanding of those differences, I am deeply indebted to Jennifer Pitts's groundbreaking scholarship, which she has been kind enough to share with me. See Jennifer Pitts, "The Society of Nations, Imperialism, and the Color Line: Three Conceptions of the International," in *Rise of the International*, ed. Richard Devetak and Tim Dunne (Oxford University Press, forthcoming). See, too, Adom Getachew and Jennifer Pitts, "Democracy and Empire: An Introduction to the International Thought of W. E. B. Du Bois," in *W. E. B. Du Bois: International Thought*, ed. Adom Getachew and Jennifer Pitts (Cambridge University Press, 2021). I likewise owe a debt to Anthony Brewer's helpful, critical discussion of Hobson in Anthony Brewer, *Marxist Theories of Imperialism: A Critical Survey*, 2nd ed. (London: Routledge, 1990), chap. 4.
15. Du Bois, "The African Roots of War," 709–710.
16. In *Darkwater*, Du Bois repeats the point that, in the perspective of the white Christian, white supremacist culture shaping the new democratic nations, the raison d'être of nonwhites is to be dominated and exploited by whites, writing that "slowly but surely white culture is evolving the theory

that 'darkies' are born beasts of burden *for* white folk." Du Bois, *Darkwater*, 29–30, emphasis mine; see, too, W. E. B. Du Bois, "Of the Culture of White Folk," *Journal of Race Development* 7, no. 4 (1917): 439.

17. Considered with respect to late-twentieth- and early-twenty-first-century scholarship, Du Bois's explanation of imperialism in terms of white supremacist belief and white culture more generally has obvious affinities to William Appleman Williams's account of the importance of culture to the explanation of imperialism—and, specifically, to the explanation of American imperialism. See William Appleman Williams, *Empire as a Way of Life* (1980; Brooklyn, NY: Ig, 2007). In Williams's view, "The empire as a territory and as activities dominated economically, politically and psychologically by a superior power is the *result* of empire as a way of life. . . . a way of life is the combination of patterns of thought and action that, as it becomes habitual and institutionalized, defines the thrust and character of a culture and society" (Williams, *Empire as a Way of Life*, 12–13). In a similar vein, but more with an eye to the history of European imperialism, Du Bois's views likewise find an echo in Edward Said's contention that "neither imperialism nor colonialism is a simple act of accumulation and acquisition. Both are supported and perhaps even impelled by impressive ideological formations that include notions that certain territories and people require and beseech domination, as well as forms of knowledge affiliated with domination: the vocabulary of classic nineteenth-century imperial culture is plentiful with words and concepts like 'inferior' or 'subject races,' 'subordinate peoples,' 'dependency,' 'expansion,' and 'authority.'" Edward Said, *Culture and Imperialism* (New York: Alfred A. Knopf, 1993), 9. With respect to the particulars of Du Bois's counterfactualist, explanatory strategy, compare David Eltis's explanation of *slavery*, which, reminiscent of Du Bois's explanation of imperialism, stresses that "the same system that countenanced more rights for workers in Europe (and we might add rising living standards in the long run) also ensured slavery in the Americas. The central practical distinction between the freedom to exploit others and the freedom from exploitation by others is how society defines others. . . . European conceptions of the other ensured that only non-Europeans could be enslaved." David Eltis, *The Rise of African Slavery in the Americas* (Cambridge: Cambridge University Press, 2000), 223, 280.

18. W. E. B. Du Bois, *The Negro* (1915; Oxford: Oxford University Press, 2007), 106.

19. Du Bois, "Of the Culture of White Folk," 440–441; Du Bois, *Darkwater*, 31.
20. Du Bois, *The Negro*, 106.
21. In a similar vein, Du Bois takes international socialists in Germany and America to task, arguing that they "had all but read yellow and black men out of the kingdom of industrial justice. Subtly had they been bribed, but effectively: Were they not lordly whites and should they not share in the spoils of rape? High wages in the United States and England might be the skilfully manipulated result of slavery in Africa and of peonage in Asia" (see Du Bois, *Darkwater*, 34; and Du Bois, "Of the Culture of White Folk," 443). Later, Du Bois will argue that the unfreedom to which laborers of color are subject ultimately boomerangs on and undermines the freedom that white laborers enjoy at their expense. In his manifesto for the Second Pan-African Conference, for example, Du Bois writes that, "If we are coming to realize that the great modern problem is to correct maladjustment in the distribution of wealth, it must be remembered that the basic maladjustment is the outrageously unjust distribution of world income between the dominant and suppressed peoples; in the rape of land and raw material, and in monopoly of technique and culture. And in this crime white labor is *particeps criminis* with white capital. Unconsciously and consciously, carelessly and deliberately, the vast power of the white labor vote in modern democracies has been cajoled and flattered into imperialistic schemes to enslave and debauch black, brown and yellow labor, until with fatal retribution, they are themselves today bound and gagged and rendered impotent by the resulting monopoly of the world's raw material in the hands of a dominant, cruel and irresponsible few." See W. E. B. Du Bois, *the Crisis* 23, no. 1 (November 1921). Many thanks to Adom Getachew for drawing my attention to these remarks.
22. Du Bois, *Darkwater*, 34; see too Du Bois, "Of the Culture of White Folk," 443–445.
23. On January 2, 1916, the *New York Times* published a talk that Bernard Dernburg had delivered "before a huge audience at Vienna" on December 10, 1915. The speech, to which Du Bois alludes, was printed under the title "'England Traitor to the Race'—Dernburg." For a valuable discussion of Dernburg's career as a colonial administrator, which argues "that colonialism offered the possibility of cooperation between the representatives of the colonial movement and those they persecuted" (like Dernberg, who was himself of Jewish descent), see Christian S. Davis, *Colonialism, Antisemitism, and Germans of*

Jewish Descent (Ann Arbor: University of Michigan Press, 2012), chap. 4. In his influential *The Rising Tide of Color Against White World-Supremacy*, which appeared just four years after the *Times* published Dernberg's talk, and the same year as *Darkwater*, Lothrop Stoddard likewise lamented the weakening of white solidarity. Interestingly, in chapter 1 of his book, Stoddard quotes Du Bois's "The African Roots of War" as evidence of the "colored races" decreasing "fear of white power and respect," a development that to his mind made the weakening of white racial unity especially worrisome. Several years later, in 1929, Du Bois would debate Stoddard around the question "Shall the Negro Be Encouraged to Seek Cultural Equality?" See Lothrop Stoddard, *The Rising Tide of Color Against White World-Supremacy* (New York: Charles Scribner's Sons, 1920), 13–14. For an insightful discussion of the events leading up to Du Bois's debate with Stoddard, see Ian Frazier, "When W. E. B. Du Bois Made a Laughing Stock of a White Supremacist," *New Yorker*, August 2019.

24. Karl Marx, *Capital: A Critique of Political Economy*, vol. 1, trans. Samuel Moore and Edward Aveling, ed. Frederick Engels (New York: International, 1967), 714.
25. Du Bois, "The African Roots of War," 713.
26. Hilferding and Luxemburg published their books on imperialism in 1910 and 1913 respectively. See Rudolph Hilferding, *Finance Capital: A Study of the Latest Phase of Capitalist Development*, trans. Morris Watnick and Sam Gordon (1910; London: Routledge, 1981), 319; and Rosa Luxemburg, *The Accumulation of Capital*, trans. Agnes Schwarzschild (1913; New Haven: Yale University Press, 1951), 370. V. I. Lenin wrote *Imperialism, The Highest State of Capitalism* in 1916, and the pamphlet was published in 1917. Nikolai Bukarin, another prominent Marxist theorist, wrote *Imperialism and the World Economy* in 1915, but it was not published until 1917 (regarding these dates, I follow Brewer, *Marxist Theories of Imperialism*, 109).
27. Du Bois, "African Roots of War," 713.
28. For the material quoted in this paragraph, see "Record of the Proceedings of the First Universal Races Congress, Held at the University of London, July 26–29, 1911. Pub. for the Executive Council" (London: P. S. King and Son, 1911), 42–44. Much thanks to Jennifer Pitts for alerting me to the existence of this document.
29. See Du Bois, "The African Roots of War," 711. In the 1892 preface to the English edition of *The Condition of the Working Class in England*, Engels

included an article that he initially published in the March 1, 1885, issue of the London *Commonweal* with the title "England in 1845 and England in 1885." The trade unions, the article argues, "form an aristocracy among the working class; they have succeeded in enforcing for themselves a relatively comfortable position, and they accept it as final." In the Marxist tradition, the notion of a labor aristocracy is most famously associated with Vladimir Lenin's writings, and Lenin makes explicit reference to the 1892 preface to Engels's book. On this point, see Frederick Engels, *The Condition of the Working Class in England* (Oxford: Oxford University Press, 2009), 317, 321; and Vladimir Lenin, *Imperialism: The Highest Stage of Capitalism*, in *Essential Works of Lenin*, ed. Henry M. Christman (New York: Dover, 1987), 252–253. For Karl Kautsky's earlier use of the concept of a labor aristocracy, see Karl Kautsky, "Trade Unions and Socialism," *International Socialist Review* 1, no. 10 (April 1901): 597. Chad Williams has also noted the possible influence of Kautsky's writings on Du Bois, and, in particular, the possible influence of Kautsky's 1914 essay "Imperialism and the War" on "The African Roots of War." In this connection, see Chad L. Williams, *The Wounded World: W. E. B. Du Bois and the First World War* (New York: Farrar, Straus and Giroux, 2023), 220–221.

30. For the material quoted in this paragraph, see Charles L. Lumkins, *American Pogrom: The East St. Louis Race Riot and Black Politics* (Athens: Ohio University Press, 2008), 1–2.
31. For the material quoted in this paragraph, see *Darkwater*, 67–68.
32. For the material quoted in this paragraph, see *Darkwater*, 71–72. Note the words elided from the Washington Square Press edition, p. 72.
33. *Darkwater*, 68.
34. *Darkwater*, 76.
35. Du Bois explicitly argues that the manipulation of race hatred to divide workers along racial lines is widespread: "Eastward from St. Louis lie great centers, like Chicago, Indianapolis, Detroit, Cleveland, Pittsburg, Philadelphia, and New York; in every one of these and in lesser centers there is not only the industrial unrest of war and revolutionized work, but there is the call for workers, the coming of black folk, and the deliberate effort to divert the thoughts of men, and particularly of workingmen, into channels of race hatred against blacks. In every one of these centers what happened in East St. Louis has been attempted, with more or less success." See *Darkwater*, 74.

36. *Darkwater*, 75–76.
37. Part of the point of my account of Du Bois's moral and political economy of racial oppression during the era of the Great War is to show that, already then, some twenty years before *Black Reconstruction* appeared, Du Bois was contributing to the theorization of what we now call "racial capitalism"—by which, following Liam Kofi Bright and Olúfẹ́mi O. Táíwò's brief but elegant account, I mean "theorizing" about "a system in which race and capitalism are mutually supporting." See Liam Kofi Bright and Olúfẹ́mi O. Táíwò, "A Response to Michael Walzer," *Dissent*, August 7, 2020.

4. BEAUTY

1. The most famous example is the movement from the second to the third paragraphs of the first chapter of *The Souls of Black Folk*; from Du Bois's description of experiences he had as a black child growing up in Great Barrington to his description of the appearance of "the Negro" on the stage of world history as a sort "seventh son." See W. E. B. Du Bois, *The Souls of Black Folk*, ed. David W. Blight and Robert Gooding-Williams (1903; Boston: Beford, 1997), 37–38. For commentary, see Robert Gooding-Williams, *In the Shadow of Du Bois: Afro-Modern Political Thought in America* (Cambridge, MA: Harvard University Press, 2009), 77–78.
2. W. E. B. Du Bois, *Darkwater: Voices from Within the Veil* (1920; New York: Washington Square Press, 2004), 171. Hereafter cited as *Darkwater*.
3. For Du Bois's "Close Ranks" editorial, see W. E. B. Du Bois, *The Crisis* 16, no. 3 (July 1918): 111. For all other material quoted in this paragraph, see *Darkwater*, 171. For a thorough account of the circumstances and aftermath of Du Bois's decision to publish "Close Ranks," including his nomination for a captaincy in the War Department's Military Intelligence Branch and the "furious reaction" of the African American public to the editorial, see Chad L. Williams, *The Wounded World: W. E. B. Du Bois and the First World War* (New York: Farrar, Straus and Giroux, 2023), 66–82.
4. See *Darkwater*, 171–173, for all the material quoted in the paragraph. In the last line quoted, the emphasis is mine. "A Day's Pleasure" was released in December 1919. It was Chaplin's fourth film for First National Films.
5. *Darkwater*, 173–174.
6. For an account of Du Bois's thinking about the relation between beauty and ugliness that resonates with the one offered here, see Eric King Watts,

Hearing the Hurt: Rhetoric, Aesthetics, and Politics of the New Negro Movement (Tuscaloosa: University of Alabama Press, 2012), 129–130.

7. Watts, 189.
8. For the philosophical development and persuasive defense of the view that "something's salience to you . . . aligns with your evaluation that it matters," see Sophie Archer, "Salience and what Matters," in *Salience: A Philosophical Inquiry*, ed. Sophie Archer (London: Routledge), 117–118.
9. See Edmund Burke, *A Philosophical Enquiry Into the Sublime and the Beautiful*, ed. with an introduction and notes by Paul Guyer (Oxford: Oxford University Press, 2016), 90–92. For helpful discussion and criticism of Burke's "causal" account of beauty, from which I have benefited, see Hannah Ginsborg, "Kant on the Subjectivity of Taste," in *The Normativity of Nature* (Oxford: Oxford University Press, 2015), 19–21.
10. In relativizing inquiry in aesthetics to socioeconomic perspective, including the perspective of the subaltern subject, Du Bois anticipates Sylvia Wynter's adaptation of Pierre Bourdieu's account of Kant's distinction between the taste of reflection and the taste of sense. According to Bourdieu, "Kant's principle of pure taste is nothing other than a refusal, . . . a disgust for objects which impose enjoyment and a disgust for the crude, vulgar taste which revels in this imposed enjoyment." Where the vulgar taste of sense succumbs to objects that insist on being enjoyed, the elevated pure taste of reflection expresses "the distanciating power of representation, the essentially human power of suspending immediate, animal attachment to the sensible and refusing submission to pure affect, to simple aesthesis." Wynter follows Bourdieu in correlating the opposition between the taste of reflection and the taste of sense "with the domination of the middle class over the lower class at the level of the socio-political structure of our present order." That correlation is replicated, she adds, "at the global, socio-cultural level of race." In "Rethinking Aesthetics," Wynter herself revalues the opposition between the taste of reflection and the taste of sense, now valorizing the latter at the expense of the former by representing "feeling," or what Bourdieu calls "simple aisthesis," as the driving force of a politics that contests a cultural imaginary predicated on the taste of reflection. See Pierre Bourdieu, *Distinction: A Social Critique of the Judgment of Taste*, trans. Richard Nice (Cambridge, MA: Harvard University Press, 1984), 488–500; and Sylvia Wynter, "Rethinking 'Aesthetics': Notes Towards a Deciphering Practice," in *Ex-iles: Essays on Carribbean Cinema*, ed. M. Cham (Trenton: Africa

World Press, 1992), 238–279. For an earlier discussion of the perspectival orientation of Du Bois's aesthetics, see Darwin Turner, "W. E. B Du Bois and the Theory of a Black Aesthetic," in *Harlem Renaissance Re-Examined*, ed. Victor A. Kramer and Robert A. Russ (Troy, NY: Whitson, 1997), 45–63.

11. *Darkwater*, 189–190.
12. For these locutions see W. E. B. Du Bois, "The Art and Art Galleries of Modern Europe" (1896?) and "The Spirit of Modern Europe" (1900?) in Herbert Aptheker, ed., *Against Racism* (Amherst: University of Massachusetts Press, 1985), 35, 43, 56.
13. Neither, strictly speaking, does the rain, as when Du Bois writes of seeing how the rain "rises and blushes and burns and pales and dies in beauty" (*Darkwater*, 190).
14. In the W. E. B. DU BOIS PAPERS, at the University of Massachusetts, Amherst, the relevant notes are dated as having been written in 1925, but their clear connections to the argument of "Of Beauty and Death" strongly suggests that they date from a time prior to the publication of *Darkwater* in 1920. See https://credo.library.umass.edu/search?q=beauty+and+death&fq=FacetCollectionID%3A%22mums312%22&search=.
15. In what follows, I use "fulfill" and "complete" and their corresponding cognates interchangeably.
16. *Darkwater*, 189–190.
17. In one of his jottings, written on the back of *Crisis* stationary, and to which I allude in note 14 above, Du Bois explicitly associates birth per se with ugliness and pessimism.
18. Du Bois seems to think that ugliness, like original sin, is a taint on human nature at birth, and that the *telos* of human life is to rid oneself of that taint. For the Calvinist roots of much of Du Bois's thought and artistry, see Arnold Ramperdad, *The Art and Imagination of W. E. B. Du Bois* (Cambridge, MA: Harvard University Press, 1976), 5–6; and David Levering Lewis, *W. E. B. Du Bois: Biography of a Race, 1868–1919* (New York: Henry Holt, 1993), 48–50. Thanks to my former colleague Lydia Goehr for conversation about the religious and, perhaps, Augustinian dimension of Du Bois's aesthetics.
19. See Max Weber, "Science as a Vocation," in *The Vocation Lectures*, ed. and with an introduction by David Owen and Tracy B. Strong, trans. Rodney Livingston (Indianapolis: Hackett, 2004), 13.

20. Weber, 13.
21. In distinguishing between "life-stages" and "satisfactory shape" conceptions of a complete life, I follow Helen Small, *The Long Life* (Oxford: Oxford University Press, 2007), 95–96.
22. See W. B. Gallie, "What Is a Story," in *Philosophy and Historical Understanding* (New York: Schocken, 1968), 27.
23. My reading and adaptation of Gallie's views in this paragraph follow Paul Ricoeur's reading and adaptation of the same: "The "conclusion [of a story] is not logically implied by some previous premises. It gives the story an "end point," which, in turn, furnishes the point of view from which the story can be perceived as forming a whole. To understand a story is to understand how and why the successive episodes led to the conclusion, which, far from being foreseeable, must be finally acceptable, as congruent with the episodes brought together by the story." Paul Ricoeur, *Time and Narrative*, vol. 1, trans. Kathleen McLaughlin and David Pellauer (Chicago: University of Chicago Press, 1984), 66–67.
24. Quoted in Small, *The Long Life*, 53.
25. Aristotle, *Nicomachean Ethics*, trans. Christopher Rowe (Oxford: Oxford University Press, 2011), 105.
26. *Darkwater*, 154–155.
27. For all the material in the paragraph quoted from "Of Alexander Crummell," see W. E. B. Du Bois, *The Souls of Black Folk*, ed. David Blight and Robert Gooding-Williams (Boston: Bedford, 1997), 164–171.
28. Northrop Frye, *Anatomy of Criticism* (Princeton: Princeton University Press, 1957), 215.
29. Readers of *In the Shadow of Du Bois* (Harvard University Press, 2009) will notice that the argument of this paragraph repeats a line of analysis that initially appears in chapter 3 that book.
30. See Wallace Stevens, "Sunday Morning," in *The Collected Poems: The Corrected Edition* (Vintage: New York, 2015), 71–75; and Keith Lehrer, *Art, Self and Knowledge* (New York: Oxford University Press, 2012), 107.
31. Lehrer, *Art, Self and Knowledge*, 107.
32. Suppose I were telling a fictional story, based generally on Glorya's life, except that the ending involved kidnapping and murder. Ending the story in that way would seem far-fetched, and thus inapt.
33. *Darkwater*, 155.

34. Lehrer, *Art, Self, and Knowledge*, 108.
35. Lehrer, 108.
36. Lehrer, 108.
37. Du Bois, *The Souls of Black*, 170.
38. Here, Du Bois echoes Hanslick, who invokes Schelling to insist on the "sublime indifference" of the musically beautiful. See Eduard Hanslick, *On the Musically Beautiful: A New Translation*, trans. Lee Rothfarb and Christopher Landerer (Oxford: Oxford University Press, 2018), 88–89. For a philosophically informed discussion of the history of the concept of absolute music, see Lydia Goehr, *The Imaginary Museum of Musical Works* (Oxford: Oxford University Press, 2007), 211–218.
39. George Santayana, *The Sense of Beauty: Being the Outline of Aesthetic Theory* (New York: Dover, 1955), 164. For the claim that, in conceptualizing beauty in terms of death and perfection, Du Bois intended to follow Santayana, see Watts, *Hearing the Hurt*, 29. For an especially thorough discussion of the tradition of rationalist aesthetics to which Baumgarten belonged, see Paul Guyer, https://plato.stanford.edu/entries/aesthetics-18th-german/.
40. See Burke, *A Philosophical Inquiry Into the Sublime and the Beautiful*, 63.
41. Burke, 63. For commentary that highlights the political valences of Burke's concept of the sublime, and that resonates with my own account of the futural dimension of Du Bois's concept of beauty, see Jason Frank's argument that the Burkean sublime "disrupts the habitual, defies coherence, and marks an abrupt transition in experience." Jason Frank, *The Democratic Sublime: On Aesthetics and Popular Assembly* (Oxford: Oxford University Press, 2021), 104. For a related discussion of Kant's aesthetics, which emphasizes that Kant's account of the dynamical sublime moves his aesthetics beyond his analysis of the judgment of taste to the experience of being called beyond ourselves, not to the future, but to our supersensible vocation, see Hans-Georg Gadamer, "Intuition and Vividness," trans. Dan Tate, in *The Relevance of the Beautiful, and Other Essays*, ed. Robert Bernasconi (Cambridge: Cambridge University Press, 1998), 167–168. My argument in the present chapter is that Du Bois's concept of beauty incorporates elements familiar both from the modern (roughly, after Baumgarten) theorization of the judgment of beauty *and* the modern theorization (with reference to Burke and Kant in particular) of the sublime.

42. Alexander Nehamas, *Only a Promise of Happiness: The Place of Beauty in a World of Art* (Princeton: Princeton University Press, 2017), 105. The context of Nehamas's remarks about beauty, interpretation, and death is his discussion of Thomas Mann's *Death in Venice*.
43. For all the material quoted in this paragraph, see *Darkwater*, xxiii.

5. PROPAGANDA

1. Alain Locke, "Art or Propaganda?," *Harlem: A Forum of Negro Life* (November 1928), http://nationalhumanitiescenter.org/pds/maai3/protest/text10/lockeartorpropaganda.pdf; W. E. B. Du Bois, "Criteria of Negro Art," *The Crisis* (October 1926). As Ronald Judy and Elizabeth Schlabach have noted, Du Bois's understanding of the relationship between art and propaganda varied over the course of his career. Still, I focus on the 1926 "Criteria" essay, as it offers Du Bois's most detailed philosophical account of that relationship, and, more importantly, because it crystallizes a line of thought that he begins to develop in the "Postscript" of *Darkwater*. See R. A. T. Judy, "The New Beauty and W. E. B. Du Bois, or Hepheastus, Limping," *Massachusetts Review* 35, no. 2 (Summer 1994): 276n11; and Elizabeth Schlabach, *Journal of African American Studies* 16, no. 3 (September 2012): 506. For a valuable overview of Du Bois's debate with Alain Locke, see Leonard Harris, "The Great Debate: W. E. B. Du Bois vs. Alain Locke on the Aesthetic," *Philosophica Africana* 7, no.1 (March 2003): 15–39. See also, in this connection, Eric King Watts, *Hearing the Hurt: Rhetoric Aesthetics and Politics of the New Negro Movement* (Tuscaloosa: University of Alabama Press, 2012), chap. 6.
2. Du Bois, "Criteria of Negro Art."
3. See Melvin Rogers, "The People, Rhetoric, and Affect: On the Political Force of Du Bois's *The Souls of Black Folk*," *American Political Science Review* 106, no.1 (February 2012): 194–195.
4. Rogers, 195.
5. Rogers, 195.
6. Paul Taylor, *Black Is Beautiful: A Philosophy of Black Aesthetics* (Malden, MA: Wiley Blackwell, 2016), 92.
7. Taylor, 97.
8. For my thoughts regarding the significance of the placement of "Jesus Christ in Texas" in relation to "The Ruling of Men," I am indebted to

Allison Blackmon Laskey's intriguing analysis of what she takes to be the "ring composition" structure of *Darkwater*. See Allison Blackmon Laskey, "Of Forms and Flow: Movement Through Structure in *Darkwater*'s Composition," *New Centennial Review* 15, no. 2 (Fall 2015): 107–118.

9. *The Crisis* published a supplement to its July 1916 issue titled "The Waco Horror." It offered a detailed account of the burning and lynching of Jesse Washington, including photographs.
10. For the material quoted heretofore in this paragraph, see *Darkwater*, 95–97.
11. *Darkwater*, 97.
12. Edward J. Blum, *W. E. B. Du Bois: American Prophet* (Philadelphia: University of Pennsylvania Press, 2007), 157.
13. For this formulation, I am indebted to J. Cameron Carter, "Between W. E. B. Du Bois and Karl Barth: The Problem of Modern Political Theology," in *Race and Political Theology*, ed. Vincent Lloyd (Stanford: Stanford University Press, 2012), 102.
14. *Darkwater*, 99.
15. *Darkwater*, 102.
16. *Darkwater*, 102–103.
17. *Darkwater*, 103.
18. *Darkwater*, 103–104.
19. My answer to this question is a somewhat revised version of the reading of the conclusion of "Jesus Christ in Texas" that I present in Robert Gooding-Williams, "Beauty and Propaganda: On the Political Aesthetics of W. E. B. Du Bois," *Philosophical Topics* 49, no. 1 (Spring 2021): 14–21. For an extraordinarily careful critique and subsequent exchange regarding that earlier reading I am particularly indebted to Jill Frank.
20. The reference is to Isaiah 53:3.
21. In invoking Isaiah 53, and the figure of the suffering servant, Du Bois may well mean to invite us to interpret the farmer's wife's experience through the lens of the doctrine that Christ's self-sacrifice was an act of atonement, occasioned by human sin, that brought good out of evil and left the world better than it would have been had the sin never occurred. In Christian theology, this is the idea of the *felix culpa*. A further interpretive hypothesis, which I do not explore here, is that Du Bois's thinking along these lines may well have been influenced by, and involved a critical engagement with, Josiah Royce's discussion of the *felix culpa* doctrine in *The Problem of Christianity* (originally published in 1913), and by Royce's analysis there of acts of

treason in relation to acts of atonement. See, on this point, Josiah Royce, *The Problem of Christianity* (Chicago: University of Chicago Press, 1968), chaps. 6 and 8. In this connection, it is also worth noting that Royce, like Du Bois, invites us to think of the atoning deed(s) of the suffering servant in aesthetic term, e.g., as "divinely beautiful" (see Royce, *The Problem of Christianity*, 184–185). Finally, for an overview of the treatment of the idea of the suffering servant and the closely connected idea of the "Beloved Community" in twentieth-century African American thought, with special emphasis on Howard Thurman, and Martin Luther King Jr. see Allen K. Shin and Larry R. Benfield, eds., *Realizing Beloved Community: Report from the House of Bishops Theology Committee* (New York: Church Publishing, 2022), 19–61.

22. For the relevance of the figure of the "cross and the lynching tree," I am indebted to James H. Cone, *The Cross and the Lynching Tree* (Maryknoll, NY: Orbis, 2017), esp. 152–166.

23. In my discussion of Dürer's painting I follow Joseph Leo Koerner's interpretation in "The Epiphany of the Black Magus Circa 1500," in *The Image of the Black in Western Art III, Part 1*, ed. David Bindman and Henry Louis Gates Jr. (Cambridge, MA: Harvard University Press, 2010), 81–92.

24. In exploring the power of shame, self-discontent and the like to reform the actions of the perpetrators of injustice, Du Bois's thinking resonates with Abraham Lincoln's and Edmund Burke's similar reflections. On this point, see David Bromwich, "Moral Imagination," *Raritan* 27, no. 4 (Spring 2008): 15–16.

25. See Michael Fried, "Art and Objecthood," in *Art and Objecthood* (Chicago: University of Chicago Press, 1998), 148–172; and Fried, *Absorption and Theatricality: Painting and Beholder in the Age of Diderot* (Chicago: University of Chicago Press, 1980).

26. By yoking the farmer's wife's morally informed experience of terror to her apprehension of a self-contained perfection that, since Baumgarten at least (see chapter 4), conventional aesthetics associates with beauty, Du Bois here relates his conception of beauty to modern conceptions of the sublime, as he does, we have seen, in his account of the nature of beauty (again, see chapter 4, including note 41). In this respect, his portrait of the farmer's wife's experience resonates with William Blake's "fearful symmetry" and William Butler Yeats's "terrible beauty" (my thinking, on this point, follows Helen Vendler's discussion of Yeats's "Easter 1916" in Helen Vendler, *Our Secret*

Discipline: Yeats and Lyric Form [Cambridge, MA: Harvard University Press, 2007], 20, 382–383n15). For a thoughtful, alternative reading of Du Bois's description of the farmer's wife's experience, through the lens of what the author takes to be Du Bois's appropriation and revision of Santayana's account of the sublime, see Eric King Watts, *Hearing the Hurt: Rhetoric, Aesthetics, and Politics of the New Negro Movement* (Tuscaloosa: University of Alabama Press, 2012), 43–45.

27. The difficulty the farmer's wife faces here is not the hardness of a philosophical problem, but what Cora Diamond has called "a difficulty of reality . . . the apparent resistance by reality to one's ordinary mode of life, including one's ordinary modes of thinking: to appreciate this difficulty is to feel oneself being shouldered out of how one thinks, how one is apparently supposed to think, or to have a sense of the inability of thought to encompass what it is attempting to reach." See Stanley Cavell, Cora Diamond, John McDowell, Ian Hacking, and Cary Wolf *Philosophy and Animal Life* (New York: Columbia University Press, 2008), 58.
28. For the distinction between manifestational and propositional revelation, see Mats Wahlberg, *Revelation as Testimony: A Philosophical-Theological Study* (Grand Rapids, MI: William B. Eerdman's, 2014).
29. W. E. B. Du Bois, *John Brown*, ed. David Roediger (New York: Modern Library, 2001), 219.
30. For all the material quoted in this paragraph, see Du Bois, 202–203.
31. Du Bois, 204.
32. Du Bois, 213.
33. See the epigraph to chapter 7.
34. The idea here is that the revelation could be regarded as giving an audience a reason to question its ideal of ethical conduct, although, by hypothesis (see chapter 2), that questioning comes about neither through empirical scientific inquiry nor internal critique (see chapter 2). There is a difference, then, between having a reason and arriving at a conclusion through reasoning (scientific inquiry or internal critique). For this formulation, I am indebted to my colleague Akeel Bilgrami.
35. See Iris Murdoch, *The Sovereignty of Good* (London: Routledge, 1970), 84–86.
36. For my thoughts about Gadamer here, and for an excellent Gadamer-inspired, contemporary account of the power of "aesthetic world disclosure" to "pull us up short" so that we "come to see or understand what we

previously could not," see Georgia Warnke, "Virginia's Slavery Deliberations," *Philosophy of the Social Sciences* 48, no. 2 (2018): 218–236.
37. Darryl Pinckney, "Moon Over Miami," *New York Review of Books*, April 20, 2017.
38. For further development of these ideas, see Robert Gooding-Williams, "The Ferguson Report and the Practice of Policing," *Critical Inquiry* 47, no. 53, www.journals.uchicago.edu/doi/10.1086/711457.
39. Karuna Mantena, "Showdown for Nonviolence: The Theory and Practice of Nonviolent Politics," in *To Shape a New World: Essays on the Political Philosophy of Martin Luther King, Jr.*, ed. Tommie Shelby and Brandon M. Terry (Cambridge, MA: Harvard University Press, 2018), 98.
40. For all quotations from Du Bois's review of McKay and Larsen in this paragraph, see W. E. B. Du Bois, "The Browsing Reader," *The Crisis* 35 (June 1928): 202.
41. My conceptualization of moralism draws inspiration from Wendy Brown, "Moralism as Antipolitics," in *Materializing Democracy: Toward a Revitalized Cultural Politics*, ed. Russ Castronovo and Dana D. Nelson (Durham: Duke University Press, 2002), 368–392.
42. See Du Bois, "The Browsing Reader," 202.

6. PESSIMISM

1. W. E. B. Du Bois, *Darkwater: Voices from Within the Veil* (1920; New York: Washington Square Press, 2004), 173–174. Hereafter cited as *Darkwater*.
2. *Darkwater*, 177–178.
3. Du Bois, obviously, is not the first thinker in the Afro-modern tradition of political thought to engage with the theme of despair. For a discussion of David Walker's treatment of this theme, see Philip Yaure, "Hope and Despair in the Political Thought of David Walker," *The Pluralist* (forthcoming).
4. For all the material quoted in this paragraph, see *Darkwater*, 172–173.
5. In thinking through Du Bois's analysis, I have very much benefited from Margaret Urban Walker's discussion of hope and despair in Margaret Urban Walker, *Moral Repair: Reconstructing Moral Relations After Wrong Doing* (Cambridge: Cambridge University Press, 2006), chapter 2.
6. *Darkwater*, 174, emphasis added.
7. Thus, by "abduction," I do not mean what contemporary philosophers often mean—namely, inference to the best explanation. For the difference between

contemporary usage and Pierce's usage, see https://plato.stanford.edu/entries/abduction/peirce.html and https://plato.stanford.edu/entries/abduction/.

8. *Darkwater*, 176.
9. For the material quoted in this paragraph, see *Darkwater*, 175.
10. For the material quoted in this paragraph, see *Darkwater*, 176–177.
11. *Darkwater*, 176.
12. *Darkwater*, 177–178.
13. There is an irony here: Jim Crow causes withdrawal and an indisposition to travel, but one needs to travel precisely to cope with the dispiriting effects of Jim Crow.
14. Charles Sanders Pierce, "Abduction and Induction," in *Philosophical Writings of Pierce*, ed. Justus Buchler (New York: Dover, 2018), 151–152. For helpful discussion, see K. T. Fann, "Pierce's Theory of Abduction" (The Hague: Martinus Nijhoff, 1970), passim.
15. *Darkwater*, 179.
16. Du Bois's notion of a miracle is, broadly speaking, Humean. According to David Hume, "A miracle is a violation of the laws of nature." See David Hume, "Of Miracles," in *Enquiries Concerning Human Understanding and Concerning the Principles of Morals* (Oxford: Clarendon, 1975), 114.
17. *Darkwater*, 178–179.
18. In invoking the concept of mood, here, I draw inspiration from Heidegger's analysis of *Befindlichkeit* in *Sein und Zeit*, and from Stanley Cavell's remarks on "finding oneself" in *The Senses of Walden*. See Martin Heidegger, *Sein und Zeit* (Tubingen: Max Niemeyer, 2006), 134ff.; and Stanley Cavell, *The Senses of Walden: An Expanded Edition* (Chicago: University of Chicago Press, 1981), passim.
19. Note that Kant too opposes cowardice to the sense of elevation, of uplift, that is characteristic of the experience of the dynamical sublime. See Immanuel Kant, *The Critique of Judgment*, trans. Werner S. Pluhar (Indianapolis: Hackett, 1987), 121–122. For my earlier discussion of Du Bois and the dynamical sublime, and of what, following Harold Bloom, I called "the counter-sublime," as they relate to Alexander Crummell's experience of despair, see Robert Gooding-Williams, *In the Shadow of DuBois: Afro-Modern Thought in America* (Cambridge, MA: Harvard University Press, 2009), 101–115. Many thanks to Patchen Markell for provoking me to think more carefully about the issues I touch on here, and their connection to my earlier writing about Du Bois.

20. Keith Lehrer, *Art, Self, and Knowledge* (Oxford: Oxford University Press, 2012),107.
21. Alasdair MacIntyre, *After Virtue: A Moral Theory* (Notre Dame: University of Notre Dame Press, 1981), 197.
22. *Darkwater*, 174.
23. *Darkwater*, 9.
24. For all the material quoted in the paragraph, see *Darkwater*, 9–11.
25. *Darkwater*, 12.
26. *Darkwater*, 11.
27. The affinities with Hannah Arendt, here, are striking, for, according to Arendt, "sovereignty, the ideal of uncompromising self-sufficiency and mastership, is contradictory to the very condition of plurality. No man can be sovereign because not one man, but men, inhabit the earth." See Hannah Arendt, *The Human Condition* (Chicago: University of Chicago Press, 1958), 234.
28. For the material quoted in the paragraph, see *Darkwater*, 11–13.
29. *Darkwater*, 15.
30. Brian Barry, "Is It Better to be Powerful or Lucky," in *Democracy and Power, Essays in Political Theory I* (Oxford: Clarendon, 1991), 285.
31. See W. E. B. Du Bois, "Sociology Hesitant," in *The Problem of the Color Line at the Turn of the Century*, ed. Nahum Chandler (New York: Fordham University Press, 2015), 271–284. For discussion of this essay vis-à-vis Du Bois's overall intellectual development, see Robert Gooding-Williams, https://plato.stanford.edu/entries/dubois/.
32. I borrow the phrase "collectivist holism" from Vincent Descombes, *The Institution of Meaning: A Defense of Anthropological Holism*, trans. Stephen Adam Schwartz (Cambridge: Harvard University Press), xxii.
33. For the material from "Sociology Hesitant" quoted in this paragraph, see Du Bois, "Sociology Hesitant," 274–278. The language and analysis of "Sociology Hesitant" owe a debt to William James's "The Dilemma of Determinism" and, in particular, to James's conceptualization of the will's independence—its ability to choose courses of action not fixed "by parts of the universe already laid down"—in terms of the concept of chance. See William James, *The Will to Believe* (New York: Dover, 1956), 150. For a general discussion, see Jose Itzigsohn and Karida Brown, *The Sociology of W. E. B. Du Bois* (New York: New York University Press, 2020), 17–19. For a more detailed analysis, see Robert Gooding-Williams, https://plato.stanford.edu/entries/dubois/.

34. Du Bois, "Sociology Hesitant," 276. Regarding Kant, see, e.g., his discussion of causality in his analysis of the third antinomy of the first *Critique*. Immanuel Kant, *Critique of Pure Reason*, trans. Norman Kemp Smith (New York: St. Martins, 1965), 409–415: A444–A452 and B473–B481.
35. In the language of contemporary, Anglo-American philosophy, I read Du Bois as a "hard libertarian" committed to incompatibilism and indeterminism, as well as to the view that free agency involves a distinctive form of causation wherethrough agents author their actions—what Du Bois calls "indeterminate force." (See Du Bois, "Sociology Hesitant," 278.) In classifying Du Bois along these lines, I rely on the conceptual framework Gary Watson lays out in, *Agency and Answerability* (Oxford: Oxford University Press, 2009), chaps. 6 and 7.
36. Du Bois, "Sociology Hesitant," 278.
37. Du Bois, 275.
38. Du Bois, 275.
39. Du Bois, 278.
40. See Arendt, *The Human Condition*, 246. It is also worth noting that, like Du Bois, Arendt also suggests that miraculous action—for Arendt, action *as such*—escapes natural scientific explanation: "action, seen from the viewpoint of the automatic processes which seem to determine the course of the world, looks like a miracle. In the language of natural science, it is the 'infinite improbability which occurs regularly.' Action is, in fact, the one miracle-working faculty of man" (246). For insightful discussion of Arendt's understanding of action's miraculous power to interrupt the prevailing order of things and begin something new, see Susannah Young-ah Gottlieb, *Regions of Sorrow: Anxiety and Messianism in Hannah Arendt and W. H. Auden* (Stanford: Stanford University Press, 2003), 147–160; and Bonnie Honig, "The Miracle of Metaphor: Rethinking the State of Exception with Rosenzweig and Schmitt," *Diacritics* 37, nos. 2/3 (Summer–Fall, 2007), *Taking Exception to the Exception*, pp. 78–102.
41. My analysis presumes that Du Bois reifies causal laws and conceptualizes them as constraining the facts, not as emergent regularities. For a clear analysis of this distinction by a proponent of the "emergent regularities" view, see Jenann Ismael, *How Physics Makes Us Free* (New York: Oxford University Press, 2016), 109–111.
42. I am particularly indebted to Francy Russell for alerting me to the extent to which Du Bois refers to "fact" in "Of Beauty and Death."

43. *Darkwater*, 7–8.
44. *Darkwater*, 15.
45. *Darkwater*, 4. Alexander Du Bois is buried near the entrance of Grove Street cemetery, at Yale.
46. Gooding-Williams, *In the Shadow of Du Bois*, 68–70.
47. www.poetryfoundation.org/poems/45536/ode-intimations-of-immortality-from-recollections-of-early-childhood.
48. Esther Schor, *Bearing the Dead: The British Culture of Mourning from the Enlightenment to Victoria* (Princeton: Princeton University Press, 1996), 132.
49. Du Bois, *The Souls of Black Folk*, 38.
50. *Darkwater*, xxiii.
51. My account of imaginative perception owes a debt to Charles Larmore's analysis and defense of the idea of a "creative-responsive imagination," which focuses in particular on Wordsworth. See Charles Larmore, *The Romantic Legacy* (New York: Columbia University Press, 1996), 7–16.
52. As Paul Guyer reads him, Kant similarly claimed that the judgment of beauty demands agreement. According to Guyer, "what the judgment of taste [for Kant] requires as a condition of calling an object beautiful is that it occasion a pleasure which could be felt—and under ideal conditions would be felt—by any human observer of that object." See Paul Guyer, *Kant and the Claims of Taste*, 2nd ed. (Cambridge: Cambridge University Press, 1997), 144. Criticism of this interpretation has centered on the point that Guyer fails to capture the normativity of Kant's claim that judgments of beauty demand agreement. For a succinct summary of versions of this criticism, see Hanna Ginsborg's discussion in https://plato.stanford.edu/entries/kant-aesthetics, 2.3.4. Here, I leave open the question as to whether Du Bois's conception of the demand for agreement admits of a "normative" interpretation.
53. Hannah Ginsborg has persuasively argued that Kant held a similar view. See Hannah Ginsborg, *The Normativity of Nature: Essays on Kant's Critique of Judgement* (Oxford: Oxford University Press, 2015), 27–29.
54. See M. H. Abrams, *Natural Supernaturalism: Tradition and Revolution in Romantic Literature* (New York: W. W. Norton, 1971). For the material quoted in this paragraph, see Akeel Bilgrami, "The Political Possibilities of the Long Romantic Period," in *Secularism, Identity, and Enchantment* (Cambridge, MA: Harvard University Press, 2014), 181–201. See also, for clarification, Akeel Bilgrami, *Self-Knowledge and Resentment* (Cambridge:

Cambridge University Press, 2006), 253–260. For related lines of argument, pivoting around the notion of a "wider" objectivity, see Alice Crary, *Beyond Moral Judgment* (Cambridge, MA: Harvard University Press, 2009); and Alice Crary, *Inside Ethics: On the Demands of Moral Thought* (Cambridge, MA: Harvard University Press, 2016).

55. Thanks to Francey Russell for pointing out that Du Bois emphasizes the moral, not the instrumental demands that nature makes on us.
56. Gooding-Williams, *In the Shadow of Du Bois*, 123–124. At the end of the short story, Du Bois's "black John" affords us a black model of a Schopenhauerian holy man.
57. In *The Birth of Tragedy*, Nietzsche famously argues that Apollonian art, the art of the Homeric Epic, "by seducing one to a continuation of life," can counter the spirit of pessimism expressed in the "wisdom of Silenus." See Friedrich Nietzsche, *The Birth of Tragedy and The Case of Wagner*, trans. Walter Kaufman (New York: Vintage, 1967), 41–44. For a detailed account of the idea of beautiful willing that Nietzsche develops in *Thus Spoke Zarathustra*, see Robert Gooding-Williams, *Zarathustra's Dionysian Modernism* (Stanford: Stanford University Press, 2001), esp. chap. 4.
58. Kwame Anthony Appiah, *Lines of Descent; W. E. B. Du Bois and the Emergence of Identity* (Cambridge, MA: Harvard University Press, 2014), 4.
59. Appiah, 5.
60. For detailed discussion of the complexity of Mann's engagement with Schopenhauer and Nietzsche, see Philip Kitcher, *Deaths in Venice: The Cases of Gustav von Aschenbach* (New York: Columbia University Press, 2013), esp. chap. 1.
61. For my quotations from Freud's essay, see Sigmund Freud, "Appendix: On Transience," trans. James Strachey, in Matthew von Unwerth, *Freud's Requiem: Mourning, Memory, and the Invisible History of a Summer Walk* (New York: Riverhead, 2005), 215–219.
62. Max Weber, "Science as a Vocation," trans. Rodney Livingston, in *The Vocation Lectures* (Indianapolis: Hackett, 2004), 12–13. Weber first delivered "Science as a Vocation" in November 1917.
63. For a general discussion of pessimism in Du Bois's cultural milieu, at least in Germany, see Fritz Ringer, *The Decline of the German Mandarins: The German Academic Community, 1890–1933* (Middletown, CT: Wesleyan University Press, 1990).
64. Du Bois titled a never-completed and unpublished manuscript relating to blacks and World War I "The Black Man and the Wounded World." For

discussion, see Chad Williams, "World War I in the Historical Imagination of W. E. B. Du Bois," *Modern American History* (2018): 1, 3–22.
65. For the material from *Darkwater* quoted in this paragraph, see *Darkwater*, 179–184. For a Kantian reading of the aesthetics animating Du Bois's discussion of his visit to the Grand Canyon from which I have benefited, but which differs from my own interpretation in several ways, see John Claborn, "W. E. B. Du Bois at the Grand Canyon: Nature, History, and Race in *Darkwater*," in *The Oxford Handbook of Ecocriticism*, ed. Greg Garrard (New York: Oxford University Press, 2014), 118–131. Du Bois's visit to the Grand Canyon obviously invites detailed psychoanalytic interpretation, which is beyond the ken of this chapter.
66. *Darkwater*, 189–190.
67. In chapter 7, I take up Du Bois's reflections on the possible "end of the world." There, I discuss his short story "The Comet," which belongs to the final chapter of *Darkwater*, and which immediately follows "Of Beauty and Death" and *"The Prayers of God."* I will also take up the idea that Du Bois is best understood as embracing a version of what William James called "meliorism," which stakes out a middle ground between optimism and pessimism; see William James, "Pragmatism, Lecture VIII," in *Pragmatism, and Other Writings* (New York: Penguin, 2000), 119–132.

7. DU BOIS'S PLURALISM

1. See William James, "The One and the Many, cont.," in *William James: Writings 1902–1910* (New York: Library of America, 1987), 1054.
2. W. E. B. Du Bois, *Darkwater: Voices from Within the Veil* (1920; New York: Washington Square Press, 2004), 112. Hereafter cited as *Darkwater*.
3. *Darkwater*, 78, 109.
4. See W. E. B. Du Bois, "Two Novels" *Crisis* (June 1928).
5. Henry Louis Gates Jr., "Preface to Blackness: Text and Pretext," in *Within the Circle: An Anthology of African American Literary Criticism from the Harlem Renaissance to the Present*, ed. Angelyn Mitchell (Durham: Duke University Press, 1994), 245.
6. Claude McKay, "A Negro to His Critics," *New York Herald Tribune*, March 6, 1932.
7. Stanley Cavell, *Philosophy the Day After Tomorrow* (Cambridge, MA: Harvard University Press, 2005), 66.

8. See Du Bois, "Two Novels." For a discussion of the biblical roots of the conceptualization of idolatry as a form of betrayal, see Moshe Halbertal and Avishai Margalit, *Idolatry*, trans. Naomi Goldblum (Cambridge, MA: Harvard University Press, 1992), chap. 1.
9. Lawrie Balfour, *Democracy's Reconstruction: Thinking Politically with W. E. B. Du Bois* (Oxford: Oxford University Press, 2011), 99–100.
10. Shatema Threadcraft, *Intimate Justice: The Black Female Body and the Body Politic* (Oxford: Oxford University Press, 2016), 92–93.
11. For all the material quoted in this paragraph, see *Darkwater*, 127–128.
12. For all the material quoted in this paragraph, see *Darkwater*, 129, 131, 134–138.
13. For all the material quoted in this paragraph, see *Darkwater*, 128–129, 137–140, and 189.
14. For the material quoted in the paragraph, see Mary Wollstonecraft, *A Vindication of the Rights of Women* (Mineola, NY: Dover, 1996), 6–7; *Darkwater*, 140–141.
15. For all the material quoted in this paragraph, see *Darkwater*, 141–142.
16. For all the material quoted in this paragraph, see *Darkwater*, 141.
17. *Darkwater*, 143–144.
18. In effect Du Bois presents Cooper as paraphrasing and, perhaps, as elaborating a claim he has already made: "To no modern race does its women mean so much as to the Negro nor come so near to the fulfilment of its meaning. As one of our women writes: 'Only the black woman can say "when and where I enter, in the quiet, undisputed dignity of my womanhood, without violence and without suing or special patronage, then and there the whole Negro race enters with me."'" See *Darkwater*, 134.
19. Another source may have been his portrait of Alexander Crummell in *Souls*, which I have invoked as exemplifying his conception of a beautiful life (see chapter 4).
20. William Shakespeare, *Twelfth Night*, 3.4.
21. Here, my argument builds on the analyses of Beverly Guy-Sheftal and Farah Griffin, who have similarly highlighted this aspect of the argument of "Damnation." See Beverly Guy-Sheftal, *Daughters of Sorrow: Attitudes Toward Black women, 1880–1920* (New York: Carlson, 1990), 161; and Farah Jasmine Griffin, "Black Feminists and Du Bois: Respectability, Protection, and Beyond," *Annals of the American Academy of Political and Social Science*," 568 (March 2000): 29, 33.

22. For references to Hartman's book, see Saidiya Hartman, *Wayward Lives, Beautiful Experiments: Intimate Histories of Social Upheaval* (New York: W. W. Norton, 2019), 349. It is worth noting here that Hartman draws the epigraph of her book from Larsen's *Quicksand*; significantly, however the passage she quotes—"She was, she knew, in a queer and indefinite way, a disturbing factor"—captures Helga Crane's open and undecided sense of self, thus suggesting a very different reading of the novel than Du Bois offers.
23. For a philosophically insightful discussion of Afropessimism that focuses on Jared Sexton's Afropessimism, which I ignore here, see Paul Taylor, "Survival Is Not a Theory: Afropessimism Transposed," in *Black Art and Aesthetics: Relationalities, Interiorities and Reckonings*, ed. Michael Kelly and Monique Roelofs (London: Bloomsbury Academic, 2024), 263–274.
24. For an excellent review and overview of Wilderson's book as a whole, see Jessie McCartney, "On Afropessimim," *Los Angeles Review of Books*, July 2020.
25. Frank B. Wilderson III, *Afropessimism* (New York: W. W. Norton, 2020), 16.
26. For this point I am indebted to M. H. Abrams, *Natural Supernaturalism: Tradition and Revolution in Romantic Literature* (New York: W. W. Norton, 1971), chaps. 3 and 4.
27. Wilderson, *Afropessimism*, 16.
28. I borrow this example from the Stanford Encyclopedia of Philosophy essay on category mistakes: https://plato.stanford.edu/entries/category-mistakes/. Wilderson does not use the concept of a category mistake, but I have introduced the concept to clarify his argument.
29. Wilderson, *Afropessimism*, 102.
30. Wilderson, 87.
31. Wilderson, 225–226.
32. See Wilderson, 16, for Wilderson on the distinction between absence and loss, which is critical to his argument.
33. Wilderson, 225–226. As I read Wilderson, the category of the social subsumes and comprehends the categories of the moral and the political.
34. See Wilderson, 217, for Wilderson's claim that "there is no Black time that precedes the time of the slave."
35. Wilderson, 174.
36. In its essential respects, Wilderson's argument can be read as applying to the "black experience" a more general critique of the idea of historical

progress already evident in the writings of the pessimist European philosopher Arthur Schopenhauer. On this point, see, especially, Schopenhauer's essay "On History," in *The World as Will and Representation*, vol. 2, trans. E. F. J. Payne (New York: Dover, 1958). For discussion of Schopenhauer's essay and critique, see Robert Gooding-Williams, *Zarathustra's Dionysian Modernism* (Stanford: Stanford University Press, 2001), 113–114.

37. Wilderson, *Afropessimism*, 174.
38. Wilderson, 223.
39. Wilderson, 226.
40. Wilderson, 218.
41. Wilderson, 171. For Wilderson's references elsewhere to "the end of the world," see Wilderson, 103, 174, 323, and 331.
42. Unless otherwise noted, all the material quoted from "The Comet" in this paragraph and pages that follow comes from *Darkwater*, 195–209.
43. Here, I quote Arnold Rampersad, *The Art and Imagination of W. E. B. Du Bois* (New York: Schocken, 1976), 178.
44. Abrams points out that, historically, some commentators on Revelations 21 have read its reference to a new Earth to "signify not a transcendent location in the eternity of heaven, but merely a purged and renovated form of the earth we now inhabit." Abrams, *Natural Supernaturalism*, 42.
45. *Darkwater*, 78.
46. For an excellent discussion and critique of the concept of total revolution as it operates in colonial and postcolonial discourse, see David Scott, *Conscripts of Modernity: The Tragedy of Colonial Enlightenment* (Durham: Duke University Press, 2004).
47. In *Darkwater*'s "Credo" Du Bois writes, "I believe in Patience . . . patience with the tardy triumph of Joy and the mad chastening of sorrow; patience with God!" (*Darkwater*, 2). For a very different and darker reading of the story's ending, with which I here take issue, see Ronald Sundstrom, "The Prophetic and Pragmatic Philosophy of 'Race' in W. E. B. Du Bois's 'The Comet,'" *APA Newsletter on Philosophy and the Black Experience*, Fall 1999.
48. Beauty is not the only such means in Du Bois's view, but the one I focus on here and elsewhere in this book.
49. James, "The One and the Many, cont.," 1053.
50. James, 1051.

51. Roberto Mangabeira Unger, *Pragmatism Unbound: The Self Awakened* (Cambridge, MA: Harvard University Press, 2007), 113.
52. If "meta-theoretically" Wilderson is at odds with Marxism, then "meta-meta theoretically" he is at one with it.
53. See Unger, *Pragmatism Unbound*, 114. For the pluralist and meliorist, James suggests, the world can "only be saved piecemeal." See William James, *Pragmatism, and Other Writings* (New York: Penguin, 2000), 128.
54. "Manic Depression/Mantic Disposition: A Poetics of Hesitant Sociology/Black Topological Existence" is the unpublished essay of Moten's from which I have been quoting—with his permission.
55. Hartman, *Wayward Lives*, 228.

INDEX

Page locators in italics indicate figures

abductive reasoning, 139, 142–143, 235n7
Abrams, M. H., 162, 244n44
accountability, 22, 35–36, 49, 105
action: of black women, 178–179; and causal law, 145, 147, 154–156, 164; dominated by material and ideal interests, 58; as miraculous, 147, 238n40. *See also* agency
"Adoration of the Kings" (Dürer), *111*, 113, 119–122
aesthetic education, 21–24, 52, 211n57; capacity for receptivity increased by, 7, 24, 110, 169; double-edged, 130–131; integrative power of challenged, 21–22; prescriptive tendency in, 131, 170. *See also* artistic beauty; natural beauty; propaganda
Africa: Congo Free State, 57; and new imperialism, 56–71; as root of World War I, 56, 58, 61; scramble for, 5, 57, 64, 68–69, 220nn3; Stanley's explorations, 57–58
"African Roots of War, The" (Du Bois), 56–67, 71, 72, 220n4, 221n14, 224n23
Afropessimism, 26–27, 168, 170, 184–188, 195–196; apocalyptic, 26, 184, 188, 195; emancipatory narratives of redemption critiqued by, 185–187; essential antagonism between Blacks and the world, 186–187, 195; faux-equilibria, 186, 194. *See also* pessimism
Afropessimism (Wilderson), 184–188
agency: first-and third-person perspectives, 35–37, 205n34; guiding conception for studying, 35–37; "human wills," 155–156; "indeterminate force," 155, 238n35. *See also* action

America: democracy and aristocracy linked, 60; failures of democracy, 10, 12, 38, 58–59; founding commitment to democracy, 13–15, 17; moral impartiality in histories of, 32
Andreas-Salomé, Lou 165
antagonism, essential, 186–187, 195
appeal, moral: aesthetic, 36, 169; ill-will as susceptible to, 31, 36, 48–49; as plea for moral self-reflection, 31, 213n7
Appiah, Kwame Anthony, 164
apt ending: for natural event, 144–145, 157; required for beautiful life, 84–86, 88–94, 100, 101, 109–110, 193–194; in story analysis, 90, 144, 148, 229n23. *See also* beautiful event/life; completeness; death
Arendt, Hannah, 156, 209–210n49, 210n56, 237n27, 238n40
Aristotle, 90–91, 100
art, as propaganda, 105, 107, 123–124, 129–131
artistic beauty: as challenge to white supremacy, 6–7, 36, 52, 101–102, 118–121, 203n17; congitive horizons expanded by, 107–108, 110; as counter to democratic despotism, 23–24, 101–102, 105, 135, 169; ethical horizons expanded by, 107–110, 121–123, 126, 130, 234n34; moral authority unmoored from religious doctrine, 104, 113, 123–124, 126–127; "objective vision" afforded by, 127; and propaganda, 106–110, 123–124; second-person moral address achieved by, 49, 105, 121, 127; truth, goodness, and right as tools of, 106–107, 109. *See also* aesthetic education; beauty; natural beauty; propaganda
Atlanta race riots, 47

Balfour, Lawrie, 174
"barbarians," 15
Barry, Brian, 153
Barry, Peter, 40
Baumgarten, Alexander, 98–99, 230n39, 41, 233n26
Beard, Charles, 32–33
Beard, Mary, 32–33
beautiful event/life, 25, 131, 144, 169–170, 196; apt ending required for, 84–86, 88–94, 100, 101, 109–110, 193–194; black women's lives as, 170–184; "End" versus "end," 84, 86; Glorya's, 95–98, 145; inspiration, power of, 96–97, 180, 182; John Brown's, 123–126; narrative arc of, 103, 148–149, 161, 163, 185; possibilities projected by, 100, 101, 109–110; uniqueness of, 94–95; and "veiled" corner, 92–93, 96–97, 101. *See also* Coleridge-Taylor, Samuel; Crummell, Alexander; ethical life
beauty: of absolute music, 97–98, 103, 122, 230n38; astonishment by, 7, 22, 24; beautiful willing, 164, 240n57; of black women, 176–181; and death, 79–80, 84–85, 95, 172; depair and pessimism countered by, 6–7, 102, 104, 134, 139, 142, 164, 170, 184, 210n56, 240n57; and "End," 84, 86;

ethical horizons expanded by, 107–110, 121–123, 126, 130, 234n34; human beings' physical appearance, 175–179; interpretation of, 99–100; judgment of, 161–162, 239n52; numerically distinct instances of, 94–95; pedagogical power of, 6–7, 12–13; and perfection, 97–99, 103, 121, 230n39, 233n26; political impact of, 1, 6–7, 36; possibility of subverting racial oppression through, 23–24, 31, 36, 113, 135, 147, 169, 193–194; promise of future possibilities in, 98–101, 109, 146, 163; and sacrifice, 79–80; temporally bipolar nature of, 25, 85, 100, 121, 146; transience of, 165; two criteria of, 83–84, 95, 100–101, 121, 172; ugliness thwarted by, 81–83, 101, 109, 133, 139–141, 167–168; unexpected and unfamiliar revealed by, 7, 14–15, 22, 83–84, 94–100, 119, 145; universal theme of, 82, 164; white supremacy combatted by, 1–2, 6–7, 23–24, 101–102, 118–119, 123, 203n17

beliefs, white supremacist: in black subhumanity, 15, 41, 43–45, 63, 75; and imperialism, 62–65

biblical references in Du Bois: Apostles' Creed, 26; Book of Revelations, 188–190; Genesis 2:23, 39; Isaiah 53, 117, 119, 124, 232n21; Mark's Gospel, 210n54; Matthew's Gospel, 17–18, 26, 93, 210n50; New Testament Parable of the Talents, 26, 93

Bilgrami, Akeel, 162–163, 205–206n34

Blackness, as Slaveness, 186

Black Reconstruction (Du Bois), 32–34, 203n15

Blake, William, 233n26

Blum, Edward, 114

Bourdieu, Pierre, 227n10

boycott, 29

British Empire, 34, 46, 223n21

British Industrial Revolution, 3

Brown, John, 113, 123–124, 218n39

Burke, Edmund, 83, 99, 229n9, 230n41

Canetti, Elias, 208–209n45

capitalism: democratic movement's success in taming, 58; economic interests, 29, 30–31, 34; humane, vision of, 220–221n6; industrial, 2–4, 60, 201n5; new enslavement of labor, 203n15; underconsumption as problem for, 59, 62

Captains of Industry, 4, 60, 201n5

category mistakes, 185, 243n28

causal/explanatory significance, 34, 37, 39–40, 48, 55

causal law, 145, 147, 154–156, 164, 238n41

Cavell, Stanley, 173, 206n37

chance, 151–156, 196

charity, hatred compatible with, 45–46

child, figure of, 20, 159, 210n56

Christianity: contradictory understandings of, 52; crowd aligned with, 49; metaphysical issue of, 39, 51; tragedy as a prelude to comedy, 93–94. *See also* white Christian culture

Christianity's American Fate (Hollinger), 51–52
"circle of concern," 23–24, 52–53, 102, 103, 110, 130
citizens, black: black women, 170–171, 174–175; feminist theory of, 174–185; possibility of subversion seemingly precluded for, 23–24, 135–137; receptivity to the possibility of subversion, 22–24, 135, 169
citizenship, democratic, 7–9, 103. *See also* citizens black; crowd, the; mob, culture of; white Christian culture
civic virtue, 7, 21, 211n57
Civil War: as duel between two industrial systems, 3
"Close Ranks" (Du Bois), 79–80, 136, 226n3
Coleridge-Taylor, Samuel, 15, 91–93, 95, 144
collectivist holism, 154
colonialism: expansion into Africa, 56–71; ideological formations of, 222n17. *See also* imperialism
"Comet, The" (Du Bois), 188–194, 244n47
completeness: apt end, required for beautiful life, 86, 88–94, 100, 101; congruity needed for, 90, 144, 229n23; "End" versus "end," 84, 86; incompleteness of ugliness, 84–87; "life-stages" concept, 88–89, 100; in natural beauty, 145–146; required for beauty, 22, 24–26, 110, 229n32; and unexpectedness, 83
Comte, Auguste, 154

Cooper, Anna Julia, 181, 242n18
criminal, figure of, 13, 14, 15, 171, 191, 207n40
Crisis (journal), 153; "Christmas Crisis" issue, 111–112, *112*, 119–120
"Criteria of Negro Art" (Du Bois), 102–103, 106–108, 130
crowd, the, 12–21, 169, 206nn34, 37; Christianity aligned with, 49; democratic conception of, 208n40; episodic, 17–18, 182; "hunting pack," 208–209n45; mob contrasted with, 13, 15, 17, 192, 208n40; open and closed, 208–209n45; polity shaped by, 14–16, 19–21; receptivity to the unfamiliar, 7, 14–15, 17, 22–23, 52, 110, 169, 192, 194; sans culottes, 13–14, 209nn47, 48
Crummell, Alexander, 26, 92–94, 96–97, 101, 127, 144, 145, 182, 194
culture: as explanation for American imperialism, 222n17

"Damnation of Women, The" (Du Bois), 26, 131, 174–183, 196
Darkwater (Du Bois), 1–2, 221–222n16, 241n67; beauty explicated and exemplified in, 2, 11–12; as call to arms, 30; "The Immortal Child," 20; "The Comet," 188–194, 244n47; "Credo," 26, 193, 244n47; "The Damnation of Women," 26, 131, 174–183, 196; East St. Louis race riots in, 72–76; explanatory frameworks for racial oppression in, 30; "The Hands of Ethiopia,"

40–41, 213n7; "The Immortal Child," 92; "Of the Ruling of Men," 110, 174, 183, 202n6; "Of Work and Wealth," 213n7; "Postscript," 102–103, 106, 141, 183; "The Princess of the Hither Isles," 20, 213n7; questions posed by, 20–21; "The Second Coming," 17–20, 192, 210n50; "The Shadow of Years," 149–154; "The Souls of White Folk," 30, 33–34, 37, 39, 41, 67, 123. See also "Of Beauty and Death" (Du Bois)

death: and beauty, 79–80, 84–85, 95, 172; Priam's as incoherent, 91, 95; self-understanding thwarted by scientific progress, 88–89, 92; ugliness defeated by, 84–88. See also apt ending

Death in Venice (*Der Tod in Venedig*) (Mann), 165

democracy: America's founding commitment to, 14–15, 17; contesting Christian contradictions as critical to, 52; democratic ideal, 2, 7–12, 25, 110; Du Bois's method of philosophical inquiry modeled on method of, 11; economic, 61; exchange of ideas, 204n24; exclusions from, 2, 4–6, 7–8, 12, 36, 53, 56, 59, 64, 76–77; failures of method, 10, 12; inclusiveness required by, 8–11; interpretive, 205n28; labor republican tradition, 201n5; normative notion of, 7; philosophy of, 3–4, 202n6; as "rule of all," 8, 11; semantic, 205n28; as way of life, 206n37; women's voices critical to, 171

Democracy in America (Tocqueville), 10, 12

democratic despotism, 5, 12; artistic beauty as counter to, 23–24, 101–102, 105, 135, 169; in East St. Louis, 71–76, 135; fragility of, 192; majority, tyrannies of, 10–11, 16, 204n25; philosophical paradox of, 60–61

democratic development, 169; restriction of darker peoples', 2, 4–6, 12, 36, 53, 56, 59, 64, 76–77; role of beauty in, 6; of white working class, 5, 64

democratic ideal, 2, 7–12, 25, 110

democratic movements: 1877 as pivotal year for, 5, 203n14; darker peoples suppressed by, 5; failure to halt imperial expansion, 58–59; increase in beneficiaries of government, 61; not applicable to nonwhites, 63–64; as product of the eighteenth century, 2; self-interested resistance to, 3; success in taming capitalism, 58

Dernburg, Bernard, 67, 68, 223–224n23

Descartes, René, 48

despair, 235n3; in Afro-modern thought, 235n3; beauty as counter to, 6–7, 102, 134; defined, 137; moral psychology of, 136–138; as no answer to ugliness, 134. *See also* pessimism; pessimistic despair

despotism, democratic, 205n31; terror of, 21

Dewey, John, 108, 204n24
Diamond, Cora, 234n27
disequilibrium, 185–187
distributive justice, 71–72
double-consciousness, 208n44
doubleness (twoness), 218n39
Dovidio, John, 217n31
Dred Scott decision, 65–66, 216n27
Du Bois, Alexander, 158, 160
Du Bois, Alfred, 158–160
Du Bois, W. E. B.: black audiences addressed by, 85, 213n7; counterfactual reasoning of, 58, 64, 70, 151, 220n5, 222n17; democratic ideal, 2, 7–12, 25, 110; epistemic humility, commitment to, 170, 172, 182; explanatory frameworks for racial oppression, 29–30, 33–34, 139, 222n17; as expressivist, 108–109; Grand Canyon visit, 241n65; as "hard libertarian," 238n35; hermeneutical improvisation of, 11–12, 14, 15, 21–22, 82, 120, 148, 164, 175, 205n28; "intellectual milieu" of, 164–165, 168; method of philosophical inquiry modeled on method od democracy, 11; moralism of, 26, 130–131, 170, 184, 235n41; as moral realist, 33; natural places, visits to, 103, 134, 140; normative notion of democracy, 7; personal experience in writings of, 79–81, 143, 149–153; phases of intellectual development, 30–31, 149–154; *The Philadelphia Negro*, 184, 196; pluralism of, 170; politics of compromised by philosophy of beauty, 26, 170, 172–175, 181–183; as rhetorician, 107–108; romanticism of, 104, 157, 158–163; travels of, 103, 134, 140–142, 147, 154, 157, 163, 166–167; *Works:* "The African Roots of War," 56–67, 71, 72, 220n4, 221n14, 224n23; *Black Reconstruction*, 32–34, 203n15; "Close Ranks" editorial, 79–80, 136, 226n3; "Criteria of Negro Art," 102–103, 106–108, 130, 231n1; *Dusk of Dawn*, 1–2; *John Brown*, 26; "A Litany of Atlanta," 20, 47; *The Negro*, 64; "Of Beauty and Death," 20–21, 79–100, 109; "Of the Coming of John," 208n40; "Of the Culture of White Folk," 37, 64–67, 69; "The Second Coming," 17–20, 192, 210n50; "Sociology Hesitant," 154–155, 157, 194, 195, 237n33; *The Souls of Black Folk*, 208n40. *See also Darkwater* (Du Bois); "Jesus Christ in Texas" (Du Bois); "The Souls of White Folk" (Du Bois)

Dürer, Albrecht, *111*, 113, 119–122
Dusk of Dawn (Du Bois), 1–2; explanatory frameworks for racial opresion in, 29; unconscious in, 31

East St. Louis, Illinois, 71–76, 135, 167; Great Migration to, 74; labor aristocracy in, 73–74; race riots, 73, 75, 225n35; and World War I, 74
economic democracy, 61
economic interests: armed national associations of labor and capital,

61, 66, 70, 72, 75; and ill-will, 29, 30–31, 34; nation as agent of, 59–61, 67–70; profit motive, 40, 41, 59; stabilized by white supremacy, 36; wealth inequality, 4, 223n21
education, "practical immortality" through, 20
Eltis, David, 222n17
emancipatory narratives of redemption, 185–186
Engels, Frederick, 72, 225n29
England, 34, 46, 67–68, 72, 96
entrenchment thesis, 6
ethical conduct, 123, 126, 234n34
ethical horizons, expanded by beauty, 107–110, 121–123, 126, 130, 234n34
ethical life, 32, 36, 52, 91, 108. *See also* beautiful event/life
etiquette, 14, 16, 206n34
Europe: amoral, antidemocratic expansion into black territories, 58; exploitation of the world's darker peoples, 31, 34; Franco-Prussian War, 57; human decency of, 207n38; white culture of, 38. *See also* British Empire; England
expressivism, 108–109

Fanon, Frantz, 188
"Feast of Blood" (Patterson), 47, 49
felix culpa doctrine, 232–233n21
first-person and third-person points of view, 35–37, 45–53, 205–206n34; relevance of to contemporary debates, 49–50
"First Universal Races Congress" (University of London), 56, 71

Flag and the Cross, The (Gorski and Perry), 50–51
franchise (suffrage): and French Revolution, 201–202n6; and permanent majorities, 10–11; perversion of universalization, 10–11; reasoning for exclusion, 7–8; universal, 2, 7–8, 170–171, 202n6
freedom: emancipatory narratives of redemption critiqued, 185–187; and exploitation, 222n17; "practical immortality" through education, 20
French Revolution, 3, 4, 201–202n6; Terror, 21
Freud, Sigmund, 165, 168
Fried, Michael, 122
Frye, Northrop, 93

Gadamer, Hans Georg, 127, 234–235n36
Gallie, W. B., 90, 144, 229n23
Gates, Henry Louis, Jr., 172
Gorski, Philip S., 50–51
governance, 5, 62–64
Grand Canyon, 166–167
Great Migration, 73
guiding conception, 35–37
Guyer, Paul, 239n52

habits of mind, white supremacist, 6, 23–25, 30, 40–41, 73, 212–213n3; causal/explanatory significance of, 55; combatting, 1, 25, 76–77, 104; racial oppression explained by, 33–37. *See also* moral psychology; white supremacists

Hartman, Saidiya, 27, 183–184, 196, 243n22
hatred: and affective disposition, 42–43, 73; benign forms, 44; as cause of European jealousies, 67, 70; as distraction, 4; and economic exploitation, 5–6; ill-will versus, 84, 217–218n37; Indian-haters, 45–46; not seen as incongruity by white Christians, 38–39, 45–46, 50–51, 117, 123; simple and malicious, 218n37; used to divide workers, 223n21, 225n35. *See also* ill-will
Hegel, G. W. F., 108
Hilferding, Rudolph, 70, 224n26
historically and self-consciously situated hermeneutical improvisation, 11–12, 14, 15, 21–22, 82, 120, 148, 164, 175, 205n28
historical stillness, 185–186
Hobsbawm, Eric, 3
Hobson, J. A., 55, 56–57, 59–62; at "First Universal Races Congress," 56, 71
Hollinger, David, 51–52, 105
Home to Harlem (McKay), 129–131, 172–174, 184
Honneth, Axel, 202n6
Houston race riot, 167
"how possibly" question, 48–49
Huguenot religious minority, 16
human flourishing, conditions of, 86
Hume, David, 236n16
humiliation, fear of, 138
Hursthouse, Rosalind, 217n30

ideal conceptions, 35
ignorance, 29
Iliad, 91
ill-will, 215–216n27; and capitalist economic interests, 5–6, 29, 30–31, 34; complex of motivations for, 40–44; hate versus, 84, 217–218n37; and imperialism, 70; as susceptible to moral appeal, 31, 36, 48–49. *See also* hatred
imagination, 102–103; reality disclosed by, 160–162; truth and goodness as tools of, 106–107
imperialism: as competition among multiple new democratic nations, 67–68; empire as way of life, 222n17; Euro-American, 36; ill-will as explanation for, 70; impetus to, 58; industrial, 2, 4; labor aristocracy theories, 55, 72–77, 225n29; Marxist theories of, 70, 224n26; nation as agent of, 59–61, 69–70; "new," 56–71, 72; "open-door" trade policy, 67–69; and primitive accumulation, 69–71; Roman idea of, 57; "root idea of empire," 57; and white supremacist beliefs, 62–65; white supremacy as "switch," 59, 69–71, 220n5; and world views, 55, 58–59, 220n5. *See also* colonialism
improvisation. *See* historically and self-consciously situated hermeneutical improvisation
inclusiveness, 8–11
Independent, 37

Indian-haters, 45–46
"indivisibility, thesis of," 194
industrial capitalism, 2–4, 60, 201n5
inspiration, power of, 96–97, 180, 182
international governance, 5, 64
"Intimations of Immortality" (Wordsworth), 20, 159–160

Jacobson, Matthew Frye, 46–47
James, William, 26, 170, 194, 209n45; meliorism of, 195, 241n67, 245n53
"Jesus Christ in Georgia" (Du Bois), 111–113, *112*
"Jesus Christ in Texas" (Du Bois), 26, 217n30, 231–232n21, 232n19, 233–234n26; farmer's wife's experience, 115–123, 233–234n26, 234n27; Jesus as nonwhite in, 114–115, 117; lynching in, 117–120; moral authority unmoored from religious doctrine in, 113, 126–127; propaganda as art in, 123–124; as tribute to beauty, 103
Jim Crow: as binary caste system, 47; pessimism as response to, 134–138, 142; and travel, 139–142, 147, 236n13
John Brown (Du Bois), 26, 123–126
Journal of Race Development, 37
justice, inclusiveness required for, 8–11

Kant, Immanuel, 48, 147–148, 155, 227n10, 230n41, 236n19, 239n52
Kautsky, Karl, 72, 225n29
Keats, John, 24
King, Martin Luther, Jr., 128–129

Kipling, Rudyard, 203n15
Kobes Du Mez, Kristen, 52, 105

labor aristocracy, 55, 72–77, 225n29. *See also* white working class
labor republican tradition, 201n5
Larsen, Nella, 26, 129–131, 170–174, 181–182, 184, 243n22
Lehrer, Keith, 95–98, 145, 148
Lenin, Vladimir I., 224n26, 225n29
Leopold II of Belgium, 57, 203n14
Letters on the Aesthetic Education of Man (Schiller), 21–22
life morality, 124–126
"life-stages" concept, 88–89, 100
"A Litany of Atlanta" (Du Bois), 20, 47
Locke, Alain, 106
loopholes, moral, 65–66, 76
Louis XIV, 13, 14, 16, 206n36, 209n47
Lumpkins, Charles L., 73
Luxemburg, Rosa, 70, 224n26
lynching, 42; of Jesse Washington, 111, *112*; in "Jesus Christ in Texas," 117–119
lynch mob, 15–19, 47, 73, 117–120, 127, 190, 192, 208–209n45

majority, tyrannies of, 10–11, 16, 204n25
Mann, Thomas, 165
"Man of the Crowd, The" (Poe), 14–16, 208n40
Mantena, Karuna, 128–129
Marx, Karl, 69, 108
Marxist theories, 55, 70, 187, 195, 224n26

McKay, Claude, 26, 129–131, 172–174, 184
meliorism, 195, 241n67, 245n53
Melville, Herman, 45–46
Mill, John Stuart, 10
Mills, Charles, 217–218n37
miracle, 145, 147, 236n16, 238n40; and chance, 151–153; emancipatory significance of, 156–157; invoking of not justified, 149–157
mob, culture of, 15–21, 29, 169, 209nn48, 49, 210n54; and beauty of women, 177; combatting of, 23, 192–193; crowd contrasted with, 13, 15, 17, 192, 208n40; episodic and dispositional, 16–19, 49, 192, 209–210n49; and figure of stranger, 13, 17, 19, 191; human nature constrained by, 15, 20, 23, 52; lynch mob, 15–18, 47, 73, 117–120, 127, 190, 192, 208–209n45
monism, 194–195
Montego Bay, Jamaica, sunset, 103–104, 134, 142–143, 146–147, 154, 157, 161, 163, 165, 167
Moonlight (movie), 128
moral authority: second-person moral address, 49, 105, 121, 127; unmoored from religious doctrine, 104, 113, 123–124, 126–127
moral character: alternative conceptions of, 52–53, 122, 135–136; of white supremacists, 1, 37–39, 41, 44–45, 55, 58–59, 70, 77, 101, 135
moral psychology: first-person perspectives, 35–36, 45–53; historical explanations, 32–34; of pessimistic despair, 136–138; portrait of white supremacist, 39–44; social-scientific explanation of racial oppression, 32, 35–36, 55; third-person perspectives, 35–36; white moral character and white Christianity, 37–39; of white supremacy, 2, 25, 29–53, 212–213n3. *See also* habits of mind, white supremacist; "The Souls of White Folk" (Du Bois)
moral vice, 36, 40, 75–76, 214n10, 215–216n27
Morris, Aldon, 208n44
Moten, Fred, 27, 195–196
Mount Desert Island, Maine, 140–142
Murdoch, Iris, 127
music, absolute, 97–98, 103, 122, 230n38
mutual intelligibility, 206n37

NAACP, 152–153
narrative arc, 103, 148–149, 161, 163; of black life as flat line, 185
natality, 87, 210n56
nation, as agent of economic interests, 59–61, 67–70
nationalism, white Christian, 50–52, 105
natural beauty: as antidote to pessimism, 26, 103–104, 135–136, 142, 161, 169; and apt ending, 144–145, 157; call to fight for justice, 146–147; judgment of as demanding agreement, 161–162; miracle concept not justified, 149–157; miracle found in, 143,

145–147, 236n16; and poetic license, 158–163; racial oppression countered by, 6, 24–25, 140–142, 203n17; subjective and objective experience of, 143, 147, 161–162; sunset image, 103, 140, 143–147, 154, 157. *See also* aesthetic education; artistic beauty; beauty

natural supernaturalism, 26, 162–163

"negative capability," 24

Negro, The (Du Bois), 64

Nehamas, Alexander, 99–100

Nietzsche, Friedrich, 164–165, 168, 240n57

Nussbaum, Martha, 23, 52

"Ode" (Wordsworth), 20

"Of Beauty and Death" (Du Bois), 20–21, 79–100, 109, 130, 165, 178; beautiful life in, 86, 88–94, 100, 101, 124, 179; beauty opposed to pessimism in, 85–86, 133; universal themes in, 164

Ofili, Chris, 128

"Of the Culture of White Folk" (Du Bois), 37, 64–67, 69

"Of the Ruling of Men" (Du Bois), 110, 174, 183, 202n6

On Liberty (Mill), 10

On the Aesthetic Education of Man (Schiller), 21–22, 211n57

"On Transience" (Freud), 165

Packenham, Thomas, 220n3

Park, Robert, 208n44

Patterson, Orlando, 47, 49, 105, 186

Peirce, Charles Sanders, 139, 142

Perry, Samuel L., 50–51

pessimism: beauty as counter to, 104, 139, 142, 164, 240n57; as cowardice, 134–138, 142, 147, 236n19; defined, 137; despair induced by, 6–7; European, 165, 168; natural beauty as antidote to, 26, 103–104, 135–136, 142, 161, 169; possibility of subversion seemingly precluded, 23–24, 135, 136–137; receptivity as counter to, 22–24, 135, 169; and resignation, 164; ugliness associated with, 85–86. *See also* Afropessimism; despair

pessimistic despair, 26, 135; as fear of oneself, 137–138; first- and second-order, 138, 139; humiliation, fear of, 138; moral psychology of, 136–138

Philadelphia Negro, The (Du Bois), 184, 196

philanthropy, 4, 42

"Philosophy of Democracy," 3–4, 202n6

Pinckney, Darryl, 128

Plato, 211n57

Pliny the Elder, 56, 57, 219–220n3

pluralism, 26–27, 170, 184, 194–195, 245n43

Poe, Edgar Allen, 14–16, 207n40

practical deliberation, 32, 214n7

"practical immortality," 20

praise, false, 26, 173, 183, 184

"prestige" of white race, 67, 68

Priam's death, 91, 95

primitive accumulation, 69–71

prison-house, racial, 159–161

Problem of the Color Line at the Turn of the Twentieth Century: Essential Early Essays (Du Bois), 201–202n6
progress, historical, 186–187, 243–244n36
propaganda, 29; art as, 105, 107, 123–124, 129–131; and artistic beauty, 106–110, 123–124; and dignity, 128–129; theatricality of protest, 128–129. *See also* aesthetic education; artistic beauty

Quicksand (Larsen), 129–131, 170–174, 181–182, 184

racial capitalism, 226n37
racial categorization, 114
racial oppression, 212n1; anti-Black violence as totalizing, 187–188; cognitive component, 41–42, 67, 217n31; combatted by struggles against capitalism, 76–77; explanatory frameworks for, 29–30; labor of dark workers kept cheap, 5, 67, 69–70; natural beauty as counter to, 6, 24–25, 140–142, 203n17; and new imperialism, 56–71; and overwork, 91–92; possible subversion of through beauty, 23–24, 31, 36, 113, 135, 147, 169, 193–194; social-scientific explanation of, 32, 35–36, 55; white folks' habits of mind as explanation for, 33–37; whites as owners of Earth, 41–44, 67–68, 117; white working class share in spoils of exploitation, 60–66, 72, 73
rational inquiry, 29, 31, 49, 102
reality, disclosed by imagination, 160–162
reason, 234n34; "abduction," 139, 142–143, 235n7; white supremacists as recalcitrant to, 31, 34, 47–48
receptivity: black, to the possibility of subversion, 22–24, 135, 169; of crowd, 14–15, 52, 110, 169, 192, 194; increased by aesthetic education, 7, 24, 110, 169; lacking in white Christian, 23, 52; to stranger, 14–15, 17, 22, 52, 110, 121, 191; to women's voices, 171, 173, 183
"Recessional" (Kipling), 203n15
reconciliation, 45, 211n60
Reconstruction, 2, 4–5
relativism, aesthetic, 179, 181
"religious right," 24, 50
republican political thought, 21
"respectability" ideology, 130
"responsibility-right," 42
revelation, 123, 126, 234n34
Riddle of the Sphinx, 124
Rilke, Rainer Maria, 165
Ringer, Fritz, 220n5
Rise of American Civilization (Beard and Beard), 32–33
Rodin, Auguste, 128
Rogers, Melvin, 107–110
Romanticism, 185; natural supernaturalism, 26, 162–163
romantic love, racist ideals of, 128
Rome, 57

Rousseau, Jean-Jacques, 201–202n6
Royce, Josiah, 231–232n21

Said, Edward, 222n17
salience, 23, 79, 82, 227n8
sans culottes, 13–14, 16, 209nn47, 48
Santayana, George, 99, 230n39
Schapiro, Tamar, 35–36
Schiller, Friedrich, 21–22, 211nn57, 59, 60
Schopenhauer, Arthur, 164–165, 168, 244n36
science, Du Bois's philosophy of, 154–155, 160–161, 163
"Science as a Vocation" (Weber), 88–89, 92
scientific progress, 88–89, 92
"Second Coming, The" (Du Bois), 17–20, 192, 210n50
self-reflection, 31, 49, 138, 213n7
self-understanding: thwarted by scientific progress, 88–89, 92
"Shadow of Years, The" (Du Bois), 149–154, 157–159
Sharpe, Granville, 34
"Short Entry on the Possible" (Hartman), 196
Siegel, Susanna, 16–17
Simmel, Georg, 14–15, 207n39
Simpson, Lorenzo, 205n28
slavery: mechanistic explanations of, 32–33; other, concepts of, 222n17; revolt against, 3; shaken by John Brown, 123–126; Slaveness, Blackness coterminous with, 186

slave trade, 3–4, 40–41, 57, 176
Smith, Hampton, 19
social death, and Black life, 186
socialist groups, 60, 202n6
social-scientific analysis, 32, 35–36, 55
sociology, 145, 154–157, 161, 183
"Sociology Hesitant" (Du Bois), 154–155, 157, 194, 195, 237n33
sorrow songs, 164
Souls of Black Folk, The (Du Bois), 2, 93, 208n40, 226n1; beauty and rhetoric in, 107–108; "Of the Coming of John," 164
"Souls of White Folk, The" (Du Bois), 30, 33–34, 39, 41, 67, 123; two versions of, 37–38; white Prometheus figure in, 37
sovereignty, 151–153, 237n27
Spencer, Herbert, 154
Spillers, Hortense, 185
Spivak, Gayatri, 211n60
Stanley, Henry Morton, 5, 57–58, 203n14
Stevens, Wallace, 95
Stoddard, Lothrop, 224n23
story analysis, 90, 144, 229n23
stranger, 13–19; receptivity to, 14–15, 17, 22, 52, 110, 121, 191. *See also* "Jesus Christ in Texas" (Du Bois)
"Stranger, The" (Simmel), 14–15, 207n39
sublime, 99, 230nn38, 41; "counter-sublime," 236n19; dynamical, 147–148, 167, 230n41, 236n19
success, elements of, 153

sunset image, 103, 140, 143–147, 154, 157; as exercise in poetic license, 158–163; narrative arc of, 103, 148–149, 163
"switches" metaphor, 59, 69–71, 220n5

Taney, Roger, 65–66, 216n27
Taylor, Paul, 108–109
Thinker, The (Ofili), 128
Threadcraft, Shatema, 174–175
Tocqueville, Alexis de, 10, 12, 205nn31, 33
Tolstoy, Leo, 88–89, 100
trade unions, 60, 71–74, 225n29
travel: black traveler, 140–142, 147, 236n13; and Jim Crow, 139–142, 147, 236n13; spirit revived by, 103, 140–142, 161–162, 163
Turner, Mary, 19

ugliness, 228n18; defeated by death, 84–88; as eternal, 84–85, 87; as expected, 94; great, 164–168; incoherence of, 90; incompleteness of, 84–87, 94; little hatefulnesses and thoughtlessnesses of race prejudice, 139, 140, 165; persistence of, 191–193; pessimism associated with, 85–86; thwarted by beauty, 81–83, 101, 109, 133, 139–141, 167–158
unconscious, 29, 31, 216n8
understanding: interpretation of beauty, 99–100; *Verstehen*, 33
"unequal rights," philosophy of, 50–51
unfamiliarity: beauty's revelation of, 7, 14–15, 22, 83–84, 94–100, 109–110, 119, 145; crowd's receptivity to, 14–15, 52, 110, 169, 192, 194; and moralism, 172
Unger, Roberto, 24, 194, 195
universal themes, 11, 82, 164

Van Gogh, Vincent, 96
"veiled" corner, metaphor of, 11–12, 105, 109, 183; and beautiful life, 92–93, 96–97, 101; and beauty, 82–83, 101; and black traveler, 140–142; and black women's experience, 171–172; and human physical beauty, 175, 177; and salience, 82
Verstehen, 33
virtue, moral, 40, 126, 130–131; attributed by Du Bois to black women, 170, 172–182; white supremacy as, 45
vocation, moral, 146–148, 165–166

Waldron, Jeremy, 42
Walker, David, 213n7
Washington, Jesse, 111, *112*
Wayward Lives, Beautiful Experiments (Hartman), 183–184, 196
Weber, Max, 33, 55, 100, 165, 220n4; "switches" metaphor, 59, 70, 220n5; world views concept, 55, 58–59, 220n5; *Works:* "Science as a Vocation," 88–89, 92
white Christian culture, 37–39; artistic beauty as challenge to, 6–7, 36, 52, 101–102, 118–121, 203n17; "circle of concern," 23–24,

52–53, 102, 103, 110, 130; as a culture of the mob, 15–20; democratic development inhibited by, 12; dis-integrated by aesthetic education, 24; first-person point of view, 45–53; "new religion of whiteness," 38, 45; racial hatred not seen as incongruity by, 38–39, 45–46, 50–51, 117, 123; receptivity lacking in, 23, 52; revision resisted by, 6; as syncretic, 38; white supremacist vice as moral virtue, 45. *See also* habits of mind, white supremacists; white supremacists; white supremacy

white folk, souls of: in Du Bois's "middle period," 215–216n27; training in racist feelings, 115, 216n28, 217n30

whiteness: as English and Teutonic races, 218n42; hierarchically ranked white peoples, 46–47; modern "discovery" of, 41; "new religion of," 38, 45; as ownership of Earth, 41–44, 67–68, 117; racial categorization of, 114

white supremacists: aesthetic education's effect on self-understanding, 23–24; affective dispositions, 42–43, 62–63, 73; belief in black subhumanity, 15, 41, 43–45, 63, 75; cognitive traits, 41–44, 67; Du Bois's portrait of, 37, 39–44; life morality of challenged, 124–126; moral blame of as justified, 34; moral character of, 1, 5, 37–39, 41, 44–45, 55, 58–59, 70, 77, 101, 135; portrait of, 39–44; as recalcitrant to reason, 31, 34, 47–48. *See also* habits of mind, white supremacist; ill-will; white Christian culture

white supremacy, 221–222n16, 223–224n23; beauty as vehicle for combatting, 1–2, 6–7, 23–24, 101–102, 118–119, 123, 203n17; as complex of motivational, cognitive, and affective dispositions, 40–44; moral psychology of, 2, 5, 25, 29–53, 212–213n3; as moral vice, 40, 75–77; as "switch" that accounts for imperialist expansion, 59, 69–71, 220n5'; whites degraded by, 46. *See also* white Christian culture

white working class, 223n21; advancement of, 64–65; competition encouraged between black and white unskilled labor, 72–73; democratic development of, 5; race hatred encouraged in, 74–75, 225n35; share in spoils of exploitation of darker races, 60–66, 72; slavery of, 32. *See also* labor aristocracy

Whitman, Walt, 209n45

Wilberforce, William, 34

Wilderson, Frank B., 184–188, 194–195, 243–244n36, 243n28, 245n52; social theory of, 185–187

will, the, 164, 237n33, 240n57

Williams, William Appleman, 222n17

Wollstonecraft, Mary, 177
women, black: backward-looking account of, 182–183; Cooper's view of, 181, 242n18; Du Bois's typologies of, 175–176; efficiency as an aesthetic value for, 178–179; false praise of, 173, 183, 184; feminist theory of citizenship, 174–175; freedom contemptuously thrust upon, 180–181; idolization of as antidemocratic, 173; lives of idolized by Du Bois, 170–184; moral virtue attributed to, 170, 172–182; receptivity to voice of, 171, 173, 183; and "specious homage," 177, 181–182
Wordsworth, William, 20, 159–160

world views, 55, 58–59, 220n5
World War I: Africa as root of, 56, 58, 61; black colonial fighters in, 68; call for black soldiers, 79–80, 147, 165–166, 226n3; carnage caused by, 79; economic order shaped by, 36; November 1919 armistice, 30; ties strengthened between capital and labor aristocracy, 73; world robbed of beauty by, 165
World War I era (1910–1920), 1–2, 6
Wynter, Sylvia, 227n10

Yeats, William Butler, 233n26
Young, Charles, 166

Zerilli, Linda, 205n37